Moreton Morrell Site

£14·95

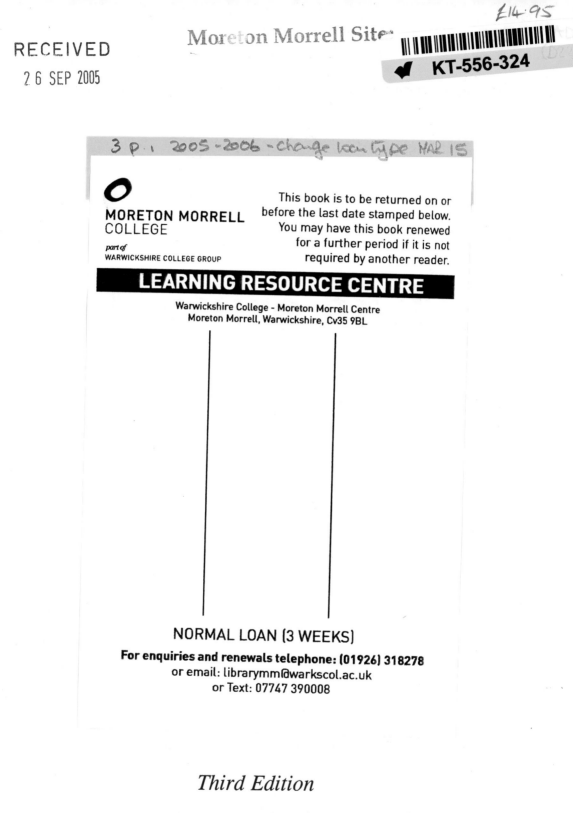

3 p. 1 2005-2006 - change loan type MAR 15

Third Edition

Business Education Publishers

©Ian Adams and Andrew MacMullen 2000

ISBN 1 901888 20 7

First published in 1990
  Reprinted 1991
Second Edition 1994
Third Edition 2000

Cover design by Tim Murphy Creative Solutions

Published in Great Britain by
Business Education Publishers Limited
The Solar Building
Doxford International
Sunderland

Tel. 0191 5252410
Fax. 0191 5252426

British Cataloguing-in-Publications Data
A catalogue record for this book is available from the British Library

Printed in Great Britain by Athenaeum Press, Gateshead

To Our Families

The Authors

Ian Adams is a teacher of very wide experience, and is presently Lecturer in Politics at Durham University. He has been teaching and researching into the relations between government and leisure for some years. Dr Adams is also the author of *The Logic of Political Belief* (Harvester-Wheatsheaf, 1989) and *Political Ideology Today* (Manchester University Press, 1993).]

Andrew MacMullen is Lecturer and Postgraduate Director in Politics at Durham University. He has been teaching and researching European government and administration, especially in the field of EU institutions, for many years. His recent work has appeared in Neill Nugent (ed) *At the Heart of the Union* (Macmillan, 2nd edition 2000), and the journals *Parliamentary Affairs*, *Diplomacy and Statecraft*, and *Crime, Law and Social Change*.

Preface

This book is primarily designed for students of leisure studies who need to understand the crucial role of government in the area of leisure. It assumes no knowledge of government on the student's part, and begins by providing a comprehensive introduction to the workings of our political, central and local government systems and how they relate to leisure in general.

The main part of the book, however, deals with those major areas of leisure where government's role and influence is particularly important. These are Broadcasting, the Arts, Countryside, Sport, Tourism and Heritage. For each area there is an account of its history in relation to government, and a description of the governmental bodies involved, including central government departments, quangos, local authorities and various regional bodies. In addition, there is a discussion of a variety of issues facing each of the areas of leisure: such things as football hooliganism, business sponsorship of the arts, the deregulation of broadcasting, and the impact of '1992' on travel and tourism.

Many people have helped me in the preparation of this book. I have been given information and advice from local and national politicians, civil servants and officers of various national bodies, local government officers, pressure groups, as well as colleagues and friends. There are too many to name, but I am very grateful to all of them. However, I would particularly like to thank my colleagues Joyce Liddle and Paul Callaghan , whose assistance has been invaluable throughout, and my employers New College, Durham for financial assistance with research expenses. In spite of all this help there are no doubt many mistakes and gaps, responsibility for which is entirely my own. Suggestions for improvement for future editions will be most welcome.

Ian Adams
New College Durham, July 1990

Preface to the Second Edition

Leisure is such a rapidly developing area that there has been a host of changes since the first edition of this book was published. But it is the creation of the Department of National Heritage, together with the National Lottery and the Millennium Fund, that has made a new version essential, since these have changed the whole framework of policy and organisation in this field. In producing this revised edition I have been helped by a great many people to whom I wish to express my thanks. I would like to particularly express my appreciation for the help I received from the staff of New College Durham Library and the Official Publications section of Durham University Library.

Ian Adams
New College Durham, June 1994

Preface to the Third Edition

The pace of change has not slackened under a 'New' Labour government since 1997. There have been important developments in the structure of government, both central and local, as well as many in the diverse areas of leisure policy. While the fact that some reforms are still incomplete produces uncertainties, we have tried to give a reasonably clear description of the situation in the middle of July 2000. The basic structure and much of the content of the book is that established by Ian Adams, while Andrew MacMullen has taken the lead in the up-dating and revising process so both authors associate themselves with the final joint production.

Ian Adams and Andrew MacMullen
University of Durham, October 2000

Table of Contents

Chapter 2   Local Government and Leisure

Chapter 3   The Department for Culture, Media and Sport

Chapter 4 Broadcasting and Government

Chapter 5 The Arts and Government

Chapter 6   Countryside and Government

Chapter 7   Sport and Government

Leisure and Government

Chapter 1

The Role of Central Government

Introduction

Leisure is now an important, if very diverse, industry, making a major contribution to the economy and to the life of the country. Central government is a key factor, both in the development of the industry and in determining the environment in which it operates. There is an obvious sense in which the activities of government influence this industry like any other. This is in its handling of the economy. The leisure industry will flourish if the economy as a whole is flourishing. However, the significance of central government is more direct than this.

It is important in at least three main ways:

(a)   providing a legal framework for leisure activities

(b)   setting up institutions that provide, assist and supervise leisure services

(c)   determining, and putting into effect, leisure-related policies.

We will look briefly at each in turn.

Legal Framework

Virtually every aspect of our social life is regulated by law. There is a host of laws concerning marriage, work, education, running a business and many other things, including various aspects of leisure. To take some simple examples:

- Licensing laws lay down that we may only drink in public houses and bars between certain hours.

- Children below a certain age cannot see certain kinds of films in public cinemas; while other laws govern the kinds of videos that can be sold.

- Theatres, dance halls, hotels, football grounds and other public buildings are covered by various kinds of legal regulations, such as those concerning safety, and can be closed if they do not conform.

All these laws need to be passed by Parliament, and central government is ultimately responsible for seeing that they are administered by local government or other agencies.

Institutional Framework

Secondly, where there is public provision or regulation it is central government that creates the necessary institutional framework. That is, by means of legislation passed by Parliament, government sets up the various bodies that do the providing or regulating, such as the Countryside Agency, tourist boards, the BBC and the Independent Television Commission (ITC). In the same way, it is central government that creates local authorities and then requires them to provide certain services (such as libraries) and allows them to provide others if they wish (such as sports centres).

Policy Making

Thirdly, and most importantly, central government is the centre of national policy making. All the previous examples, such as licensing laws, the creation of the ITC, the functions of local authorities, and so on, are all outcomes of the policy-making process. Many of these decisions also involve questions about spending public money in these areas - whether to do so and how much. These processes usually involve debate and disagreement: for example, between some who think licensing laws ought to be strict, and others who would have them liberalised or abolished altogether, or between those who disagree on whether public money should be spent to develop a British film industry. There is a process of consultation and compromise: interested groups may be pressing both sides of the case, and the political parties could be in vigorous conflict over the issue.

The process is rather messy and complicated because it is a democratic process. People are entitled to press their different points of view, and the aim is to decide among competing arguments what is best for the country as a whole. It is *our* government and its policies should therefore reflect *our* opinions. But on most matters, public opinion is a very complex and difficult thing to pin down, with various parties and pressure groups representing different aspects of it.

If we are to have a full understanding of the leisure industry in this country, then we need to know something about its public dimension. That in turn requires some knowledge of the political and governmental system within which public leisure policy is arrived at. It is important to remember that the UK does not exist in isolation in managing its own affairs. Over many years successive British governments have entered into membership, involving a wide variety of agreements, with international organisations such as the United Nations (UN) and the European Union (EU). In some cases the government has to negotiate with major multinational corporations such as oil companies and media groups.

Democracy and Elections

The Constitution

A constitution is the basic set of rules by which any human association is run. It lays down what institutions there will be, such as executive and rule-making bodies; what offices there are and how holders are chosen; who can be a member of the association and what their rights are; and the means by which the constitution can be changed. Much the same elements will be found in any constitution, whether it be a complex modern state or an amateur dramatic society. In states, for example, we have cabinets and parliaments, while local societies have executive committees and annual general meetings.

States, and every other kind of organisation, normally have their constitutional rules written down in a single document. The United Kingdom is practically unique among modern states in having no such document. Our constitution has to be looked for in a variety of sources. Principally these are Acts of Parliament (such as the Acts that lay down our right to vote) and constitutional conventions. These conventions are simple unwritten rules that have no legal force but nonetheless are observed by all who are engaged in politics. There is no law, for example, that says we have to have a Prime Minister or Cabinet.

States normally acquire written constitutions at some great turning point in their history, such as independence or a great revolution, when a fresh start has to be made. Britain has never had such a permanent break, and so its constitution has evolved gradually over many centuries, progressively changing from a mediaeval monarchy to a modern democracy. The central principle which became generally acknowledged in the nineteenth century was the supremacy of parliament as the ultimate source of laws which would prevail over all other rules and institutions within Britain. Membership of the EU has reduced the importance of this doctrine, and the Human Rights Act 1998 will have a long term effect in giving citizens rights which may not be so easily changed as previously by parliament.

Democracy

The United Kingdom is a democracy. It is not a democracy in the way the ancient Greeks understood it, where all the citizens would gather in the market place and participate directly in all the decisions of government. That would not be possible in modern conditions. In the western world we have, instead, various forms of 'representative democracy', which means that the people have a say in who shall make the decisions on their behalf. In the British system we have regular general elections (at least once every five years) when all citizens over eighteen years have an opportunity to vote for who will represent them as their Member of Parliament.

The Electoral System

The origins of our electoral system is very old indeed, in some respects going back to the Middle Ages. However, only a small fraction of the adult population could vote before the middle of the 19th Century; and it was not until 1918 that all men over 21 could vote, and 1928 before all women had the same right. The age limit was reduced to 18 years in 1969.

Our electoral method is quite simple. The country is divided up into constituencies, and every citizen has one vote in one constituency. In each constituency the candidate who gains the most votes wins. The system is called 'simple majority' or 'first-past-the-post'. It would appear to be eminently fair, but a closer look calls this into question. The crucial fact is that when the vast majority of people vote they are not really concerned with who the actual candidates are. What matters is their party. In effect, people are voting for the government they want. The electoral system undoubtedly works in favour of the two major parties and against the smaller ones. A striking example was in 1983 when votes and seats for the main party groupings were as follows:

	Votes	% share of vote	MPs
Conservatives	13,012,602	42.4	397
Labour	8,460,860	27.6	209
Alliance	7,776,065	25.4	23

On this occasion the Conservatives won a huge overall majority with only 42.4% of the vote. The Liberal/Social Democrat Alliance won almost as many votes as Labour but won only 23 seats compared with Labour's 209. Had the Alliance won seats in proportion to their vote, they would have had around 165 seats. More importantly, in this situation no party would have won an overall majority of seats and the Alliance would almost certainly have formed part of a coalition government. The supporters of smaller parties regard this possibility as a very good thing, and very much more democratic than the present system. However, this system, by producing a big bonus of parliamentary seats to the leading party, also normally produces single party government with a clear majority claiming a mandate to govern the country for up to five years.

The alternative would be some system of proportional representation (PR) which would ensure that parties gained seats in proportion to the size of their vote. Those who support the present system say that under PR no party having an overall majority would be the usual outcome of elections, and this is just what would be wrong with a new system: we would always be getting coalition governments, with backroom deals and compromises. They argue that at least the present system gives us strong, stable government. Since the election of the Labour government in 1997 the issue of electoral reform has been under consideration, but so far without any clear decision for change at the parliamentary level. However, elections to the newly created Scottish Parliament and National Assembly for Wales, along with the Northern Ireland Assembly use various forms of PR, as do the most recent (1999) elections to the European Parliament and the Greater London Authority in 2000.

Voting Behaviour

Most people, in choosing who to vote for or whether to vote at all, are concerned with a general view of the competence of a party to govern, or broad issues like the economy, unemployment, defence or education; unless their personal interests are directly involved. For example, someone working in a local authority leisure centre may vote Labour because that party is committed to the maintenance and expansion of local government services, whereas the Conservatives are committed to privatising and otherwise reducing local services. On the other hand, the same person may choose to vote Conservative, believing they will run the economy better than Labour and therefore there will be plenty jobs for them even if they lose their present one. Sometimes a voter will not vote out of self-interest but may feel so passionately about a specific issue - like conservation, or the abolition of bloodsports - that this will completely determine the way they vote. But whatever the decisive factor may be, it remains true that the great majority of people vote for parties without much thought about the actual candidates and with only limited knowledge about specific policies.

Parties, Beliefs and Policies

The Need for Parties

Politics in the modern world is dominated by political parties. Elections are party elections, Parliament divides along party lines and government is party government. Yet historically parties are a relatively recent phenomenon, which provokes a question as to how we managed before they existed? In earlier centuries the norm was hereditary monarchy and it was kings, and sometimes queens, who were expected to actually run the country. When monarchs eventually stepped out of politics parties were needed to provide continuity and coherence. If there were no parties and we simply elected our MP just as a local representative, we would end up with a Parliament of 651 MPs who had no connection with each other. It would be impossible to form a government out of them that would have a coherent programme or much prospect of it being enacted.

With parties it is possible to vote for a government at the same time as a local representative. Each party presents us with a set of leaders, and a set of policies set in its election manifesto. We therefore can have a clear choice when we vote, and know what we can expect of the party that wins. It should be noted that we do not vote for a government directly. We vote for a Parliament, and it is from the majority party in Parliament that the Prime Minister and the rest of the government is formed. It is different in other countries. In the USA, for example, there is one set of elections for their parliament (the Congress) which votes the laws and budget, and a quite separate election for the President, who is in charge of the executive branch and has special powers in foreign affairs and defence.

For most of the past two centuries, British politics has been dominated by two main parties. Other parties have usually existed, but it has been the leading two which have tended to alternate in power. Since 1945 the two dominant parties have been Conservative and Labour, with the Liberals in third place and nationalist parties playing an increasingly prominent part in Scotland and Wales. Our system of elections has been a major factor in sustaining the two party duopoly, although from time to time the results of elections such as 1983 and to a lesser extent 1997, have led some to speculate that two-party dominance is coming to an end.

Party Beliefs and Policies

Political parties in Britain tend to stand for certain things, and to subscribe to systems of belief called 'ideologies'. These ideologies, such as conservatism, socialism and liberalism, can be a major influence on government policy. On the other hand, parties have to win power and policies, and sometimes ideologies need to change and adapt to popular opinion to gain electoral success. Since the mid-1970s both the Conservative and Labour parties have changed their policies and outlook a good deal.

After the Second World War both main parties accepted the need for considerably more government activity than in the past. The government managed the economy with the aim of maintaining full employment; it set up and ran a range of nationalised industries and it maintained a great range of welfare policies (education, housing, social security, health, etc.) known collectively as the welfare state. These policies were popular among all parties, and the general public, until the economic recession of the mid-1970s. This recession was a world-wide phenomenon, but Britain suffered particularly badly. The old economic policies no longer seemed to work as they had in the past, and people began to look for new solutions.

The Conservatives and Thatcherism

Mrs Thatcher became leader of the Conservatives in 1975 with new policies and a new version of conservatism that soon became known as 'Thatcherism'. Traditional Conservatives have always placed great stress on tradition and continuity, only changing things when absolutely necessary. Mrs Thatcher was not like this at all. She was a self-confessed radical who wanted to change everything overnight. Her analysis of Britain's problems saw many of the post-war policies as a mistake, giving the government far too much power and control, necessitating very high taxes and a massive bureaucracy to run it all. The total effect was to diminish the free market and suffocate the free enterprise system. Her solution was to put all this into reverse: to reduce state ownership and control, reduce taxes and bureaucracy and encourage the free market, free enterprise and wider consumer choice wherever possible. The main task of government, she thought, was to create the conditions in which the free market could flourish.

In 1979 the Conservatives won a General Election and began to put these ideas into effect. Virtually all the policies of the 1980s and 1990s have reflected the basic themes of encouraging the free market, reducing the role of the government and increasing consumer choice. These include: privatisation; 'contracting out' of government services; the sale of council houses; reducing government expenditure, both national and local; cuts in taxes and the increased priority given to fighting inflation; encouraging small businesses, enterprise zones and urban development corporations; and reducing the power of the trade unions. Even in areas where there was no free market, such as the National Health Service and state education, the policy was to make these areas as much like the free market as possible with hospitals competing for patients and schools for pupils, as though they were private businesses.

Government policy on various aspects of leisure has also been influenced by these ideas. Attempts have been made to make sports and the art organisations more businesslike and entrepreneurial, and for business sponsorship to replace public subsidy as far as possible. Much more competition has been introduced into the television industry; state grants for tourism projects have been phased out. There are other examples, as we shall see.

In 1990 Mrs Thatcher was replaced as Conservative Party Leader and Prime Minister by John Major. He carried forward similar policies to Mrs Thatcher, with more privatisation, fighting inflation as a top priority, and so on. He was, however, more sympathetic towards state intervention in some areas, especially sport. Since 1997 William Hague has had to reflect on the lessons of the Conservative electoral defeat and establish a style of leadership and policy which can compete with Tony Blair's 'New Labour' which has accepted many of the achievements of the previous Conservative governments.

Labour and Socialism

The Labour Party's response to the 1970s' economic crisis and the Conservative victory in 1979, was initially to become more Socialist in its outlook. This meant more nationalisation, state planning and control of the economy. But when these policies were put to the electorate in 1983, Labour was very heavily defeated. The election in 1983 of a new leader, Neil Kinnock, was followed by a shift away from left-wing policies and this was accelerated by a further defeat in 1987. In the process, Labour more or less abandoned nationalisation and state planning, accepted limitations on the power of trade unions and accepted the priority of reducing inflation and making the free market work more efficiently. To traditionalists this meant an effective abandonment of the Socialism the party is supposed to stand for. But in our system, parties have to adapt to new circumstances if they want to be elected. Labour lost again in 1992, but by a much narrower margin that the previous elections against Mrs Thatcher. Finally, in 1997 under the leadership of Tony Blair, 'New' Labour was able to exploit an increasingly wide-spread public mood that it was time for a change after 18 years of Conservative government and won a convincing victory.

Labour has moved a good way closer to the Conservatives on policies that have been popular, but there are still some differences between them. Conservatives tend to see solutions to problems in terms of the free market, while Labour tends to try to solve things through government, but stressing the idea of public-private partnership where government sets standards and provides significant financial resources. Thus, in the case of the arts, as we shall see, the Conservatives see the need for more funds in terms of business sponsorship and arts groups becoming more commercial, while Labour sees progress in terms of increased government grants in collaboration with private sector partners and with more local authority involvement. Which approach prevails depends on which party we choose to elect, but even then there may be some considerable continuity. When Labour was elected in 1997 it was keen to impress the electorate with its financial prudence, and announced that it would follow the strict overall government spending limits previously imposed by the Conservatives. It was only after two years in government that some cautiously more expansive spending started to be demonstrated.

Parliament and Government

Functions of Parliament

The purpose of General Elections is to elect a House of Commons to represent the people in Parliament. There is a House of Lords, which is not elected, but most power effectively now lies with the Commons.

Parliament's traditional functions are:

(a)   to pass legislation

(b)   to check and scrutinise the work of government

(c)   to provide redress of grievance

(d)   to debate the nation's affairs.

All these functions go back to the Middle Ages and are still performed. However, such has been the development of our political system over the last 130 years that its performance has come to be dominated by the party battle. The traditional functions have now become secondary to Parliament's primary task of sustaining a government and passing its legislation, and sustaining an Opposition and giving it the opportunity to criticise.

Government Control of Parliament

In the middle of the nineteenth century governments were very much subordinate to the power of Parliament. Governments frequently had their legislation thrown out; were obliged to do what they did not want to do; and were forced out of office, all by the power of Parliament alone. This began to change as, later in the century, more and more people were given the vote. It soon became impossible to be elected as an MP without the backing of a political party. As a result, parties gained great power over their MPs, for unless they supported the party and its leaders then the party could withdraw its support and the MP would not be re-elected next time. This is the basis of party discipline, which is now very strict. As a result, governments control Parliament and everything it does, including what laws are passed, what information is released, and how much scrutiny of government actions there is. So long as a government has a majority it will not be forced out of office and can more or less do as it likes.

Ordinary back-bench MPs spend much of their time looking after the interests of their constituency, dealing with constituents' problems and helping to put things right if they have been badly treated at the hands of government. This last is redress of grievance, which on an important matter MPs can question a Minister in the house or refer the matter to the Parliamentary Commissioner, better known as the 'Ombudsman'. Beyond this local sphere, however, MPs have little influence on their own. They may introduce a Private Member's Bill, which could become the law of the land, but the opportunities for doing this are very small. They may have some influence as a member of a committee: either a legislative committee, which scrutinises legislation in detail, or as a member of a select committee investigating some matter. The most prestigious back bench committees are now the series of all-party Departmental Select Committees introduced in 1979. These each monitor the work of a central department; calling for documents and cross examining ministers and civil servants. They investigate particular issues and issue reports which are extremely useful sources of information (several are cited at the end of this book). However, the ambitious individual back-bench MP can have most influence by leaving the back-benches and entering the Government or Opposition front-bench team.

Most MPs, and especially government MPs, vote for their party line most of the time, but occasionally things do go wrong. For example, in 1986 the Conservative government, despite a massive majority in the Commons, was defeated on the issue of allowing shops to open on a Sunday on the same basis as the rest of the week. It was a measure that might have transformed the leisure pattern of many people. It is also the job of the House of Commons to keep a check on the government, scrutinise the nation's finances and debate the nation's affairs. Thus, for example, each year the government asks Parliament for money to spend on the arts, and this is the occasion for annual debate on government arts policy.

In addition, there is the work of the select committees mentioned earlier. In 1992 the Department of National Heritage was created and a new Parliamentary Select Committee was set up to cover its work. The first chairman was Gerald Kaufman, a senior minister in the previous Labour government, and its thirteen members included one former Prime Minister, Jim Callaghan, before he moved on to the House of Lords. When the government department changed its name in 1997 to 'Culture, Media and Sport' so too did the committee. The committee has produced a number of important reports on a number of topics, including the future of the BBC, privacy and media intrusion, the cost of compact discs , the export of works of art, sports sponsorship and television coverage, the future of international rugby, and in July 2000 is conducting the latest in a series of investigations into the Millennium Dome.

The House of Lords

The House of Lords is the oldest part of Parliament and was originally the most powerful. The House of Commons became more important after it had established that it had the right to control the nation's finances (all government raising and spending of money has to be authorised by the Commons). This still left the Lords with much power, until this was taken away by the Parliament Acts of 1911 and 1949, which left the Lords with only a delaying power of one year over non-financial legislation. The Lords is still important for scrutinising legislation and occasionally embarrasses a government by defeating a measure, although normally this is soon reversed by the Commons. The membership of the House of Lords was dominated by hereditary peers, with appointed life peers as the second largest group. In practice this provided the Conservative Party with an automatic majority. The 1997 Labour government is committed to reform of the old system. The House of Lords Act 1999 removed the automatic right of hereditary peers to sit in the upper house, but as a transitional measure 92 peers (elected by the others) were allowed to remain.

The Lords provides a number of ministers in any government, however, the bulk will come from the ranks of the majority party in the Commons. The Prime Minister, Chancellor of the Exchequer and the majority of the Cabinet have to be, by convention, in the Commons. Normally about a third of the majority party's MPs hold some sort of position in the government. Those left out are the back-benchers who are expected to vote for the government's measures and give it loyal support.

Prime Minister and Cabinet

The particular type of democratic government we have in Britain is Cabinet Government. This is in contrast to, say, the United States where they have one-person Presidential government. The Cabinet is a committee of senior ministers, which is the central decision-making body of British government. The Prime Minister chooses the Cabinet, chairs the Cabinet and sets its agenda, and is therefore a very powerful figure. It may sometimes seem that it is the Prime Minister who makes all the final decisions, and this may depend on the personalities and political situation of those involved, but it is in fact the Cabinet that has ultimate authority. All major policies must be approved by Cabinet, and by convention all members are collectively responsible for all its decisions.

The Cabinet normally has a membership of 20-25 and consists of the PM and the heads of the various departments, such as Treasury, Foreign and Commonwealth Office, Defence, Home Office, Environment, and Health. Outside the Cabinet each of these departmental heads will have several junior ministers responsible for particular areas of the department's work. These junior ministers join with their superiors in Cabinet committees where detailed policy is made and co-ordination between departments affected.

Normally, a Cabinet comes to power with the basic outline of its policies already decided. They will have been set out in the party's election manifesto. It is the

Cabinet's job to put the manifesto promises into effect by filling out the detail and embodying the policy in legislation for Parliament to pass. It might be considered wrong (although not illegal) for a government to implement a major policy it had neglected to tell the electorate about during the election campaign. It should only do the things it has said it would do. But in practice many unanticipated issues arise which require action during a government's term of office, and there are areas such as economic policy, where things go wrong and it is reasonable for a government to adopt a different policy.

The Monarchy

Government is carried on in the Queen's name. The Monarch appoints ministers, has to sign all legislation, dissolves and calls Parliament and appoints judges, senior army officers, peers, bishops and many others. Without these things being done, government simply could not function. Yet in none of these matters does the Monarch make her own choice. Everything is bound by convention. Convention dictates that the Queen choose the leader of the majority party in the Commons to be Prime Minister. Once this is done, virtually everything else is done according to the Prime Minister's advice. This procedure keeps the Monarch above party politics through the device of acting on the advice of ministers who are themselves responsible to a popularly elected Parliament.

Government Departments

The work of government is divided up among a number of different departments and each has a variety of responsibilities. The question of which responsibilities should be allocated to which departments is a surprisingly complicated one and changes from time to time, as do their names. The majority of departments are 'functional', which means that each looks after a specific area of policy: Ministry of Defence dealing with all defence matters, the Foreign Office with anything concerning our relations with other countries and so on. Many areas of policy have a European dimension, for example the Ministry of Agriculture Fisheries and Food (MAFF) carries on its own extensive negotiations with the European Commission in Brussels and representatives of other EU states. A number of responsibilities that do not quite fit anywhere else are to be found in the Home Office, which deals primarily with police, prisons and fire service, but also immigration, tests on animals, the Church of England, elections, the Isle of Man and Channel Islands, and a number of other things. The Treasury is a key department, since it has general responsibility for the annual budget, determining the level and supervising the spending of public money, so all others will have to work within the financial limits it establishes.

This pattern, however, still leaves many areas of policy which could fit with any of several departments. In 1985 responsibility for tourism was switched from the

Department of Trade and Industry to the Department of Employment; but it could have gone to the Departments of Transport or Environment or several others with which it has links. It became part of the Department of National Heritage in 1992 which was then re-named Department for Culture, Media and Sport (DCMS) in 1997.

The pattern of functional departments has been greatly complicated by the existence of a number of territorial departments based on an entirely different principle. In the twentieth century there developed three departments organised on the basis of geographical areas: the Scottish, Welsh and Northern Ireland Offices. The responsibilities of these departments cut across those of the functional departments, although not in a consistent way. For example, the Scottish Office was responsible for education in Scotland, whereas the Welsh Office was not responsible for education in Wales which came under the Department for Education. In consequence, many government policies, including those relating to leisure, required the co-operation of at least the functional departments concerned plus the three territorial departments.

This was administrative devolution, basing a substantial number of civil servants in big offices in Edinburgh and Cardiff. They were still controlled by a government minister and the Secretaries of State for Scotland or Wales, who were members of the Cabinet in London and who represented the majority party in the UK as a whole, not the local electorates in Scotland or Wales. The 1997 Labour government was committed to going much further than this and has now implemented a much more ambitious system of devolution, confirmed by local referendums. However the schemes are not the same in Scotland and Wales. The Scotland Act 1998 established a Scottish Parliament with 129 directly elected members; it has law making powers over a wide range of domestic policies, including most of the leisure field and some tax-varying capacity. It appoints an Executive, with 22 ministerial members headed by a First Minister (Donald Dewar), which runs a structure of departments, such as Rural Affairs, Justice, Enterprise and Life-long Learning, largely staffed by permanent officials who formerly worked in the Scottish Office. The Government of Wales Act 1998 retains more central control over Welsh affairs. The National Assembly is again directly elected with 60 members appointing an executive committee. The Assembly has only limited technical legislative powers, and while it decides to spend money it can only do so from the financial grant offered from London. Interestingly, following the use of PR in the elections, in neither body is there a single party majority, so coalition and compromise was necessary in setting up the executives and deciding on policy.

The policy making process in a sector such as leisure is further complicated by the fact that most policies have implications for a number of different government departments. A policy for preserving the countryside, for example, primarily involves the Department of the Environment, Transport and the Regions (DETR as it is currently called), the Ministry of Agriculture, as well as the devolved territorial departments, but the Department for Culture, Media and Sport (DCMS) has an interest (tourism), as does Defence (countryside under its control) and a number of others. The creation of the Department of National Heritage in April 1992, later renamed the Department for Culture, Media, and Sport (DCMS) by the new Labour government in 1997 was an attempt to bring much government policy together into one department which hitherto had been scattered across several. Its work is described more fully in Chapter 3.

Ministers and Civil Servants

At the head of each government department is a minister in the Cabinet (usually a Secretary of State) assisted by junior ministers, all of whom are party politicians. They are in charge of a department staffed by civil servants who are permanent in the sense that they do not change with a new government, as ministers do. They are there to give advice to ministers and to put the ministers' policies and decisions into effect. They prepare legislation, provide information, co-ordinate with other departments, consult with pressure groups, supervise quangos and in some cases administer a nation-wide network of regional or local offices (for example, the Department of Social Security).

There is, on the face of it, a clear division of labour between ministers who take decisions and make policy, and civil servants who carry them out. Civil servants give advice on the practicalities of policy, but it is the ministers who must finally decide and who are alone answerable to Parliament. However, the reality is more complicated than this. In the first place, most government departments are huge organisations administering a wide range of policies. Ministers simply do not have the time to master it all; they have Cabinet, Parliamentary, constituency and party duties to attend to as well as running their departments. Much of the running of the department and the detailed decision-making, therefore, has to be left to the civil servants. Furthermore, top civil servants will be much more expert about the work of their departments than ministers can be, for ministers on average spend only two years in any one post before moving on or out altogether.

Because of these factors, civil servants are in a strong position to influence policy. Ministers do bring outsiders to advise them on policy matters, but civil service influence is inevitably still there. It is also perhaps inevitable that such influence should tend towards caution and against change. Cautious policies rather than radical ones tend to reduce the likelihood of having to put policies into reverse if a General Election brings a new government to power.

There is a strong tradition of political neutrality in the British Civil Service. The idea is that the same civil servants will serve any government, of whatever political party, with equal loyalty and diligence, and may, for instance, be helping one government nationalise an industry one year and another government privatise it the next. Political neutrality of this kind is not the tradition in many countries. For example, in the USA it is usual for the top civil servants to change every time there is a new President.

With the coming of a Conservative government in 1979 with radical new policies, there was a determined attempt to change the nature of the civil service. Mrs Thatcher sought to reduce the influence and the size of the service and more than 200,000 civil service posts disappeared as a result. More importantly, there was an attempt to alter the whole civil service culture, its attitudes and way of doing things, in order to make it more like private sector management. One of the main ways of doing this was to end the tradition by which the minister is formally in charge of all the departmental day-to-day activities and at least in principle follows the convention whereby the minister takes responsibility for all that happens in the department. Thus civil servants assist but remain anonymous.

Ffollowing the so-called 'Next Steps' initiative, many parts of the civil service have been hived off into agencies, such as the Passport Office, or the Vehicle Inspectorate which is an agency of DETR responsible for annual MOT testing, each with its own budget and objectives, and under the control of a named civil service manager who will take responsibility for its administration and be paid according to how well the objectives are achieved within the budget. Ministers remain responsible only for the general lines of policy rather than management, and a smaller core of traditional civil servants remain in Whitehall departments. Much of this drive has been maintained by the 1997 Labour government. Private Finance Initiatives (PFI) by which public facilities such as NHS hospitals are built and run by private contractors continue. Public Service Agreements have been devised as a scheme by which spending departments get money guaranteed for three years in return for specifying their objectives and promising to find more efficient ways to deliver them. These changes have been partly put into effect and will take many years to be fully implemented, but if pushed through to the end they will constitute a revolution in public administration in this country.

Quasi-Government and Leisure

Quangos

The central administration of Britain is primarily carried out by government departments. Each of these is staffed by permanent civil servants under the control of a Cabinet Minister and his junior ministers who are elected politicians and are responsible to Parliament for the department's work. In addition, there are a very large number of organisations which can be said to be part of the administration of the country but are not part of the departmental structure. They belong to what is often referred to as 'quasi-government' and consist of a range of semi-independent bodies, each of which has been set up by government on an ad hoc basis to do a particular job. Their official title is 'Non-Departmental Public Body' but they are often called 'quangos'. This is a fashionable and rather misleading American term which is supposed to stand for 'quasi-autonomous non-governmental organisation'.

Bodies of this kind include the Equal Opportunities Commission, British Waterways, English Heritage, and Regional Health Authorities. Some operate services, others distribute money (such as the Arts Councils), and others are regulatory agencies which oversee privatised utility services such as OFWAT (water) to protect consumer interests. They are usually set up by statute and each is under the general supervision of a government minister who normally appoints the governing body and gives it its terms of reference, but is not responsible for the day-to-day running of the organisation. The employees of such bodies are not usually civil servants. Thus, it is a kind of government at arms-length.

The number of these bodies varies according to how they are defined. On one definition there are hundreds of them, while on a broader definition, which includes the host of bodies set up to advise ministers on various matters, there are several thousand. In practice, the degree of government control varies a great deal, but traditionally the largest and most independent are the public corporations.

Public Corporations

These were often very large organisations running a major industry such as British Coal or the Post Office. In each case they were established by Act of Parliament, then a responsible minister would lay down broad objectives, approve investment plans, etc., but the idea is to let the body manage its affairs in its own way, with the minimum of government interference. Public corporations have been set up at various times to operate public services, regulate aspects of commercial activity and run nationalised industries. The early ones were regulatory and commercial, like the Port of London Authority (1908). In each case it was thought neither necessary nor appropriate for civil servants to regulate in detail some service of a specialised and highly technical nature. Since 1945 however the best known public corporations were created to run nationalised industries, such as gas and coal and railways. It was believed that this form of organisation would allow these industries to be run by businessmen taking proper commercial decisions instead of ministers and civil servants who do not think in commercial terms.

Conservative governments since 1979 had a rather ambiguous attitude to quasi-government. The privatisation programme abolished many of the largest public corporations by turning them into commercial companies (PLCs), a number of which have now become part of large multinational corporations. While the Conservative government came to power convinced that there was too much bureaucracy and set about reducing the number of quangos, it also wanted to reduce the size of the central departments with its plans to have many of the things they do hived off to semi-independent agencies. In addition, it had to establish regulatory quangos to supervise utilities, and simply modified and set up others, some of them leisure-related. This pattern has been continued by the Blair government since 1997.

Quangos and Leisure

Many government policies on leisure have almost always been put into effect by quangos rather than directly through central departments. Thus we have the four Arts Councils, four Sports Councils, the Countryside Agency (itself recently created by a merger of the Countryside Commission and the Rural Development Commission), the National Heritage Memorial Fund, the English Tourism Council, Resource (which has just absorbed the Museums and Galleries Commission) and others. A recent example is English Heritage, created in 1984 to maintain ancient monuments previously managed directly by the Department of the Environment and its predecessors. The work of a number of quangos, nationalised industries, and privatised utilities also has a bearing on leisure without it being their principle concern. Examples would include the Forestry Commission, various development corporations, Railtrack, and Northumbrian Water.

A more complicated and interesting case of the role of quasi-government is that of broadcasting. The BBC was created as a public corporation in 1927 to provide a national radio service. Apart from the arguments relating to technical specialisation, the government wanted an arm's length approach to ensure impartiality and public confidence. People might worry that broadcasting was an instrument of government propaganda if the government ran it directly. The same considerations applied in the setting up of the Independent Television Authority (ITA) in 1954, and its successors, the Independent Broadcasting Authority in 1972, and the Independent Television Commission (ITC) in 1990. However, although the BBC and ITC are both public corporations they have very different functions. The BBC is virtually a nationalised industry with a massive output of radio and TV programmes, many made by its own staff and some by private contractors. The ITC on the other hand, is a regulatory body, making no programmes of its own but licensing and supervising the independent ITV companies. In addition to these, there is The Radio Authority, set up to regulate commercial radio; a Welsh Fourth Channel Authority; and a new public body, the Broadcasting Standards Council, set up to express public concern over undue sex and violence on television. With the expected rapid development of broadcasting and its convergence with telecommunications and the internet over the next few years it is very likely that the whole system of agencies and regulation will change. This indeed may be true of the whole leisure field.

Pressure Groups and the Policy-making Process

Government today is a huge operation. Its spending in 2000-2001 is anticipated to be over £370 billion, which is some £6,000 for every man, woman and child in the country. Government is also a massive employer, with about a fifth of the national workforce with jobs in the public sector. There are nearly half a million civil servants, to which must be added members of the armed services, those employed in local government, the health service, the remaining public sector industries and a great variety of other agencies, totalling several million. The purpose of all this expenditure and employment is to put into practice the multitude of government policies that affect almost every aspect of our lives.

Pressure Groups

As government is so powerful and its activities can affect people in so many ways, it is not surprising if people try to influence the policies and particular decisions that governments make. Political parties are too general to represent very specific interests and points of view, but individuals acting on their own cannot achieve very much. They have to work together in groups of various kinds, and these go under the general name of 'pressure groups'.

Pressure groups come in all shapes and sizes: from a small group of mothers trying to have a zebra crossing put near their village school, to a great national organisation like the National Trust, with assets and income running into millions of pounds. Some are permanent groups, such as the Council for the Preservation of Rural England, while some may be temporary, such as the campaigns in the past to stop particular sporting tours going to South Africa. Again, some groups, such as the Association of Cinematography, Television and Allied Technicians (the main technical trade union in the television and film industries), exist primarily for other purposes; in this case the usual trade union functions of bargaining with employers to improve pay and conditions, and only act as pressure groups when there is some policy of government that affects them. They contrast with such groups as the National Campaign for the Arts which tries to influence government art's policy and which is purely a pressure group and nothing else. There are also national groups and local groups, exclusive groups and groups whose membership is open to anyone. These and other characteristics make it possible to divide up and classify groups in a variety of ways. Much the most important basis of classification is between what are known as 'interest' groups and 'cause' groups.

Interest Groups and Cause Groups

Interest groups are all those groups which exist to protect the interests of their members. Almost every kind of business has its own group to further its interests: travel agents, toy manufacturers, cinema operators, racecourse owners and a host of others have their trade associations. Similarly, all trade unions are interest groups, along with professional organisations of various kinds. Then again, there are groups, like the Rambler's Association or the Jazz Society or the Football Supporters Association, that represent people with particular pastimes.

The other main kind of pressure group is the 'cause' group. This term is applied to groups of people who are campaigning for some general cause, which involves no personal benefit to them. The Campaign Against Cruel Sports, for example, is clearly not a society of foxes, hares and deer looking after their own interests, but a society of people campaigning against something that they believe is morally wrong, although some of these groups, of which Friends of the Earth is one, say they are also campaigning in the interests of humanity as a whole.

Pressure Groups Methods

How do these groups go about influencing government? Our political system has various points at which pressure groups can try to exert influence. These are:

(i)   the executive

(ii)   Parliament

(iii) the political parties

(iv)   public opinion.

A sophisticated pressure group will not neglect any of these, but groups tend to concentrate on the one at which they think they will be most effective.

The most important target is the executive - that is, ministers and civil servants - for it is at this level that the real decisions are made. Big, powerful, well-established groups often have direct access at this level. The National Farmers Union (NFU), which is not a trade union of farm employees but an association of farmers, has extremely close links with the Ministry of Agriculture Fisheries and Food (MAFF). It sits on numerous bodies to advise the minister on agricultural matters and is always closely consulted on all policy matters affecting it. Countryside conservation groups who want things done of which the NFU do not approve may have a difficult time convincing government.

For groups who do not have direct access, the second level to aim at is the political parties and MPs in Parliament. If a substantial section of a major party takes up your cause, it can in time become party policy and eventually government policy. This happened in the early 1950s when various commercial interests convinced a number of Conservative MPs and delegates to the Conservative conference, of the desirability of commercial television. This created a great wave of enthusiasm in the party that persuaded a reluctant PM (Winston Churchill) and his Cabinet to introduce commercial television in 1954. The anti-hunting lobby enjoys significant support among MPs, mainly, but not exclusively, on the Labour side.

MPs are constantly deluged with literature trying to influence in favour of this or that cause or this or that group. There are now even professional lobbying organisations who introduce their clients to influential MPs and ministers so that they may be better persuaded. For example, enormous effort and expense by lobbying and public relations firms went in to persuading the government and MPs over who should be awarded the contract to build the Channel Tunnel. That was a one-off decision, but often a policy issue is involved with groups arguing opposite sides of the case and where nothing is ever decided permanently. Sometimes groups such as the Countryside Alliance spring to prominence combining issues such as defence of fox hunting, the decline of agricultural incomes, and a variety of alleged threats to the rural way of life, such as the closure of village schools and post offices.

Finally, there is public opinion. For groups not having much success with the other two, this is something of a last resort, since the real power is elsewhere. The general idea is to persuade the general public, which will in turn put pressure on MPs and ultimately ministers, to make some change. Every group seeking to influence public opinion needs publicity for their cause, and they often go to great lengths to organise some stunt that will attract media attention - Greenpeace being a good example. The purpose of all these pressure group methods is to influence the policy-making process.

Policy Making

Policy-making is the central activity of government, and the Cabinet is the most important policy-making body. However, the process does not normally begin in Cabinet. The general outlines of policy have usually been set out beforehand in the party manifesto for the election that brought the Cabinet to power, and although a Cabinet may depart from the manifesto because of circumstances it did not anticipate (economic crisis or whatever) it tries to stay within the manifesto's broad strategy. Election promises have to be embodied in detailed policies, each one coming under the department of a particular minister. The minister will discuss the possibilities and practicalities with senior civil servants who will gather information, consult with interested parties, give advice and generally help the minister to put the policy in legislative form. Once this is approved by Cabinet, it is up to the responsible minister, aided again by civil servants, to see the legislation through Parliament, and then administer it.

This sounds fairly straightforward, but the policy-making process is a good deal more complex and various than this conventional description suggests. In the first place, the idea that it is the ministers that are the policy-makers and that others - civil servants and pressure groups - play only a subordinate role is not realistic. As advisers and providers of information, and later as administrators, civil servants are in a very strong position to influence practically any policy. Pressure groups vary a lot more in their power and influence. It may even be sufficient in some cases for the opposition of a particular group to effectively prevent a policy it does not like from working.

It is equally simplistic to assume that policies are decided on their merits, or what the participants see as their merits. There is a whole range of factors that may influence the process. They include:

- what level of power and influence and level of commitment each of the participants has

- to what extent they command all the relevant facts

- whether the policy is consistent with government policy in other areas

- whether the policy fits in with the government's overall beliefs or ideology

- whether it has, or will have, support from the party's back-benchers and the party nationally

- how much it will cost, and does it enjoy a sufficiently high priority compared with other spending objectives?

- will it take up valuable Parliamentary time?

- how popular it will be with the electorate

- any problems in relation to the EU or our other international commitments.

These and other factors can greatly affect the policy-making process. It is, therefore, a difficult matter to explain how any particular policy came about. This is hard enough when all the factors involved are known, but usually they are not. For example, it is often in the interests of some of the participants, such as the civil servants, that their influence is not publicly known; while others, such as pressure groups, may want to exaggerate the part they played. These difficulties are compounded by the fact that the decision-making process in this country is shrouded in official secrecy.

Pressure Groups and Broadcasting Policy

Some of these points are illustrated by the case of the 1988 White Paper on the future of broadcasting. There is no official account of what happened (there never is), but journalists have pieced together a broad account. It appears that the chief protagonists were Douglas Hurd, the Home Secretary at the time (and therefore the minister responsible for broadcasting) and Lord Young, the then Secretary of State for Trade and Industry. It seems that there was a good deal of disagreement over what the policy should be. On the one side, Douglas Hurd, supported by the BBC and most of the broadcasting and arts establishments, favoured measures to protect public service broadcasting, which most felt a free-market would destroy. On the other hand, Lord Young argued the free-market, deregulation case, supported by the manufacturers, the advertising industry and the new satellite broadcasters. Mrs Thatcher also took a close interest in the negotiations. She generally supported Lord Young's free-market view, which fitted in well with her government's general outlook of reducing the role of the state, encouraging the free market, privatisation, more competition and consumer choice, etc. On the other hand, she was in favour of regulation when it came to the broadcasting of unnecessary sex and violence. Various other groups had an interest in the question, made representations and argued their case as widely as they could.

A White Paper had been promised, setting out the government's policy for the future of broadcasting, but these disagreements delayed its completion several times. The White Paper, *Broadcasting in the '90's: Choice, Competition and Quality*, was eventually published in November 1988 and represented a series of compromises. However, the lobbying did not stop there. Particularly vigorous were the campaigns of those who stood to lose or gain by the proposed new system of selling ITV franchises to the highest bidder. The government did make a number of changes before the White Paper was embodied in the Broadcasting Bill that was introduced into the Commons in the Autumn of 1989. As the Bill proceeded through Parliament, interested parties were trying as hard as ever to influence the final details of the Act. Even after the Bill became an Act pressure groups continued to try to influence the way it is put into effect and press for future changes.

The European and International Dimension

Since joining the European Community, now the European Union (EU), in 1973 British membership has been an increasingly important factor in government policy-making. It is a factor that is certain to increase in importance in the future as Europe moves towards ever closer co-operation and integration.

The Idea of a European Community

The idea of an economic community in Western Europe began to be seriously discussed after the Second World War. The aims were both economic and political. One priority was to restore the prosperity of Europe within a broadly free-market capitalist system. Secondly, and ultimately more importantly, it was to bring together the nations of Europe in such a way that the wars that had plagued European history, and had just devastated the continent twice within a generation, would be prevented from ever happening again. If former enemies could be brought together in a common framework so that their economies were integrated, then armed conflict would be impossible. The first step was to rebuild Europe's prosperity by replacing economic rivalry between states with co-operation. Some enthusiasts saw the process as beginning with the creation of a common market, followed by the introduction of common economic and social policies, and culminating in full economic integration. The final step would be some kind of political union, perhaps leading eventually to a federal United States of Europe with a federal president and cabinet.

The idea of a common market is fundamental. When firms export their goods to other countries they normally have to pay import duties (tariffs) which make their goods more expensive and harder to sell. Countries have these import barriers not just to raise revenue but also to protect their own industries against foreign competition. In this situation it is a great advantage for firms to have a large domestic market in which to grow large and rich, which in turn provides a strong foundation for competing in the rest of the world. A major reason why the USA is such a mighty economic power is that it has a very large domestic market of over 200 million people Smaller countries are clearly at a disadvantage in this respect, and one way of overcoming it is for a group of countries to lower trade barriers among themselves and have uniform tariffs on goods coming from elsewhere, in order to create a customs union which can lead to a large domestic market. In the case of the present EU area this now amounts to some 350 million people.

However, the European Union version of a common market always went further than a simple customs union in having a set of institutions partly independent of member governments, charged also with running common policies such as agriculture, coal and steel, competition and regional policies. There are also common social policies, concerned with social benefits, equality of opportunity and other matters across the community. Consumer and environmental protection are also areas for common action. Moves towards a single currency and supporting common management of more general economic policies is now well under way for most of the EU states. There is also some limited co-ordination of foreign policy, however, these developments are controversial. It means governments sharing their right to make policy in ever more vital areas, which some are reluctant to do. The question is bound up with questions of national sovereignty and political integration.

So far, political integration extends largely to a harmonisation of the policy interests of what remain independent sovereign states. This can be seen as a limited pooling of sovereignty, but it may be interpreted as a much greater loss of independence. By some it is considered worth it, for the sake of greater prosperity, political stability and communal influence in the world. Others, especially in Britain, are more doubtful.

The Creation of the European Community

When the formation of the European Community was being discussed in the 1950s the leading advocates were eager for Britain to be a member. The aim of preventing further wars demanded political stability and Britain was regarded as a model of a stable democracy, as well as, at that time, one of the most powerful countries in the world. However, Britain stood aloof for a number of reasons. First of all, Britain had an Empire and Commonwealth providing her with trade advantages and cheap food. Britain also had strong economic and political links with the USA. Finally, Britain's foreign policy for centuries had been to avoid strong links with Europe. No doubt these would have been overcome if the will had been there, but there was little enthusiasm for membership among politicians or the general public. Six countries went ahead without her. They were France, West Germany, Italy and the Benelux countries (Belgium, Holland and Luxembourg); and in 1957 they signed the Treaty of Rome which set up the European Economic Community.

It was soon seen to be a considerable success, with the economies of the member states growing rapidly. The British economy declined by comparison and it was soon apparent to many that Britain had made a mistake in not joining at the outset. In the 1960s Britain's application to join was turned down because of French opposition (they did not think we were European enough), and it was not until the early 1970s that our third application was accepted and we signed the Treaty of Rome, becoming members in 1973. This was on much less favourable terms than would have been possible in 1957. The Republic of Ireland and Denmark (whose economies are closely linked with ours) joined at the same time. The nine member countries became ten in 1981 when Greece joined; twelve in 1986 with the accession of Spain and Portugal, and fifteen in 1995 with Austria, Finland and Sweden. Now the former Communist countries of central and eastern Europe - Poland, the Czech and Slovak Republics, Hungary, the Baltic republics (Latvia, Estonia, and Lithuania), Romania and Bulgaria along with Turkey, Cyprus and Malta are aiming to join as soon as their economies are sufficiently developed to stand the strain of entry and they can meet the political and legal requirements. How the EU will develop in the future is a matter of great controversy, and indeed is one of the most important issues facing the Western World. To understand what is at stake we need to know something more about how the EU is run.

The Countries of the EU 2000

Member Countries

The EU System of Governance

The Treaty of Rome and a number of subsequent treaties (especially Maastricht and Amsterdam in the 1990s) act rather like a constitution, laying down the rules of membership and the institutions through which the EU is governed. There are four such main bodies:

1. The Council of Ministers

This is most important institution for all EU decisions. It consists of 15 ministers representing the different countries, the actual individuals varying according to the decision being made. The most important decisions are made at the European Council, by the Heads of Government (Prime Ministers) who usually meet twice per year. Other decisions are made by the Foreign Ministers, or by Trade, Agriculture or other Ministers according to the question to be decided. The Council is the final legislative body, drawing up rules (regulations and directives) that have the force of law, and must also vote the annual budget. Meetings normally take place in Brussels, according to an elaborate set of procedures with the Commission making proposals and taking part.

2. The Commission

This is the body that has responsibility for running many EU policies on a day-to-day basis. It administers the policies, keeps governments informed, distributes the grants, and so on. But beyond mere administration, it also has the function of making proposals for the development of policy, drafting legislation and drawing up the annual budget for submission to the Council of Ministers. The Commission has a permanent staff which is essentially a body of European civil servants drawn from the member countries. However, the Commission itself consists of senior political figures, often former government ministers from their country of origin. Romano Prodi the current Commission President came to the post from being Prime Minister of Italy, while the British Vice President Neil Kinnock is former leader of the Labour Party and Commissioner Chris Patten had been a Cabinet minister, Chairman of the Conservative Party and last Governor of Hong Kong. There are twenty Commissioners who serve for five years. They are nominated by member governments, and must be approved collectively by the European Parliament; although once nominated Commissioners act independently. Commissioners are usually given specific briefs, such as agriculture or trade. The headquarters of the Commission is in Brussels.

3. The European Court of Justice

This court is the final authority on Community Law. The Court has fifteen judges and sits in Luxembourg. It hears disputes between member countries, between member countries and the Commission, between EU institutions, and between individuals or firms and any of these. Thus, if the Commission feels a country is not fulfilling its obligations under the various agreements, then the Commission can take that government to the Court. Governments and firms have, for example, been accused of secretly subsidising activities or hampering imports and other devices contrary to Community rules. Thus in July 2000 the German car manufacturer Volkswagen was fined £50 million for preventing consumers from buying their cars more cheaply in Italy. The earlier 'Bosman' judgement transformed the European professional football scene by overturning many of the restrictions imposed by national registration and transfer systems.

4.   The European Parliament

This is a Parliament that has gradually developed, from being a talking shop with little real power, to one which exercises increasing influence. While it elects no government it can veto the appointment of a new Commission. It has some complicated powers to hold up or in some cases to amend or veto laws before they reach the Council of Ministers. It can amend some parts of the annual budget or reject it totally, and it can dismiss the Commission as a whole. While these are drastic all-or-nothing powers that cannot be used very much, the Parliament did play an important part in the events which led to the resignation of the whole Santer Commission in March 1999 over allegations of improper behaviour by some Commissioners and staff. Since 1979 it is directly elected, and now it has a certain democratic authority. This has helped it to gain more influence on EU affairs. The Parliament has 626 members (87 of them from the UK), directly elected for five years, representing the member-countries roughly in proportion to their population. It meets in Strasbourg, Luxembourg and Brussels.

The EU is financed through a combination of import duties on foreign goods entering the union at any point, a small proportion of all VAT paid throughout the member states, and some direct contributions based on the relative prosperity of the states. The budget is still relatively small, currently running between 2-4% of national budgets. The money is spent on running the EU institutions and on financing its various programmes. The biggest and most important of these is the Common Agricultural Policy (CAP) which accounts for about 50% of the budget. The European Regional Development Fund ('Regional Fund' for short) and European Social Fund account for most of the rest. In the early 1980s Britain was in a long-running dispute with the Community over its contribution. Because Britain was a very big importer of goods from abroad, and because it has only a relatively small farming industry, Britain was paying far more into the Community than it was receiving. After a great deal of controversy a formula was eventually worked out whereby those countries that were paying 'too much' in this way were given a rebate in compensation.

The Single Market or 'Europe without Frontiers'

By the mid-1980s it was felt that the Community, which had changed its institutions and policies little since 1958, must not stand still and stagnate but must press on with more integration, both economic and political. The result was a bold plan, known as the 'Single Market', to make the common market much more of a reality, with the expectation that more ambitious commitments to integration would follow.

The Single Market programme was embodied in the Single European Act agreed by Heads of Government in 1985. The idea was to remove all barriers to the free flow of people, goods, services and capital within the EU. That is, taking the common market to its logical conclusion: a Europe largely without internal frontiers. This has major implications for many things and not just doing away with import duties and passports. It implies some standardisation and harmonisation of many technical regulations and consumer protection measures across the Community, so goods and services would be available on the same terms in the different countries within the EU. Thus Spanish electronic equipment has to meet the same safety requirements as in Belgium or any other country. It implies the mutual recognition of people's qualifications, so that the degrees, diplomas and certificates of one country are acceptable in all the others. It implies the ability of anyone to deposit and borrow money anywhere in the Community and a whole range of legislative and administrative changes to ensure a 'level playing field' cutting out unfair discrimination and competition.

In 1985 the EC decided on a dramatic attempt to set a deadline, with the hope of clearing everything by the critical date of 31 January 1992, so that from 1 January 1993 the EC would truly be a 'single market'. The Council of Ministers asked the Commission to draw up a plan. The result was the Commission's White Paper of June 1985 which listed all the barriers that could be removed, set out the legislation necessary to remove them (there were recommendations for over 300 changes), and proposed a timetable for it all to happen. All the member states worked to implement this plan. It was facilitated by the passing of the Single European Act by each of the member states in order to come into force on 1 July 1987. What this did was to amend the original Treaty of Rome in a number of ways, the most significant being to introduce majority voting in respect of single market policies to speed things up and make it more difficult for one country to drag its feet.

Everyone was committed to strive for as much change in the direction of the single market as possible by the end of 1992, and a great deal of progress was made. However, some problems to do with crime, drugs, terrorism, etc. could not be solved and barriers will still be needed for some time. There are also technical differences that will just have to remain (such as right-hand and left-hand drive cars in different parts of Europe). But many changes have been made, and we will see what all the effects will be.

What is certain is that the Single Market is a major challenge for British business, with both big opportunities and big dangers, just as is the case for every other country. There are opportunities to expand and sell more goods and services to continental Europe, but only if our goods are competitive. By the same token, goods from the rest of the EU are easier to sell in Britain, and if French and German or Italian goods are cheaper and better they will sell and put British firms out of business or else be taken over by European firms. The removal of frontier restrictions on people has increased mobility for workers seeking employment and also enhanced prospects for tourism.

The Maastricht and Amsterdam Treaties

Once the single market programme was under way, the leaders of Europe began to consider the next steps. It was felt by many that all the 1992 measures still fell short of a genuine single market. What was really needed was to have the same currency operating in the market,. This would cut out all the costs of changing money from one currency to another, reduce the risks to businesses having to deal in fluctuating currencies, and make it easier for consumers to compare prices and get the best deals for goods and services. This in turn implied co-ordinating economic policy and interest rates with a European central bank to administer it. In addition, there could be a common citizenship, with everyone enjoying the same basic civil rights; common employment rights for all workers; institutional reform with more majority voting in the Council of Ministers and more powers for the European Parliament; moves towards a common European foreign policy, and perhaps even a common European security and defence capacity.

Was this pointing towards a 'United States of Europe' with a European government? Some people, especially in Britain and Denmark were hostile to such a development. Mrs Thatcher, especially, was bitterly opposed to any loss of British sovereignty (i.e. independence). However, other European governments were much more enthusiastic and agreed to conferences which negotiated the next steps, finally decided at Maastricht (in Holland) in December 1991.

By the time these decisions came about, Mrs Thatcher had lost office (partly as a result of her attitude to Europe) and been replaced by John Major, who was much less hostile to Europe and indeed insisted that he wanted Britain to be at the centre of European policy-making. Nevertheless, he was not an enthusiast for a United States of Europe, and besides, whatever he agreed had to be acceptable to his party in Parliament, which included many who supported Mrs Thatcher. What John Major did was to negotiate a series of opt-outs, so that Britain did not participate, or could withdraw from the main proposals.

By far the most important of these proposals was a progressive movement in timetabled stages towards a common European currency. Britain was allowed to opt out at a later stage of the process if it disagreed. The second most important agreement, known as the 'Social Chapter', was to allow legislation on common workers' rights (like union membership, minimum holidays, rights to be informed and consulted by employers, etc.) Britain alone was allowed to opt out of this altogether. The other agreements were often rather minor - the European Community became the European Union, there was to be a common format for passports, and some significant increases in the powers of the European Parliament.

The British opt-outs were seen as a triumph of John Major's diplomacy but the opposition to it among some of his own party was so strong that his government was nearly brought down before the treaty was ratified by Parliament. But the controversy was far from over. Part of the Maastricht agreement was that there would be another inter-governmental conference to discuss further changes. Britain participated, but before the conclusion of this process in 1997 there was a change in government with the arrival of Tony Blair as Prime Minister. Labour had been very critical of the increasingly 'eurosceptic' tone of the Conservative government and signalled that it would enter into a more co-operative and positive dialogue with its EU partners. Although it was happy to sign up to the Social Chapter, in fact the British negotiating position did not change much in essentials. However the Amsterdam Treaty which was agreed in June 1997 and came into effect in May 1999 was a very limited measure, reflecting the fact that a number of national governments, including the French and Germans, could not agree on significant institutional changes to the Commission and Council of Ministers.

Eleven EU states (with Greece likely to join them) have now linked their currencies and are progressing towards economic and monetary union with the adoption of the 'euro' as their single currency. Britain, along with Denmark and Sweden, will have to decide whether to join this group or stay outside with a limited ability to influence future developments. The Blair government has made it clear that it favours the single currency in principle, subject to the economic conditions being right and the British people giving their consent in a referendum after the next election.

The European Union and Leisure

The European Union influences leisure in a multitude of small ways although it has only limited direct interest in areas such as culture and tourism. Some of these will be discussed in more detail later. For the moment just a few examples will be sufficient to illustrate the wider impact of the EU on leisure.

In the first place, there are a number of EU bodies from which grants and loans may be obtained. These include the Regional Fund, the Social Fund and the European Coal and Steel Community. Most of these grants and loans are designed to aid areas of high unemployment. They have provided funds for leisure projects in various parts of the country. Many local authorities have European Liaison Officers with the specific task of gaining grants and loans from European sources.

Secondly, over the last few years the Common Agricultural Policy has been made more selective, so that farmers can no longer simply grow approved crops and automatically receive EU subsidies whether the food can be sold or not (which resulted in the food mountains and wine lakes for which the European Community used to be famous). Now subsidies are frozen if there is overproduction in some areas, and there are other instruments to limit production; while at the same time there are encouragements to put some land to non-agricultural use. This has led some farmers in Britain to look to other uses for some of their land and buildings, often leisure uses.

Finally, there is the case of Britain's polluted beaches. It has been known for some time that our beaches do not meet the standards of cleanliness laid down by European regulations. Despite promises of improvement, the European Commission lost patience and threatened to take Britain to the European Court over the matter. Since then there has been a good deal of progress. In 1994 some 80% of Britain's 457 designated beaches passed the minimum EU standard; although the 20% of failures included some of the most popular ones, such as Blackpool and Brighton. There are continuing plans to improve these, although one of the problems is the increases in the charges which Britain's privatised water companies have demanded in order to fund the necessary improvements, especially in sewage disposal. The EU has other standards for high quality beaches, which include visitor facilities. These must be achieved in order to be awarded the EU's prestigious Blue Flag.

Other International Organisations

Britain has many other international links and commitments which have important implications for leisure. The specialist UN agency UNESCO deals with many aspects of culture. The system of World Heritage Sites is operated by UNESCO. Britain was also a founding member in 1949 of the Council of Europe which now includes 41 states. Although best known for the protection of human rights, it plays an important role in culture, sport, promoting youth activities etc. It has produced legal conventions on such diverse topics as promoting youth exchanges through the 'au pair' system and group visits, preventing football hooliganism, and the protection of historic cities and archaeological sites.

At a more technical level, Britain takes part in the European Broadcasting Union (which among other achievements brings us the annual Eurovision Song Contest) and the many international conferences and conventions which help to regulate telecommunications and civil aviation. In a world where travel and tourism, communications and the media are becoming increasingly interdependent, national governments have to co-operate in order to manage these activities.

There is no doubt that as globalisation develops, more and more of the policies of central government, including leisure, will be influenced. But at the other end of the governmental scale, leisure is also an increasingly important factor in the world of local government.

Chapter 2

Local Government and Leisure

Local authorities (LAs) are the main providers of leisure services in the public sector. But the world of local government is very varied and complex, and has been changing rapidly. Before looking specifically at their contribution to leisure provision, it is necessary to understand something about the nature, function and working of local government in general.

The Role of Local Government

Local Government Services

Local government has an important role in the governmental process of this country. It has been responsible for many of the vital services needed to keep a modern community going, including police, fire service, education, social services, public housing, roads, rubbish collection, road maintenance, environmental health, libraries, public transport, planning, street paving and lighting, consumer protection, and many more.

These are the more important services that LAs are required to provide by law. All LAs are multi-purpose authorities, and each type of authority has a set of responsibilities that it must fulfil. For example, every county must provide a range of schools to cater for the primary and secondary educational needs of the people within its boundaries. Similarly, each district is responsible for the public housing needs of its area. To a large extent LAs are the agents of central government, carrying out the duties that central government lays on them through Parliament. But there is a certain amount of local discretion. It is the job of an LA to provide statutory services, but in addition to this, a number of Acts of Parliament make it possible for certain types of LAs to provide various services or not, as they wish; a county, for example can establish a museum, or it may set up a sports centre and coaching schemes for young people. Traditionally, if an LA wants to provide a service for which there is no obligatory or permissive legislation, then it may gain the legal right to provide it by promoting a private Act of Parliament, giving it alone the right to do this. But the Local Government Bill, being discussed in Parliament in July 2000, may give LAs more general powers to promote economic, social, and environmental well-being in their local communities.

Legal Basis

It should be clear from this that LAs can only do what the law allows them to do. If an LA tries to do something that the law has not specifically allowed it to do then it is acting illegally, even if everyone thinks it is a good idea. It can be taken to court for acting ultra vires (i.e. 'beyond its powers'). Furthermore, local authorities have their 'authority' conferred on them by law. They are 'creatures of statute', which means they have been set up by Act of Parliament and can just as easily be abolished in the same way. There was a comprehensive restructuring of local government by the 1972 Local Government Act; a later Act abolished the metropolitan counties in 1986, and in the 1990s we have seen further wholesale changes.

Central Control

Central government exercises a great deal of control over local government. It is central government that decides what LAs there will be and what services each type will provide. Even where an LA promotes a private Bill, this has little chance of being passed if the government does not like it. Although LAs have a certain amount of discretion in the running of services, they are in many cases supervised by central government inspectors (e.g. schools and fire brigades) or have to refer important decisions to the minister (e.g. in planning matters) or are otherwise subject to government directives, or else are given advice that is hard to ignore. In some circumstances where an LA is deemed not to be fulfilling its statutory duties, central government has powers to take over an LA and run it through commissioners.

The most important means of central government control is financial. Around 80% of local government expenditure is now paid for by central grants (in the mid-1980s it was about 65%) by means of which the government is in a strong position to influence spending decisions, and persuade LAs to fall in with its economic policy. However, central government does not always have things its own way. In the 1980s, some authorities refused to make the cuts in expenditure the government had demanded. They financed their extra expenditure through high rate (local property tax) increases. The government responded by giving itself extra powers to penalise a high spending LA by reducing its grant, and to 'cap' (i.e. put a legal limit on what rates a particular LA can charge). Because of this, the degree of local independence has been greatly reduced.

Local Democracy

Many people believe that central government control is going much too far. They argue that unless LAs are left with some independence there is no point in having local government at all, and we might as well have all services provided by central government through local offices. Some feel this might be more efficient. On the other hand, it can equally be argued that central government would, if it really had to do everything, be so overburdened with work that the system would grind to a halt. Furthermore, local politicians and officials are much closer to the particular needs and priorities of their communities which do vary; and they inevitably have a stronger commitment and incentive to provide the best service for their locality. Local people in charge of a range of services also makes for more efficient co-ordination: in education and social services, for example, or planning and housing. Responding to local demand for services has enabled individual LAs in the past to pioneer new services and ways of doing things that have subsequently been taken up by the rest of the country. Recent examples of this include family planning, housing advice centres and consumer protection. However, it is the democratic element of local government that many people see as its most valuable feature.

Local government, like central government, is based on the combination of elected, and therefore democratically accountable, politicians who make policy, and permanent, professional officials who are there to advise them and put their decisions into effect. The important thing is that local government is not just part of the administrative process (i.e. running things and providing services), but is also part of the democratic process. It is part of our democratic system, the system by which all of us can participate in the running of the country's affairs. However, this democratic picture has been threatened by a combination of voter apathy and central government encroachment. In most local elections far fewer than half of those entitled to vote choose to do so; in May 1999 only 30% of the electorate bothered, and in some urban areas it was below 20%. Even the first direct election for Mayor of London (May 2000), which had enjoyed unprecedented media coverage for a year with high profile candidates such as Ken Livingstone, only produced a 34% turnout. And the model of local government allowing all of us to have a say in how many of the very important services which affect our daily lives are run - by electing local politicians with policies to implement, to deal with our complaints, and account to us for all that they do - has also been threatened by central government imposed changes. This is what is often described as the move from local 'government' to local 'governance'. This is not just an obscure change of terminology but expresses the idea of a shift from directly elected bodies with democratic accountability and direct responsibility for the execution of their functions to a much fuzzier picture. LAs which historically had a big stake in utilities such as water and gas, or health care provisions such as hospitals, have seen these taken away, in some cases right out of the public sector. More recently some activities, such as police, have been moved away to authorities made up of nominated local councillors and other central appointees; waste regulation has gone to the Environment Agency quango; education has been increasingly subject to a regime of national control and the powers of councils as local education authorities have been reduced. Services which remain may be contracted out to the private sector, or only retained 'in house' subject to competitive tendering. When the local democratic system is progressively shrunk then there seems increasingly little point in electing local representatives. Yet without genuine local government we are a less democratic country and our rights as citizens are diminished.

The Structure and Functions of Local Government

History

The continuous history of local government in Britain goes back to Anglo-Saxon times. But local government as we know it today - that is, with democratically-elected, multi-purpose councils - was a creation of the closing decades of the nineteenth century. The structure created then was extremely successful and over the next fifty years LAs were given more and more functions to perform. But by the end of the Second World War it was realised that the system was out of date and needed to be remodelled. It was twenty years before the first real steps were taken, and these were confined to London. Here a new set of London Boroughs were created, much larger than the old ones and taking in all the new suburbs that had grown up outside the old boundary. Each borough became responsible for all the direct services to the public, such as housing and social services, etc. Those services which did not involve directly dealing with people, and which needed to see London as a whole, such as planning and transport, were given to a new authority, the Greater London Council (GLC).

Creating the Present Structure

The reform of the rest of the system took even longer because there was no consensus of opinion about what the new system should look like. Eventually a new system was created by the Local Government Act of 1972, which gave us new local government boundaries with far fewer councils covering larger populations, and new local authorities with a new division of responsibilities. In the first place, a small number of areas were given special treatment because they were exceptionally large urban areas or 'conurbations'. They were designated 'metropolitan areas' and given a system like that in London, with a metropolitan county authority responsible for transport and planning, police and fire brigade; while metropolitan district councils were made responsible for personal services, such as social services, education, housing and most of the rest. There were five metropolitan areas: West Midlands (around Birmingham), Merseyside (around Liverpool), Greater

Manchester, South Yorkshire (around Sheffield), West Yorkshire (Leeds-Bradford) and Tyne and Wear (Newcastle-Sunderland).

For the rest of England and Wales there was also a 'two-tier' system with reorganised 'shire' county councils and district councils. Here the split of responsibilities was more complicated. The counties were given the same responsibilities as the metropolitan counties, plus a good deal more. Education, social services, libraries and a number of other things went to the counties; while the district authorities were given the one major responsibility of housing and a number of minor ones such as public health, local planning, street lighting, etc. Finally, there are parish councils responsible for local amenities in rural areas, while in urban areas communities can opt to set up a community town council if they wish. At the same time a new system was created for Scotland. Most of the country was given a two-tier system with functions divided between nine regional councils and fifty-three regional ones, plus three Island councils combining both levels.

This new local government system lasted only twelve years before significant modification. In 1986 the Conservative government abolished the GLC and the five metropolitan counties and transferred their responsibilities to joint committees of the boroughs in London and the districts in the metropolitan areas. There was a good deal of opposition to this move, including some from within the Conservative party, especially in defence of the GLC, but the government insisted that these councils did not have enough to do and were therefore unnecessary. The government abolished the Scottish regional councils in 1996 and transferred their functions to 32 district councils, and in Wales the system was 'rationalised' into one of 22 unitary councils.

The Conservative government also had a clear preference for abolishing the two-tier system in England, but never quite managed to do so in the 'shire' counties. In 1992 it created the Local Government Commission, charged with examining structures and boundaries, consulting widely to see what local people want, and making recommendations for change on a piecemeal, area by area, basis. The rationale was that different solutions will be appropriate in different places. The Commission is therefore free to recommend for any given area that all services be provided by the county or by districts or by a combination of the two, although where they have recommended retaining a two-tier system in one or two places the government asked it to think again. So politically the government made the mistake of initially handing over restructuring to an independent commission which discovered in its consultations that there was quite a lot of support in many areas for the existing system. The consequence has been that no uniform scheme has been adopted and the structure of LAs varies in different parts of the country. In some parts (such as Berkshire) the county council has disappeared, while many other counties have been retained, but sometimes as with Durham a district like Darlington has been carved out of its territory and given unitary status.

The impetus over this type of restructuring slowed with the election of the Labour government in 1997 with a new reform agenda. Partly because the Labour party was so strongly represented in local government it looked for a way of strengthening and raising the profile of local institutions. Several white papers were published: *Modern Local Government: In Touch with the People* (Cm.4014, July 1998), *Modern Local Government in Wales* (Cm.4028, July 1998) and *New Leadership for London* (Cm.3724, July 1997). These developed a view about reforming structures of political leadership and accountability within LAs in order to give them a higher, popular profile which could encourage a greater level of public knowledge and participation. The 1997 Labour manifesto also demonstrated an interest in adding some sort of much larger regional institutions in England for purposes of strategic planning, especially in London. Some of this has overlapped with the wider issues of devolution within the UK, and the possible regionalisation of England.

Regionalism in England

The idea of regionalism, that is establishing institutions between the traditional structures of local government and the central state, can be approached from a variety of directions and has several different aspects:

1.   A desire to divide up some of the powers and functions of the central state and put them under the control of democratic regional institutions which represent the views of a distinctive regional community. This is the same type of argument which has led to devolution in Scotland and Wales.

2.   A scheme for co-ordinating various central government activities at the regional level, providing for more effective action based upon wider consultation with local groups, economic interests, and institutions, and with some greater freedom of decision for local representatives of the centre. It is worth noting that a number of government departments, such as Environment, Transport & Regions (DETR), Trade and Industry (DTI), and Agriculture (MAFF) have had for many years regional offices staffed by national civil servants to administer policies at the local level.

3.   A belief that the traditional structure of local government does not provide units large enough to effectively carry on certain desirable activities. These might include planning of transport systems (both the networks and services), big economic regeneration schemes involving

the promotion of inward investment from large multinational companies, or supporting a regional symphony orchestra. These are all likely to be beyond the resources of a county council, and in any case these activities would spill over a much bigger area and require the active co-operation of a number of LAs.

4.   As part of an on-going rationalisation of elected local government, in which, for example, big regions would represent the upper tier and either the existing counties or districts should be eliminated to leave one lower level set of LAs.

5.   A view that following Scottish and Welsh devolution it is only fair that English regions be given greater autonomy and capacity to manage their own affairs. This view is particularly strongly held in the North of England where worries about being able to compete with better financed Scottish schemes of economic development are often expressed by local government, business and trade union leaders.

6.   A recognition that there are special arguments relating to London. The abolition of the GLC in 1986 left the local government of the capital city, itself an enormous urban sprawl, in the hands of a patchwork of separate LAs, joint boards and nominated bodies. These have failed to deal with many of the major strategic planning decisions required to run such a conurbation.

In practice, the various aspects and approaches are often combined in many of the arguments which are encountered by advocates of regionalism. It is also often common to make comparisons with the successful development of elected regional institutions in such formerly highly centralised countries as France or Spain, or the flourishing Federal Republic of Germany.

The London anomaly has been most rapidly tackled since 1997, although not without producing significant political embarrassment for Labour over the controversies surrounding the nomination of a mayoral candidate. Following a positive response (72%) in a local referendum in May 1998, the Greater London Authority Act 1999 established a directly elected mayor and 25 member assembly. Elections were held in May 2000, with a victory for the independent (dissident Labour) Ken Livingstone, former Labour leader of the GLC. The potential areas of policy where the GLA may play a role include transport, strategic planning, economic development, environment, policing, culture, media and sport, and fire and emergency services. Many of the activities of the new GLA are at a very early stage of initiation, and the relationship between the Mayor, the Assembly, and central government departments such as the Treasury, DETR, Home Office, Culture (DCMS) and others remains to be worked out.

Elsewhere in England the 1997 Labour manifesto proposed Regional Development Agencies (RDA) to promote economic development, and a system of Regional Chambers to co-ordinate activities such as EU funding, and transport. It would legislate to allow local referendums for people to choose whether they would like elected regional institutions. But the Regional Development Agencies Act 1998 has delivered only part of these promises, in spite of complaints from MPs and councillors in the normally loyal Labour 'heartlands', especially the north east. Eight RDAs came in to being in 1999; they are created and financed from Whitehall. While their members (mostly from business and LAs) come from the region, they are appointed by the minister in London. The eight Regional Chambers have been instituted on a voluntary basis, made up of nominated members (a maximum of 70% from LAs, the rest from local trade unions, business, education, business etc.) They have the right to be consulted when RDAs draw up their plans, but no right to make decisions. They have no source of finance apart from relatively small local contributions (mostly from LAs) and are essentially only talking shops. The government has taken the view that there is a limited demand for such new institutions in England, and so has devised a limited scheme which incorporates some of the aspects described above under numbers 2, 3, and 5. But there is evidence that this will not satisfy some areas of the country. In the North East an opinion poll (MORI, March 1999) came down 50% in favour of a directly elected assembly with only 27% against. A cross-party North East Constitutional Convention, representing many regional groups and institutions, has been established to draw up plans for a more ambitious approach. So there may well be further developments.

Local Government Today

Thus the programme of changes is incomplete, and the overall LA picture in England has become confusing. Two things need to be remembered. (1) There are different arrangements, depending whether one is in London, or in a 'metropolitan' or 'shire' or 'unitary' area of the country. (2) Terms such as 'city' and 'borough' (based upon the possession of a royal charter) are essentially only of historic and ceremonial significance but tell one nothing about modern powers and functions. The City of Sunderland is a metropolitan district council, as is the Borough of Gateshead, while the City of Durham is a district in County Durham as is Wear Valley District Council, while Darlington Borough Council is a new unitary authority.

We can summarise the present structure of local government in July 2000 as follows:

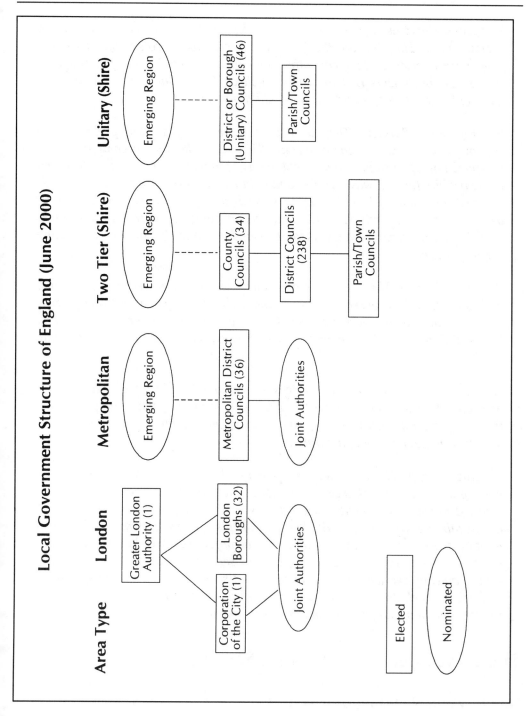

Local Government Structure of England (June 2000)

Types of Services

Local government provides a great range of services, which may be broadly classified in the following way:

Protective Services *These services are designed to protect the public in various ways. They include the fire service; consumer protection; protection from animal diseases that can affect humans; the regulation of a range of trades, establishments and activities, such as taxis, money lending, private nursing homes, theatres and cinemas, child-minders, etc.*

Environmental Services *The purpose of these services is to preserve and improve the physical environment. They include the planning system (preparation of structure and local plans, planning permission, etc.) and responsibility for highways, traffic and public transport. Also included are the various environmental health services, such as refuse collection, control of pests, safety of premises, noise and smoke control, control of nuisances associated with certain trades, insanitary and overcrowded premises, building regulations, etc.*

Personal Services *These services are concerned with the welfare of citizens, and include all levels of primary and secondary education, the career services, the various personal social services (social workers, home helps, residential homes, day centres, foster homes, etc.) and various housing services.*

Amenity Services *These are services which aim to make the area a more pleasant, desirable place to live in. They include most of the leisure services, including public parks and gardens, swimming baths and other sports facilities, museums, civic theatres, etc.*

Trading Services *These are services which aim to at least cover their costs by making a commercial charge that is not related to people's ability to pay (in contrast to such as council house rents, school meals, bus fares, etc., which are usually heavily subsidised). Services of this type range from markets and allotments to exhibition centres and civic airports. Most trading services also come under one of the other categories of services, and this is particularly true of amenity services. It is an overlap that seems likely to increase as local authorities seek to develop their amenities in the interests of attracting tourists and other kinds of economic development.*

The Development of Leisure Services

Statutory and Non-statutory Services

Leisure services and leisure-related functions are distributed in different ways among the various kinds of local authority. County councils have statutory obligations in three main areas. One is planning, where there are responsibilities for strategic planning and land use. There are additional responsibilities if part of a

National Park or Area of Outstanding Natural Beauty falls within the county's boundary. The other areas of statutory obligation are the provision of library services and education. Education is not primarily a leisure service, but is connected in several important respects: there are adult classes in colleges; there is education in terms of arts, sport, etc; and there is the use of educational facilities, such as playing fields, halls, etc., for general sporting and cultural use. District councils also have some statutory obligations (in respect of listed buildings, for example) though not as much as the counties. Unitary councils combine the obligations of counties and districts.

Most other leisure and leisure-related functions are of a permissive nature. They may also be provided by district, county, and unitary LAs. This is true of museums and art galleries, sport and recreation facilities, parks and gardens and the promotion of tourism. In some cases local authorities have promoted a Private Bill in order to provide a service not covered by existing legislation.

Evolution of Leisure Services

There is a long tradition of providing leisure amenities by local authorities. For more than a hundred years local councils have been adding to the public amenities of their towns with parks and gardens, promenades and play grounds, museums and galleries, bandstands and concert halls, and many of these in regular use today go back to the nineteenth century. Public baths, originally associated with municipal bath houses built in the interests of public health, have also long been provided in many areas. Most other sporting facilities were a later development, such as bowling greens, tennis courts, golf courses. Changes in popular taste in recent years have led to the opening of council sports centres, squash courts, skating rinks and ski slopes. These also reflect a greater affluence and the growing availability and importance of leisure in people's lives.

The greater importance of leisure for individuals is reflected in the growing importance of leisure in the economy. The shift in peoples' habits combined with the shift from a manufacturing-based economy to a service-based economy all serve to increase the economic importance of leisure. This means that leisure is becoming an increasingly important source of employment and prosperity. Thus, we see in areas where traditional industries have declined a much greater emphasis on activities to attract people in their leisure time and attract visitors to the area. Local government has played a major role in this: in the provision of modern facilities, in the promotion of tourism, in the encouragement of groups through grants and availability of premises, in support for museums, exhibitions, arts festivals, development of local places of interest, sports events, agricultural shows, garden festivals and in a host of other ways. Leisure has, therefore, become an increasingly important part of local government.

Reasons for Further Development

Despite Conservative government pressure on local government to cut expenditure, privatise and concentrate on essentials, local authorities continued to develop leisure services as much as they were able. There are several reasons for this:

1. Leisure services improve the quality of life for local people.

2. New services and facilities create employment and assist the local economy.

3. Improved amenities and new attractions help to encourage tourism.

4. Improved quality of life helps to attract business to the area. An attractive environment with good amenities is a factor in the choice of sites for factories and for business executives to live.

5. Large projects raise the profile and enhance the reputation of an area, which helps in attracting tourists and business.

6. Leisure is an area relatively free from the tight central government control that is exercised over statutory services. It gives councillors and officers greater scope for innovation and initiative.

7. Money may be available for leisure projects from outside the normally constrained sources of local government finance. Bodies such as the European Commission, tourist boards, the Countryside Agency, the Sports Council and others, all have funds available to assist approved schemes. Money may also be available from the private sector for joint projects.

8. Within the local government service there is a growing number of leisure specialists who seek to develop a comprehensive leisure service.

A good illustration of many of these points is the Riverside project in Chester-le-Street, County Durham. In 1992 Durham was elected a First Class cricket county, and began to play in the County Championship in 1993. This new status was the stimulus for a scheme to build a new county cricket ground in Chester-le-Street on a large park site on the banks of the River Wear which was called the Riverside project. The scheme includes the new ground itself and a large sports complex, together with housing, a city park, and a wildlife reservation. Chester-le-Street District Council and Durham County Council worked closely on the project, particularly on a successful bid for European funding. European Union money covered about 45% of the £6 million cost of the first phase, with half of the rest coming from the County Cricket Club, backed by commercial sponsors; but there have also been grants of £40,000 and £50,000 from the Sports Council. The remainder has largely come from the LAs, with Chester-le-Street providing the original site. The new ground, which is the first phase of the project, was ready for the 1995 cricket season, and in 1999 and 2000 the English Cricket Board awarded limited-over international matches to be played at the ground. So while local sports fans could be gratified by the opportunity to see not only their local team playing in the county championship (and be promoted to the first division for the 2000 season) they could also see international matches involving England, West Indies, Australia, Pakistan and Zimbabwe. The town, county and indeed North East region achieved substantial national and international media exposure, especially through the televising of matches.

On the other hand, in some cases there may be conflicts between improving the quality of life and encouraging economic development. For example, a major project, such as the building of a major leisure complex, may require a site that is presently an amenity for the local people. They may band together to fight the project, believing that protecting a local beauty spot is more important than new jobs. The Chester-le-Street project faced some protest over the loss of a much loved and much used local amenity area of open space. Another problem may be that new projects may bring in outsiders to do the important work, while local people are left with a few menial jobs.

However, despite problems of this kind, it is likely that leisure services will continue to be an expanding sector of local government for as long as the political and financial climate will allow. There are limits, through the constraints on local spending imposed by 'capping' local taxes and other government measures; the requirements on authorities to put leisure services out to competitive tendering to obtain best value; and Treasury restrictions on capital expenditure. But it is clear that the 1997 Labour government is cautiously positive, especially where its priorities such as 'social inclusion' and preferred methods of public-private partnerships are clearly identified.

Inner City Regeneration

One area of local government to see a future expansion of leisure facilities is in the run-down inner city areas, given priority by the Conservative Government since the 1980s and carried on even more strongly by Labour since 1997. It is recognised that improving leisure facilities can be a significant factor in bringing life back to areas of this kind. The Department of the Environment study *Developing Sport and Leisure: Good Practice in Urban Regeneration* (1989) stated:

"Sport and leisure might, at first sight, appear to be unlikely contributors to the process of regeneration. Leisure, after all, is often regarded as the 'icing on the cake', part of the product of affluence, rather than its producer.

However, as the projects discussed in this report show, sport and leisure have a positive part to play in many aspects of urban regeneration. These include:

- The upgrading and re-use of derelict land and buildings.

- The conversion of premises from redundant previous uses.

- Visual and environmental improvements.

- Contributing to the quality of life of individual residents and of urban communities as a whole, including underprivileged groups, through the provision of local facilities and opportunities for their enjoyment and well-being.

- The generation of local employment opportunities and revenue.

- The generation of community cohesion and community spirit.

- The development of tourism potential." (P.1)

The report went on to describe a variety of examples of good practice and imaginative innovation that others might follow. Various grants are available to help urban renewal, usually requiring matching funding from the local authority or other sources. Under Labour, following the Social Exclusion Unit (part of the Cabinet Office) report *Bringing Britain together: a national strategy for neighbourhood renewal*, the Department of Culture led an interdepartmental 'Action Team' which looked at the contribution of arts and sports to neighbourhood renewal, and produced a report showing the valuable contribution that could be made through lowering long-term unemployment, crime, health problems, and in providing opportunities to acquire better qualifications. LAs have been able to apply to participate in the New Deal for Communities programme, led by the DETR with input from DCMS.

Councillors, Officers and Committees

Politicians and Officials

Democratic government in Britain, at both national and local level, consists of policy and decision-making being in the hands of elected representatives, with a body of non-elected officials to put the policies and individual decisions into effect. The elected representatives may come and go and may not necessarily be knowledgeable about the work of the council departments they are responsible for, whereas the departmental officials have expertise and are permanent. Nevertheless, it is the elected politicians who are in charge. Officials advise them, but in the end it is the duty of officials to carry out whatever the representatives decide upon, to the best of their ability. This system is designed to produce an effective combination of democratic accountability and expert knowledge.

In this area, as in so many others, there are very recent changes starting to work their way through the internal structures of LAs. Traditionally there were some differences between national and local level. In Whitehall, Ministers and MPs are full-time professional politicians, while local councillors do not have salaries and are normally part-time politicians. On the other hand, Cabinet Ministers, on average, hold a given post for about two years, in contrast to councillors who may be on the same committee (and perhaps be chairman) for a great many years. This touches on another difference. National government is run by the Cabinet, a team of ministers belonging to the same party, each responsible for the policies of a department, whereas at local level, policies and decisions have been the task of a committee (reporting to the full council) which will contain councillors in appropriate proportions from different parties. Thus, 'opposition' parties participate in local government decision-making in a way they do not in national government. There are also differences between officers at different levels. Top civil servants are 'generalists', which means that their education and training will have been of a general intellectual kind and not directed towards one particular area of policy, and this enables them to move from department to department during their career. But the tradition in local government is different in this respect, in that senior officers will usually have made their career in one particular field, such as housing or social services.

These important differences apart, the relationship between elected politicians and permanent officials was much the same nationally and locally, both in theory and in practice. At both levels the theory is simply that the elected representatives make the decisions and the officials carry them out. But nationally and locally, practice is more complicated than this, and for much the same reasons. It is the duty of senior officials to advise their political masters and such is their experience and expert knowledge that such advice is very difficult to ignore. Officials must also prepare information on which decisions have to be made, and the way such information is presented will tend to reflect the officials' own view of the best course of action. The way policies are put into effect will also tend to reflect these views. Consequently, senior officials inevitably have an influence on policy and on particular decisions, and the line between policy or decision making and administration is difficult to draw.

In the second half of the twentieth century, largely due to the increasing professionalisation of local government, there was much more delegation to officials than in the past. However, there was no single pattern for all LAs. The degree of delegation and officer influence will vary from authority to authority and from committee to committee because of a number of factors. These factors included the traditions of the authority or committee; the issues involved (e.g. officials tend to have more influence in relation to decisions that are technical rather than those involving members of the public); the personalities of the officers and councillors concerned; and also the party balance. It is thought that officials generally had more influence in non-party LAs, than in party controlled ones where councillors have been elected with a definite line of policy already having been decided upon. They are also said to have more influence where no party has an overall majority, i.e. a 'hung council'. But although local government officers worked closely with councillors (especially committee chairmen and vice-chairmen) and had influence, in the end they have a duty to carry out the councillors wishes, whether they think them wise or not.

Party Politics

The influence of officials is to some extent offset by the influence of political parties. Their role in local government has steadily increased over the last forty years, so that today there are few councils not dominated by parties. Some people feel that this is a bad thing, that councillors should deal with local problems on their merit, and not follow the party line. They also feel people should vote in the same way. It is certainly true that the minority of the electorate who do vote in local elections tend to be influenced by how the parties happen to be doing nationally rather than by distinctly local issues. On the other hand, a council dominated by a majority party will have a definite programme and sense of direction, and voters do have a clearer idea of what kind of policies will be pursued if a given party is elected. Councillors stand for election every four years. Some councils are elected one third at a time so that there are partial elections three years out of every four, but most councils have all their councillors elected at the same time. Local elections always take place on a particular Thursday in May.

Committees

Traditionally, most of the important work of the local authority, where policies are given detailed form and major decisions are made, is in committees. It is here that the day-to-day decision-making takes place and where councillors and officials work together. It used to be the case that there was one committee for every department, that every committee was an independent entity responsible for the work of an equally self-sufficient department and paying little attention to what other parts of the authority were doing. Consequently, there was a marked lack of co-ordination and a great deal of duplication and inefficiency. Some authorities introduced new ways of doing things in the late 1960s. But it was the big reorganisation of 1974 that gave the opportunity for a radical change of practices. With the new system in prospect an inquiry was set up into the most efficient means of managing the new local authorities. This produced the Bains Report of 1972, which reflected the way that some of the more progressive authorities had already been going.

Corporate Management

In particular, the report advocated what was known as the 'corporate approach'. What Bains did was to apply to local government the ideas and techniques of corporate management to be found in big industry (one of the members of the committee was a senior ICI executive, but might equally have been from any other large corporation). The essence of this new corporate approach was seeing all the Las' services as a co-ordinated whole and subject to an overall plan, instead of as a collection of departments, each responsible for a separate service. The corporate approach underlies all of Bains's specific recommendations.

A new committee structure was suggested. In the first place committees should be based on 'programme areas'. That is, having fewer committees, with each covering a group of related departments to facilitate co-ordination. Furthermore, each LA should have a Policy and Resources Committee (P&RC), to be responsible for overall planning and co-ordination, and to control the LAs major resources - finance, manpower, land and buildings - each with its own sub-committee of the P&RC. The P&RC's control of resources gives it the power to supervise and co-ordinate the work of the other committees and integrate their work into an overall plan. A fourth sub-committee of the P&RC, the Policy Review Sub-committee, would have the task of monitoring the work of the programme area committees in relation to overall planning objectives.

Bains also advocated the appointment by each LA of a Chief Executive Officer (CEO) as senior manager and head of the local service. The CEO should be without departmental responsibilities, and should supervise and co-ordinate the work of the other chief officers. The management team of chief officers, led by the CEO, should ensure that the corporate approach prevails. It is important to realise that this approach is not just a form of organisation but is equally an attitude of mind. It is everyone seeing their work as related to everyone else's, as part of a greater whole. A housing manager, for example, when making decisions, must bear in mind their likely effects on other departments. The corporate approach lies behind all the Bains proposals. The P&RC is the chief instrument of centralised direction and planning. The CEO, through his management team, ensures the corporate approach is put into practice. Programme area committees each co-ordinate several departments and makes sure that their plans are integrated. The plans of these committees are in turn integrated into the LA's total plan, drawn up by the P&RC, which plans the development of all the local authority's services, sets objectives and supervises their implementation. If everyone has a part to play in the overall plan, then there is a criteria for measuring how each department is making its contribution; how efficient it is. This is monitored by the Performance Review Sub-committee.

Local Examples

As to what programme area committees there should be, Bains insisted that there was no single pattern for all LAs of the same type. But the committee structure of Durham County Council, Durham City District Council and Sunderland Metropolitan District Council were each fairly typical of their respective type. Each had a Policy and Resources Committee (called the 'Management Committee' in Sunderland) and sub-committees more or less in the Bains manner, and then a set of subordinate programme area committees reflecting their differing range of responsibilities. Thus Durham County's programme area committees were: Education; Arts, Libraries & Museums; Social Services; Public Protection; Environment, Contract Services; and Police. Durham City had the following programme area committees: Environment, Health and Transportation, Development Services, Amenities and Leisure, and Housing Services. Sunderland had the following committees: Leisure, Social Services, Housing and Estates, Education, Environment, and Public Health.

It is interesting, from our point of view, to consider the place of leisure in these structures. Both Sunderland and Durham City had Leisure committees of one kind or another, while Durham County did not. As a county, Durham County Council does not have the range of amenities, such as playing fields, public baths, leisure centres, halls and theatres and the like, that can form the core of a leisure department in the way that a district has. In consequence, leisure services tend to be divided up among several departments: museums, libraries and the arts have their own committee; while countryside conservation, recreation, planning and tourism come under several departments responsible to the Environment Committee. Thus in the case of museums, a section of the Education Department is responsible for the Bowes Museum at Barnard Castle and the Durham Light Infantry Museum in Durham City; the museum of lead mining at Killhope Wheel, on the other hand, is the responsibility of the planning department, while the Beamish Folk Museum is the joint responsibility of Durham County and a number of neighbouring LAs.

Transforming Political Leadership

The whole way in which elected councillors work within LAs is now in the middle of a dramatic set of changes. These were explained in several white papers published by the Labour government: *Modern Local Government: In Touch with the People* (Cm.4014, July 1998), *Modern Local Government in Wales* (Cm.4028, July 1998) and *New Leadership for London* (Cm.3724, July 1997). These argue in favour of strengthening and raising the profile of local institutions by reforming structures of political leadership and accountability within LAs in order to give them a higher popular profile, which could encourage a greater level of public knowledge and participation. The old style committee system was seen as slow and cumbersome, wasting the time of elected councillors on trivial administrative matters which could be better dealt with by officials. The whole system of political leadership and accountability was considered to be confusing to the public, who could not identify those who should be articulating policies and taking responsibility for their implementation. The fact that policy-making was normally made within the controlling party group, but then had to be formally decided in a series of specialist committees and the full council, was seen as obscuring the true nature of the process.

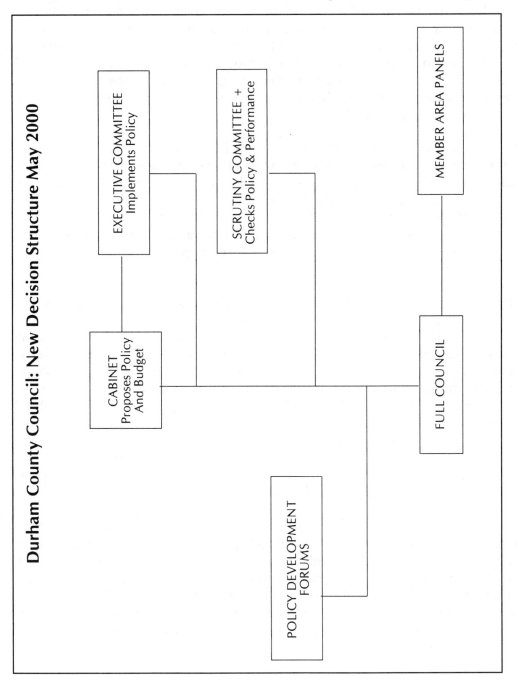

Durham County Council: New Decision Structure May 2000

EXECUTIVE COMMITTEE
Implements Policy

SCRUTINY COMMITTEE +
Checks Policy & Performance

MEMBER AREA PANELS

CABINET
Proposes Policy
And Budget

FULL COUNCIL

POLICY DEVELOPMENT
FORUMS

So the white paper, and the Local Government Bill (which in July 2000 is still being considered by Parliament) lays out a different approach. This is based on establishing a clear political executive within each LA. There will be three models to choose from: (1) a directly-elected mayor, operating with an executive made up of from 2-10 councillors; (2) a directly-elected mayor, operating with a professional council manager; (3) a council leader, elected by the council, operating with an executive made up of from 2-10 councillors. There would be a local referendum to decide whether to move to an elected mayor system. There would be separate 'overview' and 'scrutiny' committees to keep a check on the executive, whichever particular system is adopted. The 'strong mayor' options borrow characteristics of local government which are quite familiar in many parts of the USA and for example, France in continental Europe, but will represent a major change in local political practice in Britain.

The necessary legislation for mayoral elections has so far only been implemented with respect to the Greater London Authority. However, many LAs have already made changes ahead of the legislation, essentially to move to the third option, either as a transitional measure or as being closest to their preferred option. This has had dramatic effects. Durham County Council for example, an authority with a single party majority, at a meeting on 3 May 2000 adopted a radical new structure. The old committee system described above has been swept away and replaced with something like this, as follows.

There is now a 10 person 'Cabinet' which meets every two weeks, to consider major strategic and policy issues. It is made up of ten Labour councillors including the Leader and Deputy Leader of the Council. These 10, along with Liberal Democrat, Conservative and Independent councillors, sit on a 13 member Executive Committee which is empowered to take decisions. Many other decisions, which used to be made within the old specialist committees, are now being delegated to senior permanent officials. There is an all-party Scrutiny Committee and three Scrutiny Groups at which Cabinet members and officials can be questioned. There will also be all-party 'policy development forums' which can make recommendations to the Cabinet. The full council will continue to set the budget and will in some sense oversee the cabinet. Ordinary councillors will also sit in groups of 3-6 members on newly instituted territorially defined 'Area Panels' to consider local problems and to hold meetings with representatives of local community groups and organisations. Councillors will have small personal budgets of about £6,000 per year to spend on their area. Since all this is new it is difficult to know how it will operate in practice. In many respects, in streamlining procedures and concentrating powers in the hands of leading councillors and officials, it may only be recognising the reality of much existing practice. Whether it actually represents an improvement which will increase public knowledge and accountability remains open to question. Unkind critics may suggest that it reflects the sort of 'presidentialisation' which has already taken place nationally within No 10 Downing Street.

Planning and Pressure Groups

One of local government's key responsibilities, and one which bears upon leisure in a number of ways, is planning. A Comprehensive planning system was introduced in this country by the Town and Country Planning Act of 1947. We still use the same basic system with only minor modifications, although present planning law is mainly based on the Local Government and Planning Act of 1971.

Planning is basically about controlling changes in land-use. It may involve large scale change, such as proposals to build a factory or a housing estate on what is now farming land; or smaller scale development, such as turning a house into a workshop, or extending a home so that a former garden becomes a garage. All such changes require planning permission.

Planning Authorities

Planning permissions are granted by local authorities of certain kinds. In metropolitan areas it is the districts (usually called 'boroughs'), while in the rest of the country responsibility is either shared between county and district, or taken by a unitary district. Decisions over mining and quarrying and over waste disposal sites, for example, in a two-tier area, are dealt with by the county council, whereas the districts deal with most of the rest. However, there is an appeals system, and all appeals are finally decided by the Secretary of State for the Environment. This means that the system is ultimately controlled by central government.

Local Plans

In dealing with planning applications LAs are guided by a number of policies and considerations. The most basic of these are local development plans, which come in two forms. First of all there is the County Structure Plan, which every county is required by law to draw up. This involves extensive public consultation, but the result has to be approved by the Secretary of State for the Environment. It sets out the broad policy for land-use in the county, showing which areas are suitable for industrial development, which for housing, amenity and so on. Once approved, these plans embody local land-use policy so that, for example, it becomes very difficult to gain approval for a factory development in an area marked out for amenity. In addition to Structure Plans there are Local Plans. These cover a much smaller area - a district, or more usually a town - though in more detail. They may deal with all aspects of planning or just one: mineral extraction or a city-centre redevelopment. Again there is public consultation and ministerial approval, but such plans are not required by law (except in Scotland).

Where appropriate, these plans embody various national policies which also guide the planning process. They include National Parks and Areas of Outstanding Natural Beauty (AONB); Green Belts; scheduled monuments, listed buildings and conservation areas; tree preservation and control of advertising hoardings. If the land of a National Park or AONB falls within a county, then Structure Plans, and where appropriate, Local Plans, must take these into account. In North Yorkshire, for example, planners have a responsibility to protect two National Parks, the Dales and the North York Moors, as well as a number of AONBs. In such areas most kinds of development are considered 'unsuitable' and planning permission is extremely difficult to obtain. Much the same is true of green belts. These are different in that they are decided upon locally, although with ministerial approval. Land designated green belt is supposed to remain so in perpetuity. However, there may be loopholes which a developer can exploit if a minister is sympathetic. It is, for example, possible to interpret 'unsuitable development' in different ways. Then there are certain types of site that are normally exempt from usual planning controls, such as pre-existing quarry sites. An example in the 1980s was a Secretary of State for the Environment, Nicholas Ridley, giving approval for an entire new town at Foxley Wood in a green belt area of Hampshire, on a large site formerly occupied by a quarry. However, his successor, Chris Patten, reversed the decision in 1989.

Protected Monuments and Buildings

'Scheduled monuments' are important archaeological sites and unoccupied structures (such as Stonehenge, Caernarfon Castle and Fountains Abbey) which are specially protected by law; while listed buildings are normally occupied and are of historic or architectural value. Conservation areas are usually districts of towns with a special character that deserves preserving. All of these are specially protected by law and cannot be altered or destroyed without ministerial permission, and planners must take them into account. Within some of our ancient cities, such as Lincoln, Durham and York there are scheduled monuments, listed buildings and conservation areas, all concentrated together. In addition, there may be a World Heritage Site (such as Durham), which means that it has international recognition from UNESCO and its protection is monitored by an international committee.

All of these policies, together with some minor ones relating to advertising hoardings and tree preservation, must be given consideration when local planning departments deal with applications for planning permission. They are part of an elaborate procedure through which all planning application must go. This may be broken down in to a number of stages.

Planning Procedure

The first step is a properly presented application with the correct documents and plans (usually four copies of each) accompanied by the correct fee. These are the first things a planning department will check. If this is satisfactory the process continues along several parallel lines. The business of checking by planning officers divides into two forms. First, there is the technical detail. That is, the proposal must conform to building regulations and other regulations of various kinds. Secondly, the proposal is checked against the various plans and policies outlined above to see that it falls within council and government policies that are set out in legislation, development plans, DoE circulars, etc. At the same time as these investigations are going on, the process of consultation, both formal and informal, begins.

Planning authorities have a statutory duty to inform and consult those who will be affected if the planning permission is granted. This does not include the general public or local residents, unless the proposed development involves a particular nuisance. However, it is customary for planning authorities to publicise proposals of any size in local newspapers and there is a statutory duty to make proposals available for inspection by the public.

It is at this point that much of the informal side of the planning procedure goes on. Officers receive representations of various kinds - letters of protest, delegations, etc. - while councillors, especially those on the planning committee, are lobbied by fellow councillors, constituents and interested parties. Objectors need a good grasp of the technicalities, and present a well-argued case. On the other hand, pressure of a more political kind may be put on councillors, who are always sensitive to the level of their popularity.

There is, however, a time limit on all this discussion. A decision must be made within a time limit. Usually this is eight weeks; although the time can be extended by mutual agreement. If this is not agreed by the applicant, or if no decision is made within a reasonable time, the applicant is free to assume that delay amounts to rejection and can therefore appeal to the Secretary of State.

When all the checking and consultation is complete, the planning officers submit their recommendation to the Planning Committee, where it is the councillors on that committee who will make the final decision. Whereas the officers are purely concerned, at least in theory, with technical and other objective criteria such as conformity to regulations, the councillors may take wider considerations into account. These involve evaluative judgements about benefit to the community and popular opinion, and no councillor is likely to support a decision either way that could cost them their seat at the next council election.

Appeals

If planning permission is granted, then that is usually the end of the matter. It will then be extremely difficult for objectors to overturn the decision or have it reviewed. If, on the other hand, planning permission is refused, then there may be more stages to go if the applicant is determined. A refusal must be accompanied by reasons and the applicant normally has an opportunity to discuss with the authority how the plans might be altered in order to be successful. If this is not possible then the applicant may challenge the reasons given for rejection by appealing to the Secretary of State who may deal with the appeal in a number of ways. The Secretary of State may decide after written representations from both sides, or may call for all the documents and ask a DETR inspector to study them and make a recommendation before a final decision is made. Or the Secretary of State may choose to hold a full-scale public inquiry chaired by a DETR inspector. In this case all interested parties may give evidence and be legally represented. The inspector then makes a report with a recommendation, although this may be ignored. The Secretary of State always has the final say.

Assessing the System

The justification for all these stages, all this checking and consultation and appeals procedure, is to ensure that developers have sound proposals; that everyone has an opportunity to have their say and all views are considered; and that the needs of the community and the freedom of individuals to pursue their objectives are held in proper balance. Thus, in order to be successful, applications for planning permission have to satisfy a variety of criteria. They must satisfy a host of legal regulations concerning the safety and general adequacy of the building or other development. The development must not result in an eyesore or other nuisance, or involve damage to countryside or valued structure that ought to be protected. It must fit in with development plans: at least structure plans and possibly local plans, together with the various planning policies which they embody. In general it must be of benefit to the community, or at least not be detrimental to it.

However, it is possible that these considerations may conflict with each other and a difficult judgement has to be made. For example, there may be a development that is a nuisance for those close to it, but which benefits the wider community (a waste dump, for example). This is what is often described as the NIMBY ('Not in my back yard') situation. Or it might be a development that would normally be considered unsuitable in attractive countryside, but which will provide employment in an area that badly needs it. This often sets opposing groups of local residents against each other. People who live and work all the year round in national parks are often in favour of activities such as quarrying, modern forestry or military training which provide employment, and are opposed by short term visitors and owners of second homes who value rural silence and charm. Ultimately these are political decisions, and it is politicians (that is, local councillors and in the last resort the Secretary of State for the Environment) who have to make them in the best interests of the community.

On the other hand, the system can be criticised in a number of respects. It could be said that, while planning is clearly an example of local decision-making, this has to be qualified by the fact that any decision can always be overridden by central government. It could also be said that although there is opportunity for all to have their say, the system is none-the-less weighted in favour of the developer rather than the community. The community's right to prevent a planning decision being made is more restricted than many would like. However, a community threatened by a planning proposal it does not like can maximise its influence if it can organise itself effectively as a pressure group.

Local Pressure Groups

Not all local pressure groups are concerned with planning decisions. Closing a school, levels of local taxes, and many other issues may preoccupy such groups, including both temporary and permanent ones. However, planning is a major and continuing concern for many permanent groups - such as civic societies and environmental groups - and planning proposals call forth more ad hoc groups than any other type of issue. It is through the latter type of group - that is temporary and related to a specific decision - that many people become directly involved in politics for the first, and perhaps only, time. How these groups are formed, how they operate and to what extent they are successful is an important feature of local government and politics today.

Local pressure groups are often started by one or two people who feel strongly about some proposal they have heard about but are not sure exactly how to proceed. The first step is to find out how many other people feel the same way. This might be done in several ways: by word of mouth, by letter to the editor of a local paper, or by a local advert asking people to write in with their opinions. Sometimes local branches of organisations such as the National Trust, RSPB, RSPCA etc may act as a recruiting ground. However, at some stage there must be some kind of public meeting at which people can air their views and discuss the matter. What happens at this meeting, and how it is handled is often crucial to the success of the subsequent campaign. A well-attended and enthusiastic meeting is a good start, but the enthusiasm has to be maintained and channelled effectively.

If possible, the initial public meeting needs to do several things:

(a)   create an organisation

(b)   elect a committee to run the campaign on a day-to-day basis

(c)   make provision for funding

(d)   give the volunteers something to do

(e)   agree a plan of campaign, at least in outline.

If a campaign is to be successful there must be good organisation. Any organisation needs a constitution. This need only be very elementary, needing only to set down:

- the name and purpose of the organisation

- an executive committee and officers (chair, secretary, treasurer, etc.) and how they are chosen (usually by election, annually if that is appropriate)

- a periodic meeting and AGM

- any membership conditions, such as payment of membership fee.

Usually an executive committee is elected at the initial meeting. The initiators are often elected. It is a good idea for such groups to have prominent local people involved as closely as possible. It is quite common to ask local clergy to serve in this way. A lawyer, such as a local solicitor, is an extremely useful person to have, as is anyone else who can provide technical expertise relevant to the campaign. The involvement of local politicians is also a great help. Indeed, the more politicians the better, from parish councillors to MPs. If the community is lucky enough to have a local celebrity, who is known regionally or nationally, persuading them to be involved would greatly enhance a campaign.

Campaigning against a planning proposal can be very expensive, and it important for such groups to raise as much money as possible. This can be done with membership fees, events like jumble sales, appeals for donations, etc. This is something that volunteers can be getting on with. Often at the initial meeting there is maximum enthusiasm, and this has to be exploited. If people are willing to do something, but are not asked, they may soon lose interest and drift away. Volunteers need to be identified and given some task that will further the campaign. Finding new members and raising funds are just the kind of tasks that can involve everybody.

Campaigning

Local campaigns have several aspects that need to be pursued as the same time. In the case of a campaign against a planning proposal there is a primary focus for all effort, which is the planning authority's final decision. It is crucial for a campaign to master the planning procedure and the decision-making processes of the local authority concerned that result in that decision. It is also important to master the technicalities of the proposal and present a good case, and this is why good professional advice can be very important. Sometimes contact with other groups pursuing similar campaigns elsewhere may be helpful in this respect, especially if they are, for example, established conservation groups which are used to dealing with the technicalities. This is the stage in the process, when there is consultation with affected parties, that local pressure groups must make their pressure count. Ideally they should follow the correct channels, talk to the right officials and committees, and make a good case on the right kinds of grounds. Good grounds essentially show that the proposed development is demonstrably bad for the community. Objections based, for example, on the alleged poor character of the applicant will not get very far.

Although technical considerations are an important factor, the decision is essentially a political one. This is why it is important to have as much political support as possible. Local politicians who cannot be persuaded to join the campaign need to be lobbied. The local MP should be involved if possible and lobbied if not. An MP can be extremely useful in putting pressure on government ministers who may be involved, especially the Secretary of State for the Environment who may be called upon to make the final decision. There may also be other public agencies an MP may approach, such as British Coal if the proposal is for an open-cast mine.

Alongside dealing with officials and politicians, the group needs to be running a public campaign to gain publicity and popular support. Membership drives, poster campaigns, petitions, demonstrations and many other techniques are possible here. The point is to attract support and good publicity. Violent acts will usually be counter productive, whereas interesting and imaginative 'events' will attract media coverage and popular interest. The point of a campaign is, of course, to influence politicians who are highly sensitive to popular opinion if their position as elected representatives depends upon it.

If, for whatever reason, the proposal is turned down by the planning authority, this may not be the end of the matter. The developer has the right of appeal to the Secretary of State, who may call for written representations or institute a public inquiry in which case, the group must renew the fight and present as professional a case as it possibly can.

If, on the other hand, the planning committee does give planning permission, then there is no comparable appeal to the Secretary of State. Similarly, if the developer wins an appeal to the minister, the possibilities of further action by the protesting group are extremely limited. One option is direct action. That is, actions such as sit-ins, of physically preventing the development work from beginning. Such actions rarely succeed and often lose popular sympathy. Occasionally, however, they are effective. Several years ago Nirex, the body charged with disposing of nuclear waste, announced that it was going to make tests in three rural areas to explore the possibility of creating underground waste dumps. Local residents in the areas concerned were incensed and local villagers physically prevented contractors from entering the proposed sites. Shortly afterwards the proposal was shelved and nothing has been heard of it since. However, such successes for direct action are very rare. What more often happens is that a group that has failed to prevent a development stays in being as a monitoring group that makes sure developers stick to any promises they have made and tries to minimise any damage the development might cause.

Paying for Local Government

Local government provides a wide range of services and is consequently immensely costly. One way or another, local government has to be paid for, and it is generally agreed that the present system is unsatisfactory. But although the system has recently been changed several times and in a number of important ways, these changes are highly controversial, and nobody has yet thought of a method that commands wide agreement.

Capital Expenditure

The present system divides local expenditure into two kinds and finances them differently. One kind is capital expenditure and consists of spending on long-term assets, such as schools, housing, civic centres, a new computer system, and other expensive items. This is largely financed through borrowing. The government has powers to control borrowing, and in most circumstances keeps a very tight control over about three-quarters of what a local authority borrows, which is related to provision of statutory services, such as school building and road maintenance. The other quarter is determined locally and can be used for things such as new sports centres and other amenities that are not statutory obligations.

However, during the 1980s some local authorities, in conflict with the government's policy of restricting their spending, used various methods of 'creative accounting' to raise money to avoid financial restrictions. Most of these were short term measures, and in some cases were judged by the courts to be illegal. Fresh sources of finance for capital expenditure have also appeared in the past fifteen years, including lotteries (for such things as sporting and cultural facilities) and income gained from asset sales; although in the case of sales of council houses the government has not allowed the money gained to be freely spent by the LAs concerned.

Revenue Expenditure

The other and more important kind of expenditure is 'revenue expenditure', which is devoted to the day-to-day running of services and covers the costs of salaries, materials, transport and all the things necessary to keep them going. The servicing (paying interest charges) of debt incurred for capital expenditure is also paid for out of the revenue account. This obviously makes up the bulk of LA spending, and the way it is financed is one of the biggest problems in local government. There are three main sources of regular income, which are, in order of importance:

1.   government grants

2.   local taxation

3.   charges.

Grants

Around 80% of the cost of all local government services is paid for by central government, mainly through grants. The bulk of this money comes in the form of the Rate Support Grant (RSG), sometimes called the 'Block Grant'. This is calculated according to the size of the local authority's area, how well off it is, size of population, and a number of other criteria; and the resulting calculation produces an overall figure for the local authority which is then paid to it as a lump sum. Successive governments have made significant modifications to this system.

Local Taxation

The rates were an ancient form of local tax going back to the Elizabethan Poor Law. It was a tax upon property, and the more valuable a person's property the more they payed. There used to be two kinds of rates: domestic rates and business rates. It was a simple tax, easy to collect, difficult to avoid, and an authority could calculate its tax yield almost to the penny. But there were difficulties that made it unpopular. The rating system had long been subject to intense criticism, and its abolition was discussed for decades before anything was seriously attempted. It survived for so long (despite many reports and government promises of reform) because there was no alternative that enjoyed wide support. The biggest complaint against the rates was that it was simply unfair. A widowed pensioner living next door to a household of six working adults would have been charged the same rates as all the six together, if they had similar houses. There was a rebate scheme, but it could not eliminate all such unfairness. Council tenants made a contribution through their rents, although there was also a rent rebate scheme. Furthermore, in the household of six adults only one of them, in effect, paid rates, while the other five enjoyed the benefits of local services free. In fact on this basis only about half the adult population paid rates. Because of this, the government argued, councils in some areas could go on raising rates without there being enough indignant ratepayers to vote them out of office. That is, councils were not sufficiently responsible to the people who provided the money.

For these reasons Mrs Thatcher determined to abolish the rating system. Domestic rates were abolished, in Scotland in 1989 and 1990 in England, while business rates were set and collected nationally. The replacement for the domestic rates was the Community Charge, and the basic idea was that it was a flat rate personal tax that every individual had to pay (even the very poor had to pay something). The new tax did overcome some of the disadvantages of the rates, but created problems of its own. It was arguably fairer to the extent that most adults paid it. It did, it was claimed, make local councils more accountable to those who provided its money. On the other hand, it was not related to people's ability to pay (to use the technical term, it is 'regressive'), which for a personal tax is unique in Britain and extremely rare in the modern world generally. It was more common centuries ago, when a tax of this kind was called a 'poll tax'; hence the popular name given to the community charge.

But whatever the rights and wrongs of the community charge it was undoubtedly a political disaster. Many people could not afford to pay it; many refused to pay on principle; and some went to prison. There were campaigns and marches and even riots. Mrs Thatcher was one of the very few in government who were enthusiastic and refused to change her mind. It was one of the factors that helped to bring about her downfall in November 1990. In fact no sooner did Mrs Thatcher leave office then the Cabinet set about finding the alternative. It was not long before they came up with the present Council Tax, which is really the old system of domestic rates slightly modernised (the business rate system was not changed back).

This is how the system broadly works. Every property in a local authority's area (with a few exceptions) is given a value, placing it within seven broad bands. In consequence, every local authority knows exactly the rateable value of its area and therefore knows how much it would raise if it charged one penny for every £ of rateable value; i.e. a 'penny rate'. Then, every year, each local authority has to estimate its expenditure for the next financial year. It deducts from this overall figure its expected income from government grants and other sources and is left with the sum which it has to raise from the rates. It is then a simple matter of working out how many penny rates will be needed to raise the necessary sum. Then everyone will have to pay that number of pence for every pound of rateable value of their property. For example, if twenty penny rates were needed then all ratepayers in that area would have been asked to pay a poundage of twenty pence for every £ of rateable value of their property, and if 150 penny rates were needed then everyone would pay a poundage of 150p for each £ of rateable value, and so on. If only one person lives in a given property, they are entitled to a rebate.

The Business Rate

When Mrs Thatcher's government abolished the domestic rates it did not abolish business rates, but reorganised them and put them on an entirely new basis, and this change remains in force. Now, instead of local authorities setting the business rate for their areas, as they used to, there is a standard level of charge for the whole country determined by central government. It has done away with having different rates for different areas. The money raised is distributed to local authorities to help cover their spending.

Charges

Charges include all LA services where the public makes some kind of payment, such as council house rents, bus fares, night school fees, library fines, school dinners, etc. Very few such charges cover the expense of the service, although there are some, like markets and allotments, that roughly break even. Only rarely do trading services make much profit, although airports, exhibition centres and a few other do. In general, charges make only a small contribution to local finances.

Europe and Government Agencies

The European Union has become an increasingly important source of funds for hard pressed LAs in recent years. Indeed, some areas with economic difficulties, such as Scotland and the South West and North East of England, have argued that Brussels is often more sympathetic to their problems than London. Many LAs (especially counties in areas of high unemployment) employ teams of European officers whose main task is to attract European funding for projects and organisations in their area. Durham County Council has such a team and is also part of a consortium of Northern LAs that maintains a permanent office in Brussels. This money has come principally from various programmes of the Regional and Social Funds, including some specially designed to help former coal-mining areas, and has been for a variety of infrastructure projects, environmental improvement schemes, setting up of industrial estates and grants and other helps for small businesses. The famous Beamish Folk Museum has received European funds, as well as the Riverside cricket ground project discussed above. The latter attracted funds from the Sports Council, and government bodies of this kind, such as the Countryside Agency and training agencies, can be a source of extra funds, especially for appropriate capital projects.

Privatisation and the Changing Role of Local Government

After 1979 the Conservative government pursued a consistent policy of curbing local government spending. Ever stronger controls were introduced, making it more and more difficult for LAs to spend more than the government deemed essential. Frustration with high spending councils was a major factor in the government's introduction of the community charge. It was also behind the government taking powers to 'cap' the amount LAs could raise through local taxation. But arguably a more effective brake on local spending has been the reduction of what local authorities are responsible for, which goes along with new ideas of the proper function of a local authority.

The Shrinking of Local Government

The Conservative government's determination to hold down local spending was related to its more general view that local government does too much and does much of it inefficiently. Since 1979 there has been an erosion of local government responsibilities. This can be seen in respect of housing, education, planning and in the general policy of privatisation. Local government's role in housing has been significantly diminished in a number of ways. Council house building has essentially come to a standstill, while recent legislation has given council tenants the right to opt for another landlord. Most public sector housing is now in the hands of housing associations, not local councils. But the earliest and most important of these policies is the right of council tenants to buy their council houses, which has greatly reduced the number of houses under council control. In education, rights were given to school governors to take their school out of local government control, while the new City Technology Colleges completely by-passed local education authorities. Institutions of higher and further education have also been taken away from local government control. In the planning area, Enterprise Zones and Urban Development Corporations all took powers away from the LAs in their areas. But in many ways it is the policy of privatisation that is the greatest threat to local government as we have come to understand it.

Privatisation

The sale of council houses is a form of privatisation, as is the compulsory sale of spare land in the council's possession. However, the most significant form of privatisation for local authorities is 'contracting out'. That is, where council responsibilities, such as refuse collection, or things the council itself needs to keep itself running, such as cleaning and catering, are contracted out to private firms or to the council's own workforce that have successfully competed for the work. The reason why this kind of privatisation is such a threat is that practically all that councils do could conceivably be contracted out to private firms. Indeed, the Conservative Secretary of State for the Environment until July 1989, Nicholas Ridley, suggested, only half jokingly, that the ideal local authority is one that meets just once a year in a private hotel to hand out the contracts. If that view of local government prevails it would not seem to have much of a future.

Some of the more enthusiastic supporters of privatisation argued that contracting out is not a really genuine privatisation, since LAs would retain ownership of the assets and be able to set targets, budgets, entrance fees and other factors. Nevertheless, it is the 'contracting out' variety of privatisation that will most effect local authority leisure services. The 1988 Local Government Act required all LAs to contract out certain specified services, such as catering and cleaning, with an additional provision for the minister to require further services to go out to contract. That is, subject to 'compulsory competitive tendering' (CCT), where existing departments would have to bid against outside competition for the work they do. Since the Act was passed, leisure was declared a service that must be contracted out in the future. Originally contracts had to be ready by 1990, but local authorities insisted that this was not possible. They argued that leisure services are especially complicated because of the variety of facilities and the complexity of contract specifications in a non-statutory and fast-changing area. The government revised its timetable so that all of the work had to go out to contract by 1993.

Once this process was underway it soon became apparent that the great majority of these contracts were being awarded 'in house' (that is to existing departments bidding in open competition) and not, as the government intended, to local businesses. Partly this was because existing staff generally had more experience and expertise in running the facilities in question, and no doubt many councils were predisposed to favour their own staff if at all possible. But another major problem was TUPE.

Transfer of Undertakings (Protection of Employment) regulations, or TUPE, are derived from a European Union directive designed to protect the conditions and pensions of workers when ownership of firms change hands. When a court ruling decided that this applied to privatisation it put LAs into something of a dilemma. In many cases firms taking over contracts agreed to re-employ existing staff, usually at lower wages and with poorer conditions and pensions. This suited both the new employer, who did not have to train new staff, and the LA who did not have find expensive redundancy payments. But TUPE meant that this could not be done. The new firms could not employ existing staff and make a profit, while the LA could not afford to make them redundant. As a consequence many contracts were awarded 'in house' by default, since nobody else bothered to bid.

The British government challenged the application of TUPE to privatisation in the European court, but this failed in June 1994, and it had to look for other means to reverse the decision. Most observers would agree, however, that the whole complicated process of CCT became an important discipline for LAs, making them more cost-conscious and efficient than in the past. In the Local Government Act 1999 the Labour government repealed compulsory competitive tendering, but has replaced it with the requirement to obtain 'best value' in carrying out LA functions. This allows in house provision, but it must be audited to demonstrate that it is the most efficient use of resources.

The Future of Local Government

These series of changes have not just involved a contraction of local government; they also manifest a changed understanding of what local government is for. This conception of local government is not the traditional one of a service-provider. Rather they are based on an idea of the local authority as an enabler and facilitator, a regulator and supervisor. In other words, the authority makes things possible and makes sure they are then done properly, instead of doing everything itself as was the way in the past.

A good example of this new view is the changes in community care arrangements laid down in the National Health Service and Community Care Act of 1990. Local authorities were given new responsibilities for community care, but encouraged to have the service itself coming from a variety of providers: its own provision, commercial agencies and voluntary organisations. Another example is education. Following the Education Reform Act of 1988 governors (including more parents) were given far greater control over the budget and running of schools As a result, others use powers once exercised by the local authority. However, the budget and overall objectives were still set by the local authority and it supervised the work of the governors, but its role was different.

A further aspect of change is the promotion of a different concept of management. Less importance is now given to the corporate management ideas of the Bains Report (discussed earlier) and more emphasis on the management methods of the private sector. Thus, authorities are encouraged to strive for "economy, efficiency and effectiveness", and develop techniques such as performance indicators, review and evaluation and 'financial management initiative'. The new concept sees councillors less as local politicians concerned with political issues, party policy and constituent's grievances, and more like the board of directors of a commercial firm, setting targets, evaluating performance, constructing business plans and designing marketing strategies to make their services more efficient and competitive.

The other side of this is the conception of the local citizen as a customer in the market place who has consumer choice as between private and public provision of services, with schools competing for pupils, housing departments and associations competing for tenants, social service departments competing for clients and leisure services competing for customers. Another aspect is the attempt to have local services paid for as far as possible by the users, as with private business. Among the most important reasons the government had for introducing the ill-fated community charge was the idea that everyone should pay something towards the cost of services which many had previously enjoyed free; at the same time it would make authorities more accountable to their customers. Pressed to their conclusion, these ideas might point to a notion of local government without politics, where councillors are managers awarding contracts to the most efficient providers. If this is the way local government is heading it would suggest that it could be far better done by a set of government appointed businessmen, rather than democratically elected councillors.

However, as we have seen, the Labour government since 1997 has made it clear that it sees local government with a key role in promoting local community development, and is keen to find ways of strengthening the political profile of its leadership and its links with the public. It stresses the public-private partnership in a relatively pragmatic way; the public sector is encouraged to borrow techniques and share resources with the private sector, but there is also a recognition that local government must both listen to the local community and then set standards and provide the leadership. And the agenda of tackling economic regeneration, social exclusion, and restoring community values, acknowledge that a simple faith in a flourishing private business sector and the use of market forces cannot deal with many of the problems which face local communities.

Local government is changing at what is for many people a bewildering pace. Back in 1988 in a report entitled *The Competitive Council* (1988), the Audit Commission observed that:

> *"Local authorities are in the throes of a revolution. The immediate cause is a wave of legislation changing their methods of raising revenue, their ways of working and the range of their functions."* (P.1)

Since then there has been little let up in the process, and there is no doubt that local government will go on changing in the future, and that this will have important implications for leisure services along with all the other functions. But how far the changes will continue along the lines just outlined it is impossible to say.

Chapter 3

The Department for Culture, Media and Sport

The most important developments in the field of government and leisure in recent decades have been the creation of the Department of National Heritage in April 1992, later renamed as Department for Culture, Media, and Sport (DCMS) by the new Labour government in 1997. For the first time much government policy was brought together into one department which hitherto had been scattered across several.

Government Departments and Leisure before 1992

As we saw previously, many of the central government departments had a direct interest in leisure. The main distribution of functions in relation to leisure were as follows:

- *Broadcasting*: the responsibility of the Home Office, although the Department of Trade and Industry (DTI) had an interest through the manufacture of televisions and videos, as well as telecommunications and the advertising industry.

- *Countryside*: principally the responsibility of the Department of the Environment (DoE), with the Ministry of Agriculture also having an interest.

- *Tourism*: Department of Employment; before 1985 the DTI was the department responsible, and has retained an interest since; the Ministry of Transport also had an interest.

- *Arts*: Office of Arts and Libraries. This was a tiny ministry headed by a junior minister, which was set up in 1979. Arts, museums and libraries were formerly the responsibility of the Department of Education and Science (DES).

- *Sport*: Education and Science 1990-92. Previously it came under the DoE, who retained an interest because of local government.

- *Heritage*: The heritage in terms of buildings and ancient monuments was the responsibility of the DoE, while the heritage in terms of libraries, galleries and museums was the responsibility of the Office of Arts and Libraries.

All of these policy areas have a regional dimension, and in each case (except broadcasting) the Welsh, Scottish and Northern Ireland Offices had important responsibilities. Various other government departments had an interest in various areas. The Foreign Office, for example, had a close interest in tourism, in our relations with international sporting and other bodies, and with such issues as football hooligans travelling abroad (also involving the Home Office), and so on. The Ministry of Defence had a particular interest in countryside protection, since many of its training facilities are sited in National Parks and Areas of Outstanding Natural Beauty.

Most departments of central government had some interest in one or other of these leisure areas, which meant a vast degree of co-ordination (involving not just the departments, but a complicated network of quangos, local authorities and other bodies). There was, however, no department to speak for leisure as a whole, making co-ordination difficult and tending to give leisure policy a low priority.

A Ministry of Leisure

During the 1980s, as the growing importance of leisure provision in the social and economic life of the nation began to be realised, questions were raised as to the role of government in relation to leisure. Should the government play a bigger role? Should leisure services be better co-ordinated? Should there be some national agency for leisure? Finally, since many government departments have a responsibility for one or more aspects of leisure, should there be a Ministry or Department of Leisure headed by a Cabinet Minister?

The local authority associations advocated such a ministry, while others have suggested various aspects of leisure policy should be given greater priority. The House of Commons all-party Select Committee for Education, Science and Arts, looking into funding of the arts in 1982, argued the need for a Ministry of Arts, Heritage and Tourism, while both the Labour Party and the SDP-Liberal Alliance in the 1987 general election were promising the creation of a new ministry based on arts and broadcasting, if they were elected. However, the Conservative government did not see the need for such a ministry, and there was, in fact, a variety of arguments on both sides of the case.

Arguments for a Ministry of Leisure

1. The social and economic importance of leisure industries and services needs to be reflected in a higher profile in government. Leisure increasingly occupies a key position in the economy, creating new businesses, wealth and employment. Furthermore, leisure provision has important social benefits in improving the quality of life and in helping to sustain and enhance communities. Such an important public benefit demands full representation at the highest levels of government.

2. Leisure was dispersed through many departments of government, with an inevitable degree of overlap, confusion and wasted effort. A single ministry would co-ordinate the government's various leisure policies far more effectively.

3. A Ministry of Leisure could do more than respond to expressed need, it could take the initiative and develop leisure policy for the future, ahead of current needs.

4. A central unifying ministry is necessary for the most efficient development of local government leisure services, overcoming the present need for local authorities to deal with a variety of government departments and agencies.

5. It is also important to have a single government focus for the private sector leisure interests, whether business, voluntary or pressure groups.

Arguments against a Ministry of Leisure

1. The idea of a Ministry of Leisure has a faintly sinister ring about it, (like totalitarian countries with `Ministries of Culture') sounding as though the government was organising people's leisure time for them. Choice of how to use one's leisure time is a personal matter. It can be safely left to the free market, without the need for a government ministry to intervene.

2. The division of responsibility for leisure among different departments means that in each department an aspect of leisure policy is integrated with other departmental responsibilities. A Ministry of Leisure would have to weaken those connections, but still have to co-ordinate with all

the departments where leisure formerly belonged. This would create as many confusions and difficulties as benefits.

3.   There are many aspects of the nation's life that could make a similar claim, and Ministries for Women, Regional Development, Europe, Food and Inner Cities are among those suggested at various times. If they all had separate departments it would be chaotic and the problems of co-ordination overwhelming. In practice such concerns are often dealt with by attaching a particular aspect to a larger department. The government argued that leisure was quite adequately served with things as they were.

4.   Leisure is not a sufficiently coherent area to be suitable for a single ministry. It is made up of too many disparate elements that have little connection with each other. A variety of departments and agencies at national and local level is the most appropriate way of dealing with the different aspects of leisure.

The growing social and economic importance of leisure made it likely that there would be a government ministry or department devoted to it eventually, but the Conservative victory in the 1987 General Election seemed to rule it out in the foreseeable future, or at least until the Conservatives lost an election. Mrs Thatcher had no interest in the area of policy and did not think it was the kind of thing governments should be involved with. She also disliked creating new departments, unlike some of her predecessors.

The Department of National Heritage (DNH) 1992-1997

Things began to change with the advent of John Major in 1990. Apart from a greater interest in this area (especially sport), he turned out to be much less obsessed with reducing government to the absolute minimum than his predecessor had been (evidenced for example by his promise of government financial support for the Manchester bid for the Olympics, something unthinkable under Mrs Thatcher).

When it came to the 1992 General Election, the Opposition parties both again promised a new government department. The Conservative election manifesto did not do so explicitly. It did, on the other hand, promise a National Lottery and a 'Millennium Fund', which perhaps implied a new ministry. In any case, no sooner had John Major won the election than the setting up of a new department was announced. It would be headed by a Secretary of State with a seat in the Cabinet.

The Prime Minister's announcement of the setting up of the DNH in April 1992 contained the following statement of the new department's responsibilities.

"The Secretary of State for National Heritage will be responsible for central areas of our national life which enhance its quality or contribute significantly to our sense of national identity. These include the present function of the Office of Arts and Libraries (the arts, museums, galleries and libraries) together with film and the export licensing of antiques, functions which are transferred from the Department of Trade and Industry. He will be responsible for broadcasting (notably the review of the BBC's Charter), the Press (including work on the recommendations of the Calcutt Committee) and the safety of sports grounds, duties to be transferred from the Home Office; sport from the Department of Education and Science; tourism from the Department of Employment; and heritage from the Department of the Environment. He will be responsible for the Historic Royal Palaces Agency.

The secretary of State will be responsible for the proposed National Lottery and, in consultation with the Home Secretary for the legislation required to create it. The Secretary of State will also be responsible for the Millennium Fund."

The new department was therefore responsible for all the main areas of leisure where government has a major role, with the exception of countryside. This remained the responsibility of the Department of the Environment. The two departments would nevertheless have to co-ordinate, since protecting the countryside related to a number of the DNH's responsibilities, such as tourism and preserving the heritage generally.

Indeed, the new department needed to co-ordinate with all the departments from which its functions were extracted. For example, concern with protecting historic buildings and monuments was still closely bound up with the planning system and local authorities, which remained the responsibility of the Department of the Environment from which the heritage function was taken. In addition, there was still a major job of co-ordination with the regional departments. The Scottish, Welsh and Northern Ireland Offices all had significant inputs in the leisure field, choosing national tourist boards, arts councils, sports councils, etc., which were done in close consultation with the central departments and thus with the DNH.

Quangos are particularly important in this area of public policy, since the government does not wish to be seen influencing what art we see, what television we watch, and so on. Its provision of funds, and the framework of administrations is therefore mainly done on the `arm's length principle', by means of quangos. Most of the leisure-related quangos, some 45 of them that were once scattered across Whitehall, became responsible to a single department. There was now the possibility of government policy in the leisure areas to be effectively harmonised, and given the higher profile which they tend to receive in other countries.

The first Secretary of State, charged with setting up the department and fulfilling its aims was Mr David Mellor. Among his previous jobs as a junior minister he had been Minister for the Arts and the Home Office minister responsible for Broadcasting (where he had been largely responsible for introducing a `quality threshold' into the ITV franchise bidding). He was an able and ambitious minister, with Treasury experience, who had a personal interest in the arts and sport. His appointment was widely welcomed in the arts, sport and broadcasting, and he was expected to do great things with his new department.

David Mellor did not have the opportunity to fulfil these expectations, since he was forced to resign in September 1992 as the result of a sex scandal. His successor was the rather less high-profile Peter Brooke, whose ministerial career most people thought had finished. This change coincided with a financial crisis (`Black Wednesday') when Britain was forced out of the European Exchange Rate Mechanism and the government's economic policy collapsed overnight. One result of this was a squeeze on government spending. When spending plans were announced in the Autumn Statement in November 1992 the DNH received less than it had been expecting (and probably less than it would have received if David Mellor had still been minister, he being a former senior Treasury minister).

Nonetheless, it was hoped that the department's level of funding would recover when the recession ended. Furthermore, the funding of arts, sport and heritage was to receive a substantial boost with the National Lottery, which the government had promised would not be used to replace previous funding. The Department also had the prospect of a concrete goal to work towards in the celebration of the millennium. This included the Millennium Fund which had implications for arts, sport, heritage, as well as tourism.

The stated aims of the DNH were as follows.

- to conserve, nurture, enhance and make more widely accessible the rich and varied cultural heritage of the countries of the United Kingdom. Working within the wider policies of the government of the day, the Department seeks to create the conditions which

- will preserve ancient sites, monuments, and historic buildings, and increase their accessibility for study and enjoyment both now and in the future

- maintain, increase, and make available the national collections of books, works of art, scientific objects and other records and artefacts of the past and of the present

- encourage the living arts to flourish - including the performing arts; the visual and plastic arts; broadcasting; film; and literature

- increase the opportunities for sport and recreation both for champions and for the general public and

- attract a wide range of people from this country and abroad to enjoy and enrich our national culture.

The Department for Culture, Media and Sport (DCMS)

Aims and Objectives

In spite of the change of name, the DCMS basically inherited the same portfolio of responsibilities and resources as the DNH. Although it tried to redefine its aims to correspond to 'New Labour' priorities, in practice many of its activities remained very similar. It is interesting to compare its current 'Aims and Objectives' (taken from the DCMS Public Service Agreement 1999-2002.)

Aim

To improve the quality of life for all through cultural and sporting activities, and to strengthen the creative industries.

The department will:

- work to bring quality and excellence in the fields of culture, media and sport

- make those available to the many, not just the few

- raise standards of cultural education and training

- help to develop the jobs of the future in the creative industries.

Objectives

The department in partnership with others, works to:

1. create an efficient and competitive market by improving obstacles to growth and unnecessary regulation so as to promote Britain's success in the fields of culture, media, sport and tourism at home and abroad

2. broaden access for this and future generations to a rich and varied cultural and sporting life and to our distinctive built environment

3. raise the standards of cultural education and training

4.   ensure that everyone has the opportunity to achieve excellence in the fields of culture, media and sport and to develop talent, innovation and good design

5.   maintain public support for the National Lottery and ensure that the objective of the Lottery Fund supports DCMS' and other national priorities

6.   promote the role of the department's sectors in urban and rural regeneration, in pursuing sustainability and in combating social exclusion.

...[it] will seek maximum value for money in using its human and financial resources, through applying the principles of efficiency and effectiveness in its sectors and in encouraging partnership with others.

Compared with the old departmental aims, while the main areas of the portfolio remained the same (with the addition of the National Lottery), the style is rather different. There are no references to 'heritage' objects and institutions. Explicit links are made to other areas of policy, such as education, training, and economic regeneration projects. And a social agenda of broadening access - as with the 'many not the few' formula - and recognising leisure activities as a weapon to combat 'social exclusion' is clearly stated. These collectively indicate a desire to place the DCMS in line with the central 'New Labour' concerns of modernisation and social inclusion utilising partnership and efficient methods without any great increase in public expenditure.

Departmental Structure and Funding

The current political leadership is provided by the Secretary of State, Chris Smith, who has held the post since May 1997. A London MP' he held various shadow frontbench responsibilities between 1987 and 1997, including National Heritage 1995-96. There are currently three junior members of the team with particular responsibilities as Ministers of State: Janet Anderson MP (Tourism, Film and Broadcasting), Alan Howarth MP (Arts), Kate Hoey MP (Sports.) Lord McIntosh, Government Deputy Chief Whip in the House of Lords acts as spokesman for DCMS in the upper chamber. The officials are headed by the Permanent Secretary (Robin Young) a civil servant since 1973 who spent much of his previous career in the Department of the Environment before a short spell at the Cabinet Office and then arriving in DCMS in April 1998.

The DCMS (like DNH before it) is a small department, with 375 full time and 14 part time civil servants (October 1999), plus another 200+ staff employed by the Royal Parks Agency. Many of its activities and much of its spending are in fact operating through the 50 quangos with which it has close working relationships. It has a modest budget of about £1 billion (out of total central government spending of £370 billion). Its main office is in new premises at 2-4 Cockspur Street, London, which is just off Trafalgar Square, with two other offices quite close in neighbouring streets.

In fact the department had in its previous form always operated on a tight set of expenditure limits. For many who thought that the creation of the DNH heralded greater government commitment to the arts, sport, etc., the government's spending plans announced in the Autumn Statement in November 1992 were a big disappointment. There was an overall increase from £23 million for the previous year but this was accounted for by the fact that the new department took over funding of the Welsh Fourth Channel Authority; and the special administrative costs of setting up a new department. There were also long-standing commitments, such as the new British Library at St Pancras, already in the pipeline. Looking at the rest, in fact only sport and film had any significant increase. The rest - heritage, museums, libraries, arts and tourism - all faced direct cuts, or else their budgets were frozen. The DNH's budget was supposed to rise modestly in the following years, but in fact 1993 was a year of severe economic difficulty and the government realised it had to do something about its mounting debts. The Budget of that year (in the autumn and including public spending plans for the first time) introduced new cuts in public spending, including the DNH and the figures were revised downwards again.

The advent of a Labour government and Gordon Brown as Chancellor of the Exchequer determined to demonstrate prudence and maintain existing spending limits meant that the resources to be gained from tax revenue stayed very similar with only marginal increases. The departmental expenditure limits (revenue and capital) are set to rise somewhat further for the year 2001-02 to £1.1 billion.

The one bright spot, and possible exception to this financial stringency, is the National Lottery, for which the first operating licence was awarded in 1994. The government originally promised that the money raised from the lottery and used for arts, sports and heritage, would be in addition to existing government funding and not a replacement for it. But this pledge turned out to be rather hollow, since if the government is cutting or freezing DNH/DCMS budgets then this is just what is happening. In addition, in 1998 the Labour government broadened the distribution to cover schemes in health, education and the environment. Some of these were undoubtedly popular causes, but this seemed to represent a further move towards using lottery proceeds as a substitute for regular tax revenue.

The National Lottery

History

The idea of Britain having a national lottery has been floating around for some time. A great many other countries have them, including most of our EU partners, and they raise a great deal of money. There have been lotteries on a nation-wide scale in this country in the past. The first was in the reign of Queen Elizabeth I, in 1566. The most famous product of a lottery is the fine classical building that houses the British Museum, built from the proceeds of a lottery specially for that purpose. There was, however, a certain amount of scandal surrounding the question of where all the money went. It was a consequence of scandals of this kind and the influence of evangelical Christians that national lotteries were banned by Act of Parliament in 1826.

In the 1980s local lotteries were permitted and many local authorities raised funds for local amenities with them. Many, particularly in the Conservative party, supported the idea of a national lottery, but Mrs Thatcher was opposed, and it was only since her fall that the Conservative government adopted the idea. It appeared in the Conservative's 1992 election manifesto. Although initially greeted with some suspicion and opposition from Labour, by the time of the 1997 Labour Party manifesto it had been fully accepted subject to a few criticisms about the distribution of the proceeds.

Not everyone is in favour of the idea. There are people who have a moral objection to gambling and believe governments ought not to encourage it. Other objections came from those who had something to lose. This included charities, many of which have seen a marked decline in income from their money raising activities since the national lottery was introduced. The fiercest opposition came from the football pools companies who (quite correctly) were fearful of losing custom to a rival form of gambling. The government's argument - that since football pools involves a degree of skill, while lotteries do not, then the two kinds of gambling would appeal to different markets and the pools companies had nothing to fear - proved to be incorrect.

Operating the Lottery

The DCMS (originally the DNH) has always been the government department responsible for the National Lottery, but does not run it. The entire operation was contracted out to private enterprise from the start. In 1994, after competitive tendering judged by the regulator (Director of the Office of the Regulator of the National Lottery - OFLOT) the licence was granted to a commercial consortium Camelot Group plc to last until 30 September 2001. (OFLOT itself was replaced as the regulator by the National Lottery Commission in April 1999.) The five

Commissioners are appointed by the Secretary of State and have the job of ensuring that the lottery is being run in a proper manner, protecting players' interests and raising as much money as possible for good causes. This involves selecting the lottery operator, setting the terms of its licence and checking that it carries them out. Negotiations are currently (July 2000) under way with a number of potential operators (including Camelot) for the next licence round, which is due to be announced soon.

The Commission also checks that all the individuals and companies involved are fit and proper, that they are not criminals or have such links, or have been engaged in dubious activities. Given the amount of money at risk and the fact that organised criminals are routinely involved with gambling around the world, this is an important consideration. It must also licence individual games forming part of the lottery operation, and ensure that the right amount of money is paid over to the designated 'Good Causes.'

Camelot, the current operator, devises and operates the lottery games, markets and promotes them, selects the retail outlets, pays out the prizes, and hands over the appropriate share of turnover to the National Lottery Distribution Fund for passing on to the six (originally five) good causes. Camelot, as a commercial concern, makes a net profit from running the lottery, which it pays to the company shareholders. Critics, such as Richard Branson, have argued that the lottery should be run by a non-commercial trust, so that such profits would also be available for the good causes. Defenders of the present system argue that a commercial company is likely to sell more tickets and be run more efficiently, so that even after allowing for the deduction of the profit element a larger sum of money is actually available for the good causes.

The system of lotteries developed by Camelot has become quite diverse. The first (November 1994) and best known was a weekly, but since February 1997 twice weekly, competition where each player chooses a six figure number (between 1-49) recorded on a computer terminal and which is put into a national draw. This in effect gambles a £1 stake for large jackpot prizes, usually measured in some millions of pounds at extremely long odds, around fourteen million to one. There have also been instant scratch cards (March 1995) for smaller prizes and the subsidiary 'Thunderball' game (June 1999.)

The lottery has established itself very successfully on the British scene. Over 70% of households seem to buy tickets in any one of the main Saturday draws. 35,000 retailers, including post offices, small shops, and supermarkets, sell tickets for commission payments. To date there have been over 900 'millionaire' winners. Along with the institutionalisation of small-scale gambling, a further side-effect has been the creation of low quality BBC TV shows featuring the Saturday and Wednesday lottery draws - a peculiarly banal contribution to the cultural scene. So the lottery not only contributes funds to the leisure sector, but is itself a commercial part of the industry.

Money for 'Good Causes'

National Lottery ticket sales from the launch to April 2000 total over £32.4 billion, and raised £8.9 billion for the good causes. These `good causes' were originally in five categories: the arts, sport, heritage, charities, and the Millennium Fund to celebrate the year 2000. In 1998 the Labour government added a sixth 'good cause' called the New Opportunities Fund covering innovative projects in health, education and the environment.

The income flow from lottery sales is divided approximately as follows:

- Camelot (operator)   5%

- Retailers   5%

- Treasury (tax)   12%

- Prizes   50%

- Good Causes   28%

The current division among the good causes:

- Arts   16.6%

- Sports   16.6%

- Heritage   16.6%

- Charities   16.6%

- Millennium   20.0% (until 31 December 2000)

- New Opportunities +   13.3%

Handing out lottery proceeds might seem like an easy way of winning popularity, but it has its political dangers. The DCMS does not do this directly, but does give overall policy direction to a network of 13 distributing bodies, which are themselves quangos. These include the four national Arts Councils and four Sports Councils, Heritage Lottery Fund, National Lottery Charities Board, Millennium Commission, the New Opportunities Fund and the National Endowment for Science Technology & the Arts (NESTA).

Ever since the process started there have been a variety of complaints, apart from those of unsuccessful applicants. The process has been described as too bureaucratic and time consuming, especially for smaller organisations and groups. There seemed to be an initial bias towards very large projects, especially those in the South East of England, some of them with a fairly elitist image or appearing to be out of touch. Funds were flowing into high visibility buildings, but the running costs of projects could not be covered. Agreement on issues of artistic taste is notoriously difficult to establish, leading to complaints of money being wasted on ugly or inappropriate cultural projects. Over the years many of these problems have been addressed; there is now much more sensitivity to a geographical spread, to small projects, to the dangers of concentrating on the bricks and mortar rather than evidence of demand and viability. And while some projects remain controversial (as we shall see with the Millennium Dome), other artistic ventures initially criticised, such as the massive open-air statue 'Angel of the North' in Gateshead, have become widely accepted.

Marking the Millennium

The Millennium Commission

While most of the lottery funding objectives operated in existing, relatively well defined sectors of activity, the National Lottery Act 1993 introduced one novelty with the Millennium Commission (MC) whose sole purpose is to use 20% of the proceeds for 'expenditure on projects to mark the year 2000 and the beginning of the third millennium.' Under the Act the Commissioners are made up of two government ministers, one of whom (the DCMS Secretary of State) is the chair, a nominee of the Leader of the Opposition, and six independent members.

Any rationales for recognising the year 2000 in any particular tangible ways are not very obviously self-evident. While the change of year from 1999 to 2000 might excite some passing curiosity (as well as provoking fears of possible computer failures), this only applies to those who use a calendar based (apparently inaccurately) on the birth-date of Christ. In any case only a small minority of the British population are practising Christians, there is no theological significance to the number 2000, and irritatingly exact-minded persons tend to quibble as to whether the millennium did not actually start at the beginning of 2001. However, the idea that there was something worth celebrating gained some general acceptance, particularly if it provided opportunities for some fun, festivities and parties. The objectives of the MC were vague, and thus left it with considerable freedom on how to spend a considerable sum of money, which has worked out at over £2.1 billion. This was a case of a goldmine seeking prospectors.

Although from the start the MC found itself committed to one gigantic project (what became the 'Dome'), it eventually put together a strategy for distributing its cash in a variety of ways. Many of these in fact overlapped with other types of lottery funding. One line was to invite proposals for major and minor (less than £100,000) capital projects from all around the country. These have to be based on 50% matching funding, so that half the overall costs have to be raised elsewhere - from sponsorship, local government, EU funding, and voluntary donations. So far 28 such major projects have been approved (although one, the National Discovery Park in Liverpool, later was withdrawn) with a variety of objectives and different degrees of success. The Earth Centre near Rotherham, an ambitious showcase for environmentalism on a disused colliery site, has so far had a disappointing attendance and staff had to be laid off and the entrance charge reduced.

But the Dynamic Earth Centre in Edinburgh and the Tate Modern in the old Bankside power station in London have both been highly successful. The Millennium Stadium in Cardiff was completed just in time to host the 1999 Rugby World Cup final, and a £42 million grant is helping the voluntary organisation Sustrans to establish a 5,000 mile national cycle network. Some projects, such as the Eden Project in Cornwall, converting a disused china clay pit into the world's largest exotic greenhouse, the Science Centre in Glasgow, and a major canal restoration in Scotland are not yet completed. Others, such as the rebuilding, extension and refurbishment of the Covent Garden Opera House have attracted bad publicity but may prove successful in the long term. Many of the minor projects have been concerned with providing green spaces and play facilities in urban areas. Including the minor projects, 187 schemes have received over £1.2 billion.

About £100 million has been spent on millennium awards and grants to individuals to do all kinds of things which have value to the community, helping the young, the old, those with various forms of disability etc. This money is channelled through about 80 voluntary groups and charities, such as Age Concern, MIND, and Raleigh International. A further £100 million will be used as a long-term endowment for such activities. Another £20 million has gone on local community festivals, whether carnivals, dance, sculpture, environmental conferences, or sporting events. Public celebrations in towns and cities to mark the beginning and end of the year 2000 get some £11 million.

The Millennium Dome

Right from the start, under the Conservative government in 1994, it was envisaged that the Millennium Commission would support a national Millennium Exhibition as the centrepiece of its strategy. This would be comparable to the mid-Victorian Great Exhibition of 1851 and the post-war 1951 Festival of Britain. Unfortunately confusions and conflicts about objectives, organisation, and financial projections have be-devilled the whole enterprise. After some limited discussion of an alternative in the Midlands, a site was chosen at Greenwich in South London which was hardly easy of access for the majority of the British population. The Conservatives originally hoped that the lead would be taken by the private sector, but this turned out to be illusory and it was necessary to establish a public sector company, the New Millennium Experience Co Ltd (NMEC) as the operator. All the shares in this company are held by a nominee government minister, at present Lord Falconer of the Cabinet Office, who has personal links with the Prime Minister.

Agreement on the innovative building (the famous Dome) and the business plan came before any clear decisions on what the building should actually contain and how it could be marketed to the public. The business plan submitted by NMEC projected a total budget of £758 million, with a contribution of £449 million from the Millennium Commission. The balance would come from participating sponsors (£175 million), and £134 million in revenue from an estimated 12 million visitors plus what could be obtained from disposal of the assets at the end of the exhibition.

When the Labour government came into office in May 1997, it appeared to contain mixed views about the project, but agreed to continue. It was reported that Deputy Prime Minister John Prescott, Chancellor Gordon Brown, and Chris Smith, the DCMS Secretary of State, were unenthusiastic, but that Prime Minister Tony Blair, Robin Cook and Peter Mandelson were strongly supportive. The use of the project to regenerate a derelict area was increasingly stressed. Considerations of the effect on national prestige (one of the commonest arguments used to continue expensive policies) seem to have been persuasive. But while the desire to use the Dome as a showcase for British design and technology was evident, the enterprise continued to suffer difficulties. Finding sponsors took time, as did identifying the nature of the zones and exhibits. There were personal conflicts within the design and management team and between it and some of the politicians concerned (especially Mr Mandelson before his resignation from DTI.) Overall there was much negative publicity, which continued through the opening events and to the present day.

After opening, it soon became clear that the attendance would not run anywhere near the optimistic projections. The entry cost was relatively high at £73 for a family of four, and of course would be increased by very substantial travel and accommodation costs for those coming any significant distance from London. The NMEC chief executive was made the scapegoat and ignominiously fired (very unfairly in the opinion of many of those in a position to know), to be replaced by an executive from EuroDisney. The potential attendance figures have been progressively revised down to an estimated maximum of 6 million, and the Millennium Commission was forced to provide extra cash, £60 million in February and another £29 million in May (in principle repayable) to cover the deficit. Negotiations are currently under way with two potential buyers to take over the Dome after the end of the year. If the sale does not produce at least £30 million then the existing budget will be even further out of balance.

Although the Millennium Dome is currently Britain's top paying tourist attraction, and 80% of visitors report high levels of satisfaction in surveys, the provisional verdict is one of relative failure. It has failed to live up to its own predictions, nor has it communicated to the public at large a clear image of British culture and achievement. To many British people, its image (however unfairly reinforced by much of the newspaper press coverage) is one of a long-running joke. The idea of a 'millennium curse' has achieved some currency, and was immediately transferred to the initial technical problems experienced by the London Eye giant wheel (temporarily) and to the unacceptable wobbles of the millennium pedestrian suspension bridge over the Thames. While supporters of the Dome decry a national tendency to knock any bold initiatives, it is also unfortunately true that its poor image has overshadowed many of the other excellent achievements brought about by millennium funding.

Chapter 4

Broadcasting and Government

Britain has been a pioneer of radio and television, and British broadcasting is widely admired as among the finest in the world. Its quality can, to a great extent, be attributed to an early commitment to what is called 'public service broadcasting', where the provision of a service that would be informative and educational, as well as entertaining, was given priority over commercial considerations. However, due mainly to technological development, broadcasting in Britain is faced with a period of rapid change. Whether things will change for the better or for the worse remains to be seen.

The Development of Broadcasting in Britain

Early Radio

The early history of public broadcasting in Britain is the history of the BBC. Radio was developed during the First World War for military purposes, and after the war the government was very reluctant to allow its development for public use. But radio was developing fast in the USA and beginning to grow in Europe. A group of business firms concerned with manufacturing wireless sets eventually persuaded the government to grant a licence to broadcast, although initially for only one hour per day. This group of manufacturers set up the British Broadcasting Company to provide a service for those people who bought their wirelesses, and to which the government (through the Postmaster General) granted a single monopoly licence to broadcast in 1922. The Company was not designed to make a profit; the profit would come from the sale of wireless sets (or radio sets as we later came to call them).

The British Broadcasting Company was run by a rather puritanical and very formidable Scot named John Reith. He saw the work of the company in terms of providing a range of programmes of the highest standard that would educate the public, keep it informed about the world and entertain it with serious music, drama and discussion. It was John Reith, therefore, who began the public service tradition of British broadcasting. This is in contrast to the way radio was developing elsewhere, particularly in America, where it was seen as a commercial enterprise devoted principally to entertainment, and financing itself and making its profits through advertising.

The government approved of the Reith approach, so that when it nationalised the British Broadcasting Company and turned it into a public corporation it retained Reith (later Lord Reith) as the first Director General. In 1927 a Royal Charter laid down the aims and constitution of the British Broadcasting Corporation, and a new licence to broadcast granted by the government also laid down conditions. Thus, the government established the framework within which the BBC was to operate, but thereafter left it to run its own affairs as it saw fit. The government does retain a legal power to intervene in the affairs of the BBC if it deems it necessary in the national interest; but these are reserve powers that are in fact never used. The government did not, and still does not, wish to run broadcasting directly, believing that broadcasting must not become, or be seen as, an instrument of government propaganda.

In 1927 there were still just over two million wireless sets in the country, which meant only the better off had them. But by the mid-30s virtually every household in the land had one. Before long there were two channels that became known as the Home Service and the Light Programme (the Third Programme was introduced after the war). Further developments came in overseas broadcasting in foreign languages, laying the foundations of the BBC's World Service, which still enjoys a unique world-wide reputation for high quality.

The Coming of Television

During the early 1930s the BBC was experimenting with television, and in 1936 the world's first public television service began operating from Alexandra Palace. However, there were at that time only a few hundred television sets, which were hugely expensive. The television service, which was only for a few hours a day, was suspended during wartime. Radio broadcasting continued and was an important factor in uniting the nation to fight the war. Television resumed in 1946, and by the early 1950s a mass television audience had been created.

A government committee of inquiry into the future of broadcasting recommended in 1951 that the BBC retain its monopoly of both radio and television broadcasting. However, there were strong pressures inside the Conservative Party to introduce commercial television, and eventually a reluctant Prime Minister (Winston Churchill, who had seen American television and did not wish British television to go the same way) along with his Cabinet, were persuaded to allow a television system based on advertising, although only under strict control. This control was to be exercised by the Independent Television Authority (ITA), set up in 1954, which would not make its own programmes but would award broadcasting licences to regional ITV companies. These companies had to comply with requirements to provide good quality television, based on the BBC tradition of public service. Commercial programmes began transmission in 1955.

The 1960s began with another official inquiry (the Pilkington Committee) into the future of broadcasting, which reported in 1962. It recommended no basic change in the structure: the BBC and ITV would retain their television duopoly and BBC its radio monopoly. But it did recommend the development of colour television (which progressed during the rest of the decade) and a new BBC television channel (BBC2 began in 1964). It was also during the 1960's that BBC radio was subject to illegal competition from 'pirate' radio stations, operating from ships transmitting from just outside territorial waters. There had always been 'Radio Luxembourg', which the government could not do much about, but steps were made to put a stop to pirate radio in 1967. However, the BBC did recognise the demand for a round-the-clock pop music service and soon introduced Radio 1. At the same time the BBC was introducing local radio on an experimental basis.

The early 70s saw the introduction of commercial radio. The old ITA was replaced by the Independent Broadcasting Authority (IBA) in 1973, and made responsible for both commercial television and commercial radio. But there was little development of television in the decade, apart from some extension of cable television. This had always been necessary in some areas because of poor reception; they could be 'cabled up' to receive the standard channels. In 1972 the government permitted the development of cable television companies, allowed to produce their own local programmes, although the growth remained slow and on a small scale.

Channel 4 and Breakfast TV

All was not thought to be well with broadcasting, so the government set up yet another inquiry into its future, chaired by Lord Annan, which reported in 1977. The Annan Report expressed dissatisfaction with the duopoly of the BBC and IBA and recommended a new, fourth channel devoted to diversity and catering for minorities. This led to the creation of Channel 4, which began broadcasting in 1983. Mrs Thatcher's Conservative government insisted that it must be a commercial channel financed by advertising.

But although financed by the ITV companies and under the control of the IBA, Channel 4 was nevertheless given a high degree of financial and editorial independence to pursue its special remit of catering for minority audiences not catered for by the other channels, and introducing innovative and experimental programming. It rapidly became a new type of standard bearer for the public service tradition. It also constituted a fresh departure in the organisation of television, in that it was the first 'publisher broadcaster'. That is, it does not make its own programmes but commissions the greater part of its output from freelance production companies, known as 'independent producers' (the rest of the output is purchased from other channels, here and abroad). As a consequence, Channel 4 has been in the forefront of the development of an industry of small-scale television programme-makers, which has now become a large and vital sector of the British television industry.

The same year as Channel 4 began broadcasting saw the beginnings of 'breakfast television', with the BBC and ITV in fierce and direct competition. A new national franchise was created by the IBA who awarded it to a new company, TV-AM. The new company was headed by a groups of distinguished journalists and broadcasters who promised the highest quality television with a particular commitment to news and current affairs, known as the 'mission to explain.' But the new company was soon in difficulties with low audiences, and therefore low income from advertising. The company went rapidly down market, most of the distinguished people left, and the station was largely 'saved' because of the introduction of Roland Rat, who was immensely popular with young, and not so young, viewers. Some people thought the IBA should have withdrawn the franchise when the commitment to high quality broadcasting was abandoned.

New Technology

It was also clear by this time that advances in technology were opening up the prospect of a revolution in television. In the first place, video recorders were becoming common, giving rise to a whole new video industry, and giving viewers new options, such as films and other material commercially sold or hired, that were not available on the standard channels. Secondly, it appeared that cable television was at last about to take off, as it had done in the USA, with the prospect of a spate of specialist channels paid for by subscription. But most revolutionary of all was satellite broadcasting, avoiding the need for a dense and expensive network of terrestrial transmitting stations, with perhaps hundreds of new channels for anyone who cared to buy a receiving dish, and with little prospect of government control. The long-term potential was very great for operators with sufficient initial investment to create services drawing upon advertising revenue and subscription channels. The question was how government would respond to all these developments and possibilities. It was known that Mrs Thatcher was a passionate advocate of the free market and consumer choice in television, as in everything else, but government would still have to provide some framework which would inevitably influence how the revolution would proceed.

With a government dedicated to free enterprise and privatisation, it was perhaps inevitable that the position of the BBC should be challenged. In 1984 the Conservative Party's advertising agency, Saatchi & Saatchi, published a document entitled *Funding the BBC: The Case for Advertising*. It argued that the licence fee was a flat rate, regressive tax that unfairly hit the poorest, as well as being very difficult to collect (ironically the very arguments later used against Mrs Thatcher's Community Charge). As an alternative the BBC should take advertisements, which would lower the price of television advertising generally and thereby give a boost to the advertising industry. Mrs Thatcher publicly sympathised with these ideas, adding the further objection that the licence fee was a compulsory levy on television viewers whether they watched BBC programmes or not. The Adam Smith Institute went still further and advocated the BBC's complete privatisation (which was Mrs Thatcher's long-term aim, although this was not made public at the time).

These arguments led to the setting up of the Peacock Committee to examine the future funding of the BBC. Since the chairman, Sir Alan Peacock, and most of the rest of the committee were known to be free-market enthusiasts, it was widely believed that the membership had been selected as the most likely to recommend Mrs Thatcher's preferred option of a BBC taking advertising and gradually becoming more and more like a commercial company. However, in its report of 1986 the committee recommended that the BBC should not take advertising, since there was just not enough advertising revenue around to support both the BBC and ITV systems. The BBC, it argued, should continue to be financed by the licence fee for the time being, but eventually be replaced by subscription. It was further recommended that Radio 1 and 2 be sold off to the private sector and that BBC television should be required, along with ITV, to have 40% of its programmes provided by independent producers by 1996. The government accepted the recommendations on funding (although Mrs Thatcher was privately furious), but only obliged the BBC and ITV to have 25% of programming from independent producers by 1994. Meanwhile, the government was working on a comprehensive review of the future of broadcasting, which was published in 1988 and established a starting point for future broadcasting policy.

Broadcasting Policy in the 1990s

The 1988 White Paper and the Broadcasting Acts 1990 and 1996

A revised approach to government broadcasting policy was set out in its 1988 White Paper, *Broadcasting in the 90s: Choice, Competition and Quality*. Its basic themes were:

1.   a dramatic increase in broadcasting, largely due to new technology, which will give the viewer greater consumer choice

2.   that this expansion should be left entirely to commercial broadcasters

3.   that government control will be much lighter than in the past; but that nevertheless

4.   the high quality of British broadcasting will be maintained.

The main controversy over the policy has been whether the last of these is compatible with the rest.

The 1988 White Paper heralded a new age of broadcasting in Britain, with a huge expansion of TV channels and radio stations, a corresponding expansion of commercial broadcasting, a shake up of ITV, a less rigorous control of commercial broadcasting, reform of the BBC, a large expansion of satellite and cable broadcasting, two more commercial channels, and the growth of local television based on new microwave technology. However, the most detailed proposals were for a reorganisation of ITV and how it is regulated. These proposals were embodied in the Broadcasting Acts of 1990 and 1996.

Changing Commercial Television

The 1988 White Paper proposed a drastic reorganisation of the ITV system. That system had been based upon the giving out of regional franchises (plus a national breakfast-time franchise) according to the quality of programming promised, by the Independent Broadcasting Authority (IBA) charged with ensuring quality and a continuance of a substantial public service element. Regional diversity and a reflection of local community interests were considered as important elements in the franchise. So long as existing franchise holders had honoured their previous commitments to provide good quality television according to the IBA's rules, their retention of the franchise was assured. They were also legally protected from the kind of commercial take-over to which ordinary companies are vulnerable. Consequently, the same companies appeared to be in indefinite possession of their franchise. Mrs Thatcher's government felt this was far too cosy and virtually monopolistic (a franchise was once famously referred to as "a licence to print money"). What was needed was a strong injection of commercialism and competition, and one which would bring tax revenues into the Treasury.

The original idea was to have much less regulation, allow television companies to respond to popular choice, let the franchises simply go to the highest bidder (i.e. the amount the company would pay each year to the Treasury), allow companies to be taken over in the normal way and allow them to be just 'publisher' companies (just buy in programmes and not make their own, as with Channel 4) if they wanted to. However, there was disagreement within the government over the retention of the public service element. Mrs Thatcher and the Thatcherites wanted everything left to market forces, and if it disappeared, so be it; while the Home Office wanted the public service tradition protected. The 1988 White Paper was something of a compromise between these two views, and so was the subsequent Broadcasting Act.

The 1990 Broadcasting Act replaced the IBA with the Independent Television Commission (ITC) and a separate Radio Authority, which would regulate broadcasting much more lightly than the IBA. One of ITC's first tasks was to supervise an auction of 16 franchises (15 areas plus national breakfast television). However, the government decided it would be a 'blind auction' with everyone making, a one-off bid in ignorance of what others were bidding. To complicate matters supporters of public service broadcasting within the government had succeeded in introducing a 'quality threshold' which bidders had to satisfy, which meant that franchises would not necessarily go to the highest bidder, although the rules for satisfying the quality threshold were rather vague. Furthermore, the bidders had to satisfy the ITC that their bids were financially viable, although this was based on forecasts of revenue (mostly from advertising) for a decade beginning in several years time. The whole process was clouded in uncertainty, and widely regarded by participants and observers alike as a farce.

The ITC announced the result of the auction in October 1991. There had been 40 bids, with 16 winners and 24 losers. In most cases existing franchise holders had their franchises renewed, but in four cases - Thames TV, TV South, TV South West and TV-AM - they were not. The result caused great anger and controversy, with some losers arguing that the decisions were unfair. Bids could fail for three main reasons:

1.   beaten by a higher bid

2.   failed to pass the quality threshold

3.   the bid was too high to be financially sustainable.

The first reason was accepted by most parties, although TV-AM was furious because although beaten by a higher bid it was a commercially successful company. (Mrs Thatcher was so shocked by TV-AM's failure that, despite having left office the year before, she sent the Chairman a letter of apology). Two companies, Central and Scottish TV, were clever enough to calculate that there would be no rival bids in their respective regions. They each won their franchises with bids of a mere £2,000 each. But it was the other two reasons that caused most controversy, since the criteria were much more subjective. North West TV vehemently objected to losing to Granada because they had failed the quality threshold. Some passed the quality threshold, put in the highest bid, and still failed to win the franchise. This happened to TV South, whose bid of £59.7 million the ITC thought was unrealistic (Meridian TV beat it with a bid of £36.5 million).

There was a curious exchange of roles between Thames TV and Carlton TV, one of the major independent producers. Carlton won the franchise from Thames, which sold some of its facilities to Carlton, shed staff and immediately set up as an independent producer. However, that was not the end of the story, since after a two year breathing space franchise holders could be taken over like any other company. Such mergers and take-overs have progressively taken place from soon after the new franchises began in 1993 - with the additional aspect that within a further two years foreign ownership of franchises was allowed.

With a much fiercer competitive environment within the world of conventional television there was also increasing competition from cable companies, still developing modestly and more importantly, from satellite. Here the big player became BSkyB, dominated by Rupert Murdoch, the newspaper proprietor of the News International group (including the *Sun*, *Times*, and *Sunday Times*.) Satellite usage was promoted by the astute observation that an investment in buying exclusive rights to televise popular live sporting events, especially football, would provide a wonderful marketing tool. The 1990 Broadcasting Act also provided for the creation of a fifth terrestrial channel but there were substantial delays in establishing it. There were doubts about the amount of advertising revenue available to support it. The Department of Trade and Industry was keen to wait for new digital technology to develop sufficiently so that it could be used. But this did not take place with sufficient speed; and when it was decided to use older analogue technology, this required a national scheme for retuning video recorders to prevent interference from the frequencies on which Channel 5 was to be transmitted. It was not launched until March 1997.

Reform of the BBC

The 1988 White Paper was principally concerned with commercial broadcasting, but also looked at the BBC. It said the BBC needed to be more commercial and take more programmes from independent producers. But the principle recommendation was that the licence fee be frozen and the Corporation look for new sources of income that could replace the licence fee after 1996. Many immediately saw great dangers in this proposal. If the BBC had to fight for audiences in order to sustain an income it would be forced to go downmarket, and reduce its serious drama and documentaries in favour of mass audience programmes. The White Paper suggested that the BBC experiment with subscription as a possible alternative to the licence fee. Objectors thought this would reduce the BBC to a small TV company instead of one of the world's greatest (if not *the* greatest) and the flagship of British broadcasting.

It is now well known that Mrs Thatcher wanted the BBC to take advertising and turn itself into a commercial broadcaster, which could then be broken up and sold to the private sector. Mrs Thatcher apparently had no sympathy for publicly owned public service broadcasting. Everything, she thought, should be left to the free market and consumer choice. However, with Mrs Thatcher's departure in 1990, those within government committed to sustaining public service broadcasting were in a stronger position. In November 1992 the new Department of National Heritage issued a Green Paper *The Future of the BBC: A consultation document*, which made it quite clear that, while the BBC would still need to change, the threat of privatisation and marginalisation had been lifted. It stated the government's commitment to the BBC remaining a major broadcaster with a special responsibility for public service broadcasting, but invited discussion on how best this might be organised and financed.

From the early 1990s there has been an almost continuous debate on the future of the BBC. This has revolved around discussions of the basic principle that the future of quality broadcasting in Britain depends upon a strong BBC supported by the licence fee, but also involves issues about the level of financing and how the BBC should react to exploit new technology in a global market place. Before considering these questions it is first necessary to examine how broadcasting is currently organised.

The Organisation of Broadcasting in Britain

At the beginnings of broadcasting in Britain, the Home Office was the central government department responsible. It was still the Home Office that drew up and published the November 1988 White Paper and put through the subsequent 1990 Broadcasting Act. However, in 1992 responsibility for broadcasting was transferred to the newly created Department of National Heritage, and since 1997 this has now passed to the Department for Culture, Media and Sport (DCMS). It is important to note that a number of current important issues in the regulation of broadcasting, such as mergers and ownership of ITV companies and access to new technology, also consumer protection, have important commercial and competitive aspects which remain the concern of the Department of Trade and Industry (DTI).

The Department for Culture, Media and Sport (DCMS)

The DCMS is now responsible for broadcasting policy and for any legislation that such policy may entail. It is answerable to Parliament for these things and for conveying to Parliament the annual reports and accounts of the various bodies directly engaged in broadcasting, including the BBC and the Independent Television Commission (ITC). The DCMS has particular functions in respect of each of these.

In the case of the BBC the DCMS is responsible for:

- the Royal Charter. This is the constitution of the BBC, which sets out its aims and organisation. But it is granted only for a limited period, and this gives the government an opportunity to make changes each time the Charter expires

- the same is true of the operating licence (known as the Licence and Agreement) which lays down certain other conditions which must be adhered to

- the Secretary of State for Culture (after consultation with the Prime Minister) chooses the Chairman and Board of Governors, who are ultimately responsible for all that the BBC does

- finally, the Secretary of State sets the licence fee, which is the licence we all pay for in order to watch television legally. It is this licence fee that provides most of the BBC's income. There is a direct, though not immediate, relationship between the licence fee and the quality of BBC programmes we watch, the number of repeats shown, and so on.

These are the ways the DCMS sets the terms within which the BBC operates. The BBC has a duty to present to Parliament an annual report and statement of accounts. Beyond these the Corporation is largely left to run its own affairs in its own way. However, from time to time the BBC has been in conflict with the government over a number of issues, when it was thought that the government was trying to interfere directly with its independence.

The ITC does not have a Royal Charter. The constitution of bodies regulating commercial television have been set out in successive Broadcasting Acts, in particular those of 1990 and 1996. The DCMS is responsible

- for seeing these acts are passed as the need arises

- for the provision of the ITC's basic remit on broadcasting issues and licences

- appointing the members of the Commission, who are the equivalent of the BBC's Board of Governors.

As with the BBC, the ITC is responsible to Parliament through the DCMS and must provide annual reports and financial accounts. Beyond this the ITC is left to carry out its functions largely unhindered. The same system is broadly followed with other broadcasting bodies: the Radio Authority, the Welsh Channel Four Authority and the Broadcasting Standards Commission.

The British Broadcasting Corporation (BBC)

The constitution of the BBC is set out in its Royal Charter, which, like the Licence and Agreement, has to be periodically renewed (the present Charter and Licence run out in December 2006). This constitution vests all powers and responsibilities in the Board of Governors, who are responsible for all that the BBC does. The board consists of twelve governors: a chairman and vice chairman; three national governors, representing Scotland, Wales and Northern Ireland; and seven others, one of whom has special responsibility for the English regions. These are not professional broadcasters, nor even full-time. They are drawn from all walks of life, have different political persuasions, and normally include figures drawn from business, universities, trade-unions, former senior civil servants, the arts, and ethnic minorities. They appoint the most senior management of the BBC staff and are responsible for ensuring that the BBC respects its charter and other obligations. In practice the Governors seem to exercise a very light touch over the running of the corporation.

The Director-General (DG) leads the nearly 20,000 professionals on the BBC staff, with a management structure based on an Executive Committee which includes the heads of the various departments. The new DG, Greg Dyke, who took up office in January 2000, has instituted a number of internal reforms designed to reduce bureaucracy and costs (and the size of the staff) and increase the emphasis on programmes. The aim is to reduce the amount of money spent on running the BBC from 24% to 15% of total income over a five year period, freeing up an extra £200 million for spending on programmes and helping meet the government-imposed target to make savings of £1.2 billion over the next seven years. The new structure is set out in the following diagram.

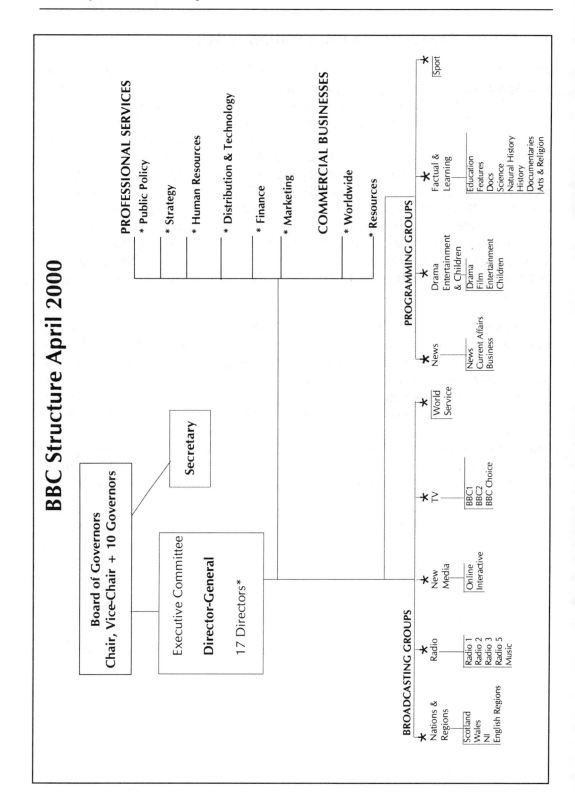

BBC Structure April 2000

Board of Governors
Chair, Vice-Chair + 10 Governors

Secretary

Executive Committee

Director-General

17 Directors*

PROFESSIONAL SERVICES

* Public Policy
* Strategy
* Human Resources
* Distribution & Technology
* Finance
* Marketing

COMMERCIAL BUSINESSES

* Worldwide
* Resources

BROADCASTING GROUPS

* Nations & Regions
  Scotland
  Wales
  NI
  English Regions

* Radio
  Radio 1
  Radio 2
  Radio 3
  Radio 5
  Music

* New Media
  Online
  Interactive

* TV
  BBC1
  BBC2
  BBC Choice

* World Service

PROGRAMMING GROUPS

* News
  News
  Current Affairs
  Business

* Drama Entertainment & Children
  Drama
  Film
  Entertainment
  Children

* Factual & Learning
  Education
  Features
  Docs
  Science
  Natural History
  History
  Documentaries
  Arts & Religion

* Sport

The BBC traditionally performs all aspects of broadcasting:

- it commissions programmes

- it makes programmes

- it transmits them.

(ITV companies do the first two, and Channels 4 and 5 mostly just the first). The Corporation also provides two national television channels and five national radio channels, plus a large local radio network. In addition, it has been developing national digital TV and radio services and a very successful online website operation. The domestic television, radio and online services are largely funded by the licence fee, which in 2000 stands at £104. Some additional income comes from commercial activities such the sales of programmes overseas, video sales, etc. which generated over £83 million in 1999-2000. The total expenditure in 1999-2000 of £2.2 billion, included as major components:

BBC 1 TV	£832m
BBC 2 TV	£421m
Regional TV	£207m
Five Radio Networks	£305m
Regional/Local Radio	£158m
New channels/digital/online	£204m
Licence fee collection	£114m

Its major external services, in particular a vast range of radio services in foreign countries in a multitude of languages as part of the World Service and a growing international TV presence, receive substantial funding from the Foreign Office.

The Independent Television Commission (ITC)

The ITC came into being in 1991, taking over the responsibilities for licensing and regulation of commercial television from the old IBA and the Cable Authority. The powers and responsibilities of the ITC are vested in the Commission consisting of ten members, similar to the BBC Board, which has a full-time professional staff to carry out the work. It is charged with licensing and regulating all commercial television services (analogue and digital) in the United Kingdom, including:

- Channel 3 (the ITV companies)

- Channel 4

- Channel 5

- cable television

- satellite television (originating in the UK)

- Teletext and other data services.

The ITC is charged with:

1. ensuring that a wide range of television services is available throughout the UK and that, taken as a whole, they are of high quality and appeal to a variety of tastes and interests

2. ensuring that there is fair and effective competition in the provision of these services

3. issuing the licences that allow commercial television companies to broadcast in and from the UK, setting out conditions on standards of programmes and advertising

4. monitoring the performance of broadcasters against the requirements of their licences and the various published codes and guidelines

5. investigating complaints and publishing its findings.

The ITC Codes are designed to protect viewers' interests on such matters as good taste and decency, political impartiality, good standards of advertising. There are a variety of penalties to ensure compliance, up to the withdrawal of the licence.

Unlike its predecessor body, the ITC does not transmit programmes, the transmission system having been privatised in 1991. Nor is the ITC as deeply involved in the scheduling of programmes as the old IBA was. This is in line with the 'lighter touch' that the 1988 White Paper sought. One major exception, and controversy, has turned on the scheduling of ITV (Channel 3) news, because the companies are required to take news from a designated provider (ITN) and broadcast it live and simultaneously. After much discussion, in 1998 the ITC allowed on a 12 month trial basis, the removal of the flagship 'News at Ten' and its replacement with an enhanced 6.30 news and a shorter 11.00 bulletin. This has continued to cause debate, and in July 2000 the ITC has been attempting to enforce a further rescheduling on the ITV companies.

In respect of the quality of programmes the ITC has been determined not to just leave things to the free market (as Mrs Thatcher had intended). It was quite stringent in its application of the 'quality threshold' when it awarded its franchises in 1991 (for ten years from 1st January 1993), and has been prepared to warn companies of poor standards when it thought necessary. In May 1994 the ITC warned several companies that the quality of their programmes was not as good as it should be. GMTV (holding the breakfast franchise) was threatened with a £2 million fine unless its quality improved, while Carlton, the largest ITV company of all, was thought not to have fulfilled its promises of new, good quality programmes (interestingly *The Sun* newspaper accused the Commission of snobbery and elitism for criticising programmes that millions of people enjoyed). But since it does not vet or preview programmes, it can only act after they have been broadcast and take any necessary action after the event. Thus Channel 4 was fined £150,000 for breaches of the ITC programme code for its 1997 documentary "Too Much Too Young: Chickens" where sequences with Glasgow 'rent boys' allegedly involving members of the public had actually been filmed using personnel from the production team.

Channel 3 (ITV)

This is made up of 15 regional licences and a national breakfast-time licence (GMTV).

Licence Holder	Area
Anglia	East of England
Border	Borders & the Isle of Man
Central	East, West & South Midlands
Channel	Channel Islands
Carlton	London weekday
Grampian	North of Scotland
Granada	North-West England
HTV	Wales & West of England
LWT	London weekend
Meridian	South & South-East England
Scottish	Central Scotland
Tyne Tees	North-East England
Ulster	N. Ireland
Westcountry	South-West England
Yorkshire	Yorkshire

The ITV companies must meet 'positive' programme requirements, including minimum percentages of 'original' and 'European' material, independent productions, and nine programme strands - drama, entertainment, sport, news, factual programmes (including current affairs), education, religion, arts, children's - and providing subtitling for deaf viewers.

The Channel 3 service is financed mainly by the sale of advertising airtime. In 1999, net advertising revenue of the regional C3 companies was £1,874 million and £65m for the national breakfast-time service. The bid made by each Channel 3 licensee is paid annually, adjusted for inflation. The payments are assessed and collected by the ITC but are forwarded to the Government. In 1999 payments totalled £419 million. Since the award of the licences, there have been a number of mergers and take-overs. This makes the regionally based system appear rather artificial, since in the summer of 2000 it seems that all the franchises are likely to be held by only two companies, Granada and Carlton. But in principle the licence conditions attached to the separate geographical areas remain in force even though the shareholders have changed.

Channel 4

This is a national service, except for Wales, which has its own Welsh Channel Four (SC4). Channel Four used to be owned by the IBA, but the 1990 Broadcasting Act reconstituted it as a statutory non-profit making corporation. The Act also changed its method of financing. Previously the other ITV companies financed Channel 4 by paying a fixed percentage of the previous year's income from advertising, but selling advertising time on Channel 4 and keeping the revenue. This arrangement was replaced by an even more complicated one. Since 1991 Channel 4 has sold its own advertising, but to ensure its viability, the ITV companies were obliged to provide extra funds if advertising revenue fell below what was needed to run the channel. If, on the other hand, revenue was more than was needed, the surplus had to be paid to the ITV companies. In fact, to the surprise of some, Channel 4 was very successful at selling its advertising, and produced a consistent surplus which it was then obliged to give to the ITV companies. Finally in 1997 Chris Smith, Secretary of State at the DCMS, made an order under his powers in the 1996 Broadcasting Act to reduce these payments. In 1999 the Channel 4 net advertising revenue was £590 million. (The Welsh SC4 continues to be subsidised by a small percentage of C4 and ITV advertising revenues.)

According to the Broadcasting Act, Channel 4 is meant to appeal to tastes and interests not generally catered for by the ordinary ITV companies, encouraging innovation and experiment at a high standard, including programmes of news, current affairs, and educational value, with a proportion which are European. This obligation was vigorously pursued by the channel's first chief executive, Jeremy Isaacs, and his successors Michael Grade and Michael Jackson. It has a special brief to cater for minority interests likely to otherwise be ignored by commercial television. Thus, there have been regular programmes for ethnic minorities, trade unionists, the handicapped and other social minorities. There is also extensive programming for minority tastes: wine lovers, jazz lovers, American football and baseball enthusiasts and a multitude of others. In recent years there has been a deliberate policy to test the boundaries relating to sex and gender issues - a move which led to some accusations in the tabloid press of C4 broadcasting pornography. It also prompted a series of interventions by the ITC about contraventions of the codes and inadequate compliance procedures - 8 cases in 1996 and 14 in 1997.

Channel 4 has been innovative in the way programmes are made and relate to the public. For example, the channel pioneered extensive use of back-up material where viewers send for free or cheap information sheets or booklets. Another example is the 'Film on Four' scheme, where a substantial part of the drama budget goes on funding (partly or wholly) the making of feature films, which will often be released in cinemas before reaching the Channel 4 screen. This has proved to be a great and much-needed boost to the British film industry, and has helped to develop new writing and film-making talent. The scheme has been responsible for over 100 films since the channel began, including such critically and commercially successful films as *Letter to Breznhev, My Beautiful Laundrette, Mona Lisa, A Room with a View,* and *Four Weddings and a Funeral.* It has been followed in 1998 by the launch of a subscription film channel 'FilmFour.'

A further major difference between Channel 4 and other companies is that it is essentially a 'publisher' company. It does not make its own programmes but commissions them from others and sees that they reach the public, just as a book publisher commissions and accepts books by independent authors and sees that they reach the bookshops and does not have them written or even printed by its own staff. As a result of this system, Channel 4 has been responsible for a flourishing of small firms making their own television programmes, known as the 'independent producers'. Subsequently the BBC and ITV companies were also obliged by government to take 25% of their programmes from the independents, and these have become a major sector of the television industry.

Channel 5

The Government's White Paper *Broadcasting in the 90s: competition, choice and quality (1988)* first proposed an additional terrestrial channel. Government studies established that coverage of 65-70% of the population could be provided on Ultra High Frequency (UHF) in the band using channels 35 and 37. These could be received by existing TV receivers, although some viewers might need a new or additional aerial. Channel 5 was planned to enlarge the choice of a majority of UK viewers and to introduce new competition to the advertising market, with a licence to be awarded on the basis of a competitive tender with a quality threshold in terms of programming. After several abortive attempts and delays, the ITC received bids in

1995 from (bid amount): Channel 5 Broadcasting Ltd and Virgin TV Ltd (each £22,002,000 - apparently a remarkable coincidence); New Century TV Ltd (£2,000,000); UKTV (£36,261,158). The ITC announced its decision to award the licence to Channel 5 Broadcasting Ltd. New Century TV (with a lower cash bid) had also passed the quality threshold, but UKTV and Virgin TV did not for different reasons comply with this requirement. Virgin TV subsequently appealed against the ITC decision and was granted leave for a judicial review of the decision in the High Court, which failed in January 1996.

The successful bidder was owned by three major shareholders, United News & Media, CLT/UFA and Pearson (since merged), each of which was a major media group. The service was launched on 30 March 1997 and has proved commercially successful with net advertising revenue in 1999 of £187 million. While it does have to meet certain ITC standards, most of its programming could be described as 'cheap and cheerful' with a recent addiction to late evening soft pornography.

The Radio Authority

Set up by the 1990 Broadcasting Act, the Radio Authority licenses, assigns frequencies to, and regulates all commercial radio in the UK (but not the BBC.) The Authority has seven members appointed by the DCMS for five years, and is supported by about forty professional staff. It has granted three national licences, awarded on the basis of cash bids along with guarantees of meeting the statutory criteria, for eight year periods; one of which under the law must be for a 'non-pop' station (Classic FM) and one a speech based service (Talk Radio), with the third going to Virgin Radio offering a rock and pop mix. The Authority also licenses local stations of various sorts, including commercial organisations, experimental and short-term community broadcasting, and restricted (e.g. hospitals and universities.) It is also responsible for cable and satellite radio licences, and the new emerging national and local digital radio services, with the first national multiplex licence awarded to Digital One, which commenced operations in November 1999.

The Broadcasting Standards Commission

This has been created by the merger of two separate bodies. The *Broadcasting Complaints Commission* was set up by the Broadcasting Act of 1981 to deal with certain kinds of complaints against the broadcasters. It considered complaints concerned with the unfair treatment of individuals or organisations in any radio or television programme, or the invasion of privacy involved in gaining information in connection with any radio or television programme. It did not deal with complaints about bad language, the portrayal of sex, violence or other matters, nor investigate cases where the complainant can seek redress through the courts. The *Broadcasting Standards Council* was set up in 1988, but given legal status by the 1990 Broadcasting

Act. It had the primary task of devising a code on the use of sex and violence in broadcasting, which broadcasters are obliged to take account of. This was done in consultation with broadcasting producers; and with the help of research, commissioned by the Council, on the effect of televised sex and violence on viewers.

The merged body thus covers two sets of complaints, involving unfair treatment of people by programme makers and also the rather more general issues of decency and taste. The part-time members are appointed by the Secretary of State, and are assisted by a small staff in the investigation of the complaints. Any person or organisation can make a complaint if they feel they have been badly treated in a programme or in the making of it. The ordinary viewer cannot use the Commission if they think someone else has been wronged. The complainant just has to write giving details and the Commission will take it up from there. Both sides are listened to carefully before the Commission comes to a decision as to whether the complaint was justified. That decision is set out in full and sent to all concerned; copies are also sent to national newspapers and to anyone who writes and asks for one. In addition, the Commission can require the ITC, BBC or other appropriate body, to publish the outcome of the adjudication (usually whether it upholds the complaint or not) in the *Radio* or *TV Times* and also broadcast it at a time similar to that at which the original programme went on the air. But beyond publicising their judgements the Commission has no further powers.

The Debate on Quality

Ever since the 1988 White Paper there has been a fierce debate about government broadcasting policy. The policy was designed to create a framework for a new age of technological change and opportunities in broadcasting, which would be based on greater deregulation and free market competition. That is, one where there is genuine competition and the viewer has genuine choice among the expanding opportunities, yet where the high standards of British broadcasting are maintained. Much of the debate turns on whether these aims are compatible with each other and what resources are required to maintain a sphere of public broadcasting.

Political Divisions and the Debate on Public Service Broadcasting

There is in fact a wide spectrum of political opinion ranging from those on the libertarian right (such as the Adam Smith Institute) that advocate complete deregulation, breaking up the BBC and selling off the pieces to private enterprise; to those on the left who want much more regulation than at present. Most opinion is somewhere in between. However, the issue became an urgent one in the early 1990s since the government had to make important decisions concerning the future of the

BBC, its Charter and Licence which were due for renewal in 1996, and there were also decisions to be made concerning the future of ITV.

The 1988 White Paper and the Broadcasting Act that followed two years later, were both the products of compromise, reflecting a division of opinion within government and the Conservative Party. On the one hand, there was the Thatcherite zeal for the free market, and a distaste for public service broadcasting. On the other hand, there were the traditionalists who believed in the BBC and its public service tradition (represented by the Home Office). The White Paper and the Act tried to accommodate both, arguably incompatible, resulting in something of a mess. Hence the ITV auction fiasco, where free market rules and a judgement of quality were mixed together in a way that produced much criticism. Policy was something of a compromise between two contrary views, and this continues to generate confusion. Within the political spectrum there are still strong free-marketeers (especially on the Thatcherite right) and those who equally firmly uphold the public service ideal. Both sides have their arguments.

International Comparisons

Those opposed to deregulation and free market ideas point to the experience of other countries. British broadcasting is often admired as among the finest in the world, which is in striking contrast to the television of such countries as the USA and Italy. The USA is an obvious comparison because, apart from being English-speaking, it is the most technologically advanced of countries and has always been a technical leader in mass broadcasting. Throughout its history, US broadcasting has never had a reputation for quality. This is generally thought to be because US television has always been run on a commercial basis, and as such has never been seen as anything much more than a medium of mass entertainment. The big national networks have always been dominated by advertising companies who effectively decide what goes on the screen. They want the most popular programmes with the biggest audiences; and if a series has low audience ratings then it will soon be taken off because its advertising space will not be sold. The result is that American national television networks are dominated by soap operas, game shows and light entertainment. Serious documentaries are rare, news and current affairs programmes are often parochial and poor quality; and serious drama is practically never attempted. In some parts of the USA there is a public service channel (PBS) but this is run almost as a charity with a very low share of the viewing market, providing a service for a small educated audience and reliant to a great extent on foreign programmes, much of it from the BBC and the other British channels.

Another example of a national broadcasting system that is often mentioned in this context is that of Italy. This started from the position of a state-run monopoly broadcasting service of rather low quality, largely because it was dominated and colonised by the governing political parties. Then in the early 1990s the Italian government decided to completely deregulate its television, and literally anyone could set up a station and start broadcasting. The result was chaotic. In the big cities, dozens of stations sprang up, often interfering with each other's transmissions, often only lasting a few months and often showing just violent and pornographic material. It is generally agreed that the lowest point was reached when the output of some small stations began to consist of little more than local housewives taking their clothes off and advertising for local shops. The country now has over a thousand channels.

In Italy there is also a worrying political dimension, since deregulation also allowed the creation of a media empire in respect of national network television. This is the Berlusconi media empire where Mr Berlusconi and his family own a large proportion of national commercial television, as well as national newspapers and the countries largest advertising agency. This concentration of media power also enabled Berlusconi to create a major national political party from scratch in a matter of months, and win the Italian general election of 1994. His success enabled him to bring Fascists into government for the first time in any European country since 1945.

The Free Market Case

There are some who believe these interpretations and fears are unjustified. They argue, for example, that a good deal of US television is now very good. This is not in respect of the national networks, where all agree that most programmes are bland and of low quality; the improvements have come in the area of highly competitive cable television, which sustains a great variety of channels catering for all kinds of tastes. These include news, sport, family and educational channels, along with minority tastes such as music and serious drama. They also argue that the British viewing public would just not stand for endless soaps, game shows, and the like, and would not go on watching if that were all the new television offered. The advertising industry is not just interested in the biggest audiences, but is often in search of the more affluent audiences that would watch high quality television, just as the huge growth of newspapers like the Sunday Times has been possible by the advertising of more exclusive products.

Finally, it is argued that British television has been dominated for too long by an elite few who decided what was good for the British public to watch. It should be for the British public to decide what it wants to watch. There are those who insist on the consumer's right to choose, and that nobody has the right to question what the market produces, no matter what that might be. In principle, broadcasting is no different from any other sector of the economy, and the best results will result from minimum regulation and the greatest freedom of action for individual enterprise.

The Case for the Public Service Element

Those against a free market in British broadcasting fear that wholesale deregulation would lead to television like the USA or Italy. They argue, first of all, that the foundation of Britain's high quality broadcasting is the BBC and its public service tradition, and that this tradition is sustained by the licence fee. If the BBC had to take advertising, or otherwise depend on an insecure form of income such as subscription, then it would inevitably become involved either in a ratings war or decline into an irrelevant sideshow. The result would be that mass popularity programmes (like soaps, game shows, etc.) would increasingly replace serious programmes. The BBC would either become just a mass entertainment organisation engaged in 'dumbing-down' its content to compete with unregulated commercial operators, or be a small elitist organisation for the few prepared, or able, to pay for expensive, high quality, minority interest programmes.

The argument cannot just depend on the *existence* of a publicly owned broadcaster which does not depend on advertising, such as the BBC. It is also vital for it to have a significant size, high quality presence in the broadcasting sector, so that it is actually watched by a mass audience and has a real impact on viewing habits. The BBC has always argued that it must present a broad portfolio of different types of quality programme, whether costume drama, documentaries, popular series such as 'East Enders', natural history, or sitcoms. By having a market share around the 40% level, it can justify its subsidised status and affect the whole 'ecology' of the broadcasting system. PBS in America has only 3%, and so has negligible impact either on the viewing public or other broadcasters. So the BBC needs the licence fee to be set at a level which can maintain its existing portfolio of activities and respond to new opportunities.

The other aspect of the argument is the valuable contribution that advertising-supported channels can make if they are properly regulated and are in competition where standards are partly set by the BBC. In this situation, where the ITC takes into account quality and diversity when awarding licences, Channels 3, 4 and 5 all contribute to ensuring that the public service element is maintained. Indeed these channels make many programmes that are as good, if not better, than the BBC - so it would not necessarily be easy for most viewers to remember which channels carried such drama series as *Jewel in the Crown, Brideshead Revisited, Pride and Prejudice, Moll Flanders, Oliver Twist* and *The Camomile Lawn*. While the new ITC has shown some determination to regulate for quality, it remains true that in the new environment the ITV companies are under fierce commercial pressure which many feel will inevitably drive them down market whatever the ITC says. There is much competition from satellite and cable. Furthermore the ITV companies must now pay many millions (according to how much they bid for their franchises) to the Treasury, which under the previous system would have gone on programmes or profits. They must deliver large audiences or their advertising revenue will fall, which means mass audience programmes; and they must make good and regular profits or they will be taken over by another company.

In other words, if the system is too deregulated and competitive, there are lower incentives to maintain quality. Good programmes, such as high quality drama series, are extremely expensive to make. Good quality programmes, such as documentaries do not command high audiences, and stand less chance of being made if revenue depends upon mass audiences. The BBC annual accounts for 1999-2000 show average production costs for drama at £531,000 per hour, entertainment £222,000, sport £90,000, and 'daytime' programming only £34,000. BBC 1 and BBC 2 spent about £650 million on original programmes, while the total for all of Rupert Murdoch's 'Sky' channels was under £100 million.

Funding the BBC

For these reasons, many feel that a commitment to good quality broadcasting requires both positive regulation and an adequately financed BBC. This has sharpened the discussions which have continued for many years about the level of the licence, and what services the BBC should be providing and on what terms. In the 1990s the Conservative government placed the BBC in a state of chronic uncertainty leading up to the renewal of its Royal Charter in 1996. Its income was shrinking in real terms and uncertain; the corporation was undergoing a drastic management upheaval; and its capacity to develop commercial activities was severely restricted.

The central problem was the size and security of the BBC's income. Even if the licence fee was secure and increased in line with inflation, there were difficulties since its costs were rising faster than inflation. Apart from dramatically cutting down its activities (such as giving up regional broadcasting or breakfast television, etc.), the most likely alternative to secure its finances was to expand its commercial activities. These include selling programmes abroad, publishing books and magazines, selling videos of its programmes, a link-up with satellite broadcasting using its old programmes (i.e. UK Gold), and World Service TV. These accounted for five per cent of BBC income. It could be much more, but this would need more investment.

These questions were partly addressed in the government's White Paper of July 1994, *The Future of the BBC: Serving the Nation, Competing Worldwide,* which at least resolved matters for the near future. Following this, the Charter and Licence were renewed early for ten years to December 2006, and the licence fee guaranteed at least until 2001 although kept under tight control. The BBC would retain all of its radio and television services and would be allowed far greater freedom to engage in commercial activity. Expansion was possible abroad, including setting up satellite channels with commercial partners - such projects must not be financed by the licence fee. A twenty-four hour television news service for Britain was subsequently launched.

The White Paper represented a triumph for the BBC, and for its Director-General, John Birt, who had been pursuing a highly controversial policy of internal reform. He introduced an internal market known as 'producer choice', where different parts of the BBC compete with each other, and buy services from each other in competition with outside providers; as well as shedding some 5,000 jobs in the process. Although the reforms caused uproar and turmoil within the BBC, it would seem that they have saved the Corporation from more drastic measures advocated by the right of the Conservative Party. Nevertheless the right were greatly disappointed with the White Paper. They criticised it for continuing to protect the licence fee, and asked why privatisation, considered by the government to be good for other industries, was not good for the BBC.

With the election of a Labour government in 1997 the climate began to change. In 1998 the Secretary of State announced that the government was establishing a review panel to consider BBC funding, starting from the assumption that the licence fee would remain the major source, and considering the future implications of technological development. It was chaired by Gavyn Davies (an economist and partner in the major financial institution Goldman Sachs) and reported to DCMS in July 1999. After further consultation following the publication of the report, including a rather hostile set of proposals to the BBC from the House of Commons CMS Select Committee, the Secretary of State announced government policy on 21 February 2000. Among the major points were:

- a strong commitment to public service broadcasting, with the BBC "the UK's most important cultural institution" at its heart

- the BBC should maintain a distinctive schedule of benchmark quality programmes and lead the drive to take up digital and on-line services

- an acceptance of the Davies view that extra funding is needed for the BBC

- a rejection of the level of the licence fee increase proposed (2-2.5% above inflation), and also of Davies' recommendation for a supplementary fee for digital TV receivers

- an expectation of more efficiency savings and more revenue generated from commercial activities

- annual licence fee increases of 1.5% above inflation

- a review of the BBC digital services, especially News 24

- a review of BBC governance in a forthcoming White Paper on broadcasting and telecommunications.

So while there has been some improvement in the political climate for the BBC, the debate will go on. It is also clear that there is some governmental criticism of the role of the BBC Governors, particularly the way in which they are alleged to have allowed expensive digital developments such as News 24 and radio to go forward without sufficiently checking the costs. The forthcoming White Paper may well have something to say about this. But the great changes occurring within global communications will perhaps not allow anything to remain settled for long and may indeed swamp any system that a national government could attempt to impose.

Broadcasting and the Communications Revolution

The world is embarking on a communications revolution as great as, some believe greater than, that associated with the coming of the railways or the motorcar or radio and television. Nobody knows where it will all lead, but it will almost certainly transform many aspects of our lives. Broadcasting will certainly play an important part in the revolution, but not the only part. At the centre of this revolution is the development of what has come to be called the 'digital information superhighway', most of the technology for which is already with us or about to appear.

The Information Superhighways

The superhighway is all about the consequences of the development and integration of three pieces of electronic equipment many of us already have in our homes. These are the television, the telephone and the personal computer (PC). Several examples of this kind of integration became commonplace in the 1990s: Fax machines using the telephone system; video-conferencing increasingly common in business; televisions for limited data services such as teletext. We can link a personal computer to the telephone system through a modem, which can link us to other computers in other parts of the world. As a result we communicate, send and download vast quantities of information through the internet. The use of the world-wide-web system has made such activities much more user-friendly. Emails and e-commerce are becoming increasingly normal. Not only the buying and selling of goods and services, but education and the whole 'knowledge economy' are increasingly being based upon these techniques. In the summer of 2000 nearly 25% of households in Britain had home access to the internet, with the figure substantially higher if access via workplace, schools, colleges etc was included.

The fundamental technological development, which drives the process, is 'digitalisation'. This means converting, storing and transmitting many different kinds of information as sets of numbers. This is what computers do in various ways; written text, diagrams and pictures, for example, are stored as sets of numbers. This can be done with sounds, as with a music CD or digital tape recorder, or with moving images. Such digital audio-visual systems produce better definition than analogue systems, with superior pictures and sound, and they also make it easier to transmit the materials and also to mix in much more information in multi-media activities. Thus digital TV signals can carry so much more information that it is possible to include a number of different camera perspectives of a football match, and allow the viewer at home rather than a TV director to decide which particular angle to use.

So the future of high technical quality TV (and radio) is digital, and although equipment is still expensive and in limited circulation, the British government is already thinking ahead to a period between 2005-2010 when the old analogue TV systems might be turned off. About 4 million homes now (July 2000) have access to digital television, mainly through Sky, ONdigital, and the cable operators NTL and Telewest. The take-up for radio has been very slow, largely because it is very expensive and offers relatively few advantages for the vast majority of listeners.

But a great deal more is possible if we integrate all three with sophisticated interactive links capable of carrying large amounts of information without delay. We already have information services through our television sets, and interaction could be vastly extended into all kinds of information and entertainment on demand: films, video games. We could have instant access to the world's libraries, databases and television channels. This is in addition to the capacity to tune in to hundreds, if not thousands, of TV channels from all parts of the globe.

As consumers of broadcasting, one particular piece of integration transforms our television watching. If the future is going to offer thousands of TV channels, this turns the need to know what is on into a serious problem. The television set can be combined with a computer to produce a 'smart screen'; that is, one that we could teach to select the kinds of programmes we like to watch (or it could learn from our choices), tosort, store and reschedule them and turn them into a package of programmes. The same could apply to advertising. We could have the computer screen out the advertisements; or it could select those relevant to our needs and tastes (for example, show only those motor car adverts that suit our financial and family circumstances). In effect, the computer would create for us our own individual television channel tailored to our personal tastes and needs. This is in fact the electronic programme guide (EPG) which two thirds of digital TV viewers now use to organise their viewing, rather than a traditional listings magazine.

Merging Technologies

Historically we have communications systems which developed separately, but are now rapidly converging in all kinds of ways. Telephone systems were based on land-based copper wire connections with limited capacity and speed, and usually operated by public monopolies which acted simply as carriers for business and private messages. Technologically advanced developments such as fibre optic cables, microwave and satellite systems are now being operated by a variety of competing utility companies. And these phone systems are being rivalled by the ubiquitous mobile which has already entered 50% of British households (and has saturated the market in Finland.) These new methods have enormous capacity to carry virtually limitless messages. TV and radio broadcasting started through land-based (terrestrial) networks and then became available through Cable (in some areas) and satellite platforms. Internet access came through PCs connected to service providers (ISP) via the commercial phone system, or in some cases (through large organisations and employers) directly through fibre optic spines. But increasingly the barriers are breaking down. Cable can be used not only for TV, but also to provide phone services and internet access. Mobiles can provide internet access through a (WAP) system without using a PC. An interactive TV set based on the right cable platform can provide internet access. TV and radio channels can be accessed through the internet. Newspaper publishers have established sophisticated web-sites.

A few years ago the home consumer of leisure could either take one's entertainment such as film or music at the time dictated by broadcast schedulers (or record a programme and play it later ~ time-shifting), or go out and buy or rent a CD or Video to take home. But digital broadcasting, whether delivered from terrestrial, cable or satellite platforms gives far greater flexibility. One could use the developing services which deliver a video through the phone line or download a music CD, possibly disregarding the rights of the copyright holder, over the internet through MP3 software.

So now there is a convergence of activity and overlap of interests in four big industrial sectors with major implications for leisure and for the whole economy. These, with a total estimated UK market capitalisation of over £500 billion in January 2000 are:

- *Audio-Visual* - terrestrial broadcasting, cable and satellite, electronic equipment, home entertainment

- *Telephony* - traditional and mobile

- *Information Technology* - hardware, software, internet, business services

- *Publishing* - newspapers, magazines, books, electronic.

The race is now on to develop the superhighways and especially to exploit their potential commercially. There is a continuing scramble to create take-overs, mergers and link-ups of various kinds between major companies in different parts of the world of media, communications and computers: computer hardware companies, software companies, newspaper corporations, film companies, cable TV companies, telephone companies, video rental companies, major TV and radio broadcasters, and so on. All this frantic activity is fuelled by the belief that only international multi-media conglomerates will be powerful enough to compete effectively in the new superhighway environment. Globally there are already some companies with massive market capitalisation such as Microsoft ($595 billion), AOL/Time Warner ($350 billion), AT&T/TCI ($170 billion), Yahoo ($121 billion), Sony ($95 billion), Viacom/CBS ($91 billion), NewsCorp ($89 billion) and Disney ($72 billion.)

British Involvement

The extent to which Britain and British companies are, or could be, involved in these developments is a complex question. The situation seems to be one of opportunity hampered by a variety of regulation, with a difficult debate over whether the regulations should be relaxed. One of the key links is the fibre optic cable. All offices and households need to be 'cabled up'. The cost, however, is vast, and cable TV which the Conservative government counted on to be a driving force in the process has not been very successful in Britain. The other main contender is British Telecom. BT uses fibre optic cables for its 'trunk routes'; but lines to homes and offices are virtually all the traditional copper wire with very little capacity beyond carrying one message going one way. However, BT would not undertake the cost of cabling everyone up unless there would be a substantial return on the investment. In effect, this means using the cable for TV. Unfortunately, when BT was privatised in the mid-1980s, it was forbidden to be involved in broadcasting before the year 2002. The point of this and other restrictions was to prevent BT becoming so big and powerful that it could crush all competition. If the cable/telephony route fails, then true mass interactive access will be delayed further.

However broadcasting companies will have a major role. If, as seems likely, we are going to end up with hundreds, or thousands, of TV channels, then there is a question of what they are all going to broadcast. No doubt there will be vast quantities of old programmes and old films, cheap soap operas and game shows and a great deal of rubbish. Good, new, well-made programmes will be at a premium. Again in this new world being created, big would seem to be beautiful. It is the big media conglomerates that have the best chance of exploiting the new opportunities. It will be the likes of Rupert Murdoch's News Corporation, Time-Warner and other huge multi-media companies that combine newspapers, film, TV, publishing etc., that will be the big players.

British commercial TV companies have traditionally not been in this league; they were simply too small. The separate regional companies could not merge, were immune from take-over and could not be owned by newspapers. Since that 1990

Broadcasting Act, and the subsequent awarding of franchises, the rules have been changed, so that there have been increasing waves of mergers and take-overs. In the summer of 2000 it appears that the way is open for the ITV channel 3 and channel 5 to be effectively owned by only two or at most three groups based upon Carlton Communications, United News and Media, and Granada. Even so, these companies are small in international media terms. And there is also the BBC which is an organisation that has a world reputation in broadcasting which it could exploit.

But while it can be argued that the future lies with very big television and/or multi-media companies, able to compete successfully in the media world market of the future, there are legitimate fears. Monopolies might abuse their power over consumers by over-pricing or restricting access to competitors. If our TV, newspapers, etc. were under the control of just a few proprietors this would be bad for democracy (as people argue is the case with Berlusconi in Italy). It is bad enough many argue that presently the Murdoch controlled group own five national newspapers and half of Sky, the main satellite broadcaster, without the creation of more media giants. Yet if much bigger companies do not emerge the companies we have may not be able to compete, and indeed be vulnerable to foreign take-over; and British media, the IT sector and other related industries could go the way of the British car industry.

These questions pose enormous problems for the government. The Department of Culture (DCMS) and the Department of Trade and Industry (DTI) have been consulting over these issues. The two departments published a joint Green Paper *Regulating Communications: the Way Ahead* in June 1999 which was sent out for discussion and feedback from interested parties. A group of experts has been established by DCMS-DTI, and a major White Paper setting out government policy and proposals for legislation is promised for autumn 2000.

Chapter 5

The Arts and Government

The arts in Britain are flourishing, they have a worldwide reputation, and they make an increasing contribution to the economy. Government support for the arts, through a number of institutions, has played an important part in these developments. However, to what extent support should continue, and in what form, has now become a matter of controversy.

The History of Government Support for the Arts

Until the Second World War, government concern for the arts was confined to the preservation of artistic treasures in museums and galleries, and the provision of art education. There was no policy of encouragement of artistic activity directly. It was only after 1939, when it might be thought the government had other things to worry about, that a policy of support began.

The Arts in Wartime

Two bodies were created to provide arts and entertainment. The more famous was the Entertainments National Services Association (ENSA), which provided mainly light entertainment for people in the services, and many of the great entertainers of the post-war world developed their talents in ENSA. The second body was the Council for the Encouragement of Music and Arts (CEMA), which provided arts for the domestic population. It began in 1939 when the Pilgrim Trust, a charitable foundation, suggested to the Board of Education that the arts must not be allowed to wither during the conflict. With money from both the government and the Trust, CEMA began to organise concerts, exhibitions and theatrical performances up and down the country, in village halls, works canteens and libraries. Sometimes it was no more than a singer and accompanist playing to a packed air raid shelter while the bombs were falling. These events were enormously popular and a great many people experienced painting or classical music or live drama for the first time in their lives because of CEMA. At the same time a network of regional offices helped to organise local tours and exhibitions and gave advice and encouragement to amateur artists.

Government supported CEMA because it was good for domestic morale, the finest quality being made available for all (CEMA's slogan was 'The Best for the Most'), while at the same time reinforcing those civilised values that the nation was fighting for. In 1942 John Maynard Keynes, the great economist, became chairman. He had been a leading advocate of government subsidy for the arts before the war, and he brought great energy and skill to his leadership of CEMA. As a result CEMA began to interest itself, towards the end of the war, in the provision and preservation of facilities. CEMA intervened to prevent the demolition of the Bristol Old Vic, one of the oldest theatres in the country and now one of our major provincial theatres. The Royal Opera House Covent Garden (leased to Mecca during the war as a dance hall) was restored to its original use and has helped to make London one of the world's major centres of opera and ballet.

Creation of the Arts Council

When the war ended it was decided to maintain a system of government encouragement and subsidy for the arts. As a result of Keynes' work, CEMA was transformed into the Arts Council of Great Britain. It was created by Royal Charter in 1945, with Keynes as the first chairman, and like CEMA it was a body of independent people with knowledge of the arts who would give grants to artists of quality, and not necessarily for the kind of art the government wanted to encourage. This was the 'arm's length principle', much like that which operated at the BBC, where the government did not wish to be seen as dictating what the people should enjoy (as happens in some countries).

The Arts Council was created at a time when there was a very strong sense that the whole nation had been united during the war and that it remained united in its determination not to return to the poverty and social ills of the pre-war years but to build a better society instead. This was the impulse behind the creation of the welfare state and government's attempts to plan and manage the national economy. The Labour Party had caught the popular mood and had won the 1945 General Election by a landslide. Government arts policy was part of a general policy of social reconstruction, of collectivist action to create a good society where the majority of people would be healthier, better educated and have good access to leisure. Increasing the availability of arts, sport and countryside was part of creating the possibility of a decent civilised life for all.

Regional Organisation

The Arts Council continued the work of CEMA as best it could with often limited funds. In the 1950's the need for economies led the Arts Council to phase out the network of regional offices it had inherited from CEMA. These had organised exhibitions and tours, and supported, advised and co-ordinated local arts organisations. They had done a good job and their disappearance was strongly opposed in the regions. Various kinds of local organisations attempted to fill the gap, usually some kind of federation of local arts groups. But it was a form of organisation developed in the north-east that eventually came to be adopted all over the country. The new kind of organisation was the Regional Arts Association (RAA), the first one being established in Newcastle in 1961 (originally confined to the north-east, but later taking in Cumbria and becoming Northern Arts). These were not formed by a coming together of artistic groups, but rather as a consortium of local authorities and other bodies interested in sponsoring the arts. They wished to maintain the 'arm's length principle' at local level by creating a kind of local arts council. The idea spread throughout the country with the encouragement of the Arts Council, which soon became their major source of financial support. But it also started to suggest that perhaps the system was too centralised and that further devolution to the regions from the national Arts Council might be desirable.

The Wilding Report

This theme was particularly examined in the late 1980s. The Minister for the Arts, Richard Luce, commissioned the retiring Permanent Secretary of the Office of Arts and Libraries, Richard Wilding, to investigate the whole funding system and make recommendations. His report entitled *Support for the Arts: A Review of the Structure of Arts Funding* was published in September 1989. The government announced its response early in the following year.

The Wilding Report was the most fundamental review of arts funding since the founding of the Arts Council in 1946. In its recommendations it aimed to create a more streamlined system, giving more power to the regions with less bureaucracy and cost. Its main proposals were:

1. to reduce the number of Regional Arts Associations in England from 12 to 7, to be achieved through mergers

2. reconstitute RAAs as statutory bodies called Regional Arts Boards (RABs)

3. chairmen of the new RABs to have permanent seats on the Arts Council, creating a 'federal structure' in which the Arts Council and the regional bodies would plan and work out budgets together

4. to create a new three-tier system of categorising clients, with the Arts Council directly responsible for some, and the regional body responsible for others, while there would be joint responsibility for a third. The Arts

Council would retain responsibility for general matters, and would widen its brief to cover commercial and amateur arts.

5.   The Crafts Council would be merged with the Arts Council.

Together these proposals were designed to make the whole system more co-ordinated and effective. They would reduce the number of bodies dealing with funding thereby saving money and reducing bureaucracy. This would make it easier for arts bodies to apply for grants. The Arts Council would be reduced in size and the regions would have more say.

The Wilding Report created great controversy in the arts world and there were vigorous campaigns to save threatened Regional Associations. In the end only two disappeared and the rest were recreated as Regional Arts Boards in 1991. It was decided keep the Crafts Council as an independent body. On the question of the balance of power between the Arts Council and the RABs, the government decided to be even more drastic than Wilding. More resources and more responsibilities for major arts organisations would be devolved upon the regions at the expense of the national Arts Council, perhaps eventually leaving it with only the major national companies, but the process was to be carried out only gradually.

The proposals were accepted by Mr Peter Polumbo, the Arts Council's Chairman, but not by Luke Rittner, the Secretary General and head of the permanent staff. Rittner resigned in 1990 since he believed that the proposals effectively meant the destruction of the Arts Council as a significant body.

Consensus and Controversy

Government intervention in society and the economy, in the form of the welfare state and government economic management, had remained popular during the 1950s and 60s under all parties. Government subsidy of the arts was part of this intervention. Under eminent figures such as Keynes and Arnold Goodman the scope and budget of the arts council steadily grew. The provision of arts and arts facilities for ever wider sections of the population was almost regarded as a branch of the welfare state, as is suggested by Arnold Goodman's remark in the Arts Council's 1969 Annual Report:

> *"Within our society there is now a widespread feeling that the provision of drama and music and painting and all culture in its broadest sense is no longer to be regarded as a privilege for the few, but is the democratic right of the entire community."*

However, the 1960s was an age of the 'New Left' and of student revolt. Rejection of authority was the fashion, and this was reflected in anti-establishment art. Many radical artists, whose art proclaimed that governments were corrupt and oppressive, nevertheless demanded government subsidy for their artistic endeavours. The Arts Council attempted to cater for this and tried to hand out subsidies without discrimination. This led to a good deal of controversy about what was good art and what was proper for the Arts Councils to be encouraging. The general consensus about what the government should subsidise was thereby diminished.

Minister for the Arts

The 1960s also saw an increase in the government's commitment to the arts. Hitherto, government money to the Arts Council and other bodies was handled by the Treasury. But 1965 saw the appointment of Jennie Lee as the first Minister for the Arts. This was not a Cabinet post but that of a junior minister in the Ministry of Education. Nevertheless, it meant that now there was a minister to argue the case for the arts in the government's policy-making process, giving the arts higher priority and more money as a result.

The End of Consensus

In the mid-1970s there was a worldwide economic crisis. The British economy was hit by a combination of rampant inflation and growing unemployment, and government spending had to be reduced wherever possible right across the board. In 1979 the Conservative Prime Minister, Mrs Thatcher, came to power convinced that Britain's difficulties were the result of excessive government spending and too much government interference in the economy generally. The consequence was a programme of public expenditure cuts, privatisation, reductions in taxation and a host of schemes to encourage free enterprise and new businesses. The arts budget was squeezed along with that of other departments, causing much distress and anger in the arts world.

However, when in due course the economy improved and the country grew more prosperous there was no corresponding growth of public arts funding. It became clear that the government was developing a new approach to the arts, more in line with the government's free enterprise philosophy. The arts did, however, gain a degree of independence, in that a tiny ministry was created, called the Office of Arts and Libraries, headed by a junior minister, who was also responsible for other things.

Meanwhile, in 1982 the all-party Commons Select Committee on Education, Science and Arts (with a Conservative majority and chairman) issued a report entitled Public and Private Funding of the Arts, in which it recommended a proper Ministry of the Arts, Heritage and Tourism and a lot more government investment in the arts. The government firmly rejected these suggestions, and although there was something of a change of atmosphere when John Major replaced Margaret

Thatcher in 1990, the government's help for the arts continued to be squeezed. There were, however, major changes under John Major of great potential significance. In 1992 the Department of National Heritage brought together the arts with heritage, broadcasting and tourism, implying greater co-ordination of policy, and since the Secretary of State was a member of the Cabinet, a higher profile in government decision making than ever before. Secondly, along with the new department came the National Lottery, offering new funds for the arts directly, and for one-off developments financed by the Millennium Fund.

Central Government and the Arts

The creation of the Department for Culture, Media and Sport (DCMS), as the DNH was renamed in 1997, has greatly simplified the co-ordination of government policy in relation to the arts. Nevertheless, there are a number of other central departments that have policies and programmes connected with the arts.

- The Department for Education and Employment (DfEE)is responsible for art education. It funds certain institutions such as the Royal College of Art and local colleges of art through the Higher and Further Education Funding Councils.

- A number of other local artistic activities, as well as libraries, fall within the local government brief of the Department of the Environment, Transport and Regions (DETR).

- The British Council, which promotes British culture abroad, is the responsibility of the Foreign and Commonwealth Office.

- Furthermore, there are departments that fund arts projects as part of their own responsibilities: for example, youth training schemes and tourism promotion in the employment and training branches of DfEE, and aspects of the film industry in the DTI.

- The devolved Scottish, Welsh and Northern Ireland executives also have a major interest in the arts of their regions.

However, the main responsibility for government arts policy at national level is now the Department for Culture, Media and Sport DCMS, which (originally as DNH) took over responsibility from the tiny Office of Arts and Libraries in 1992. The DCMS is responsible for all arts policy and the related areas of heritage, broadcasting and tourism. It controls and provides funds for a number of public bodies concerned with the arts, and also lays down the broad policies by which the National Lottery funds are distributed in these fields.

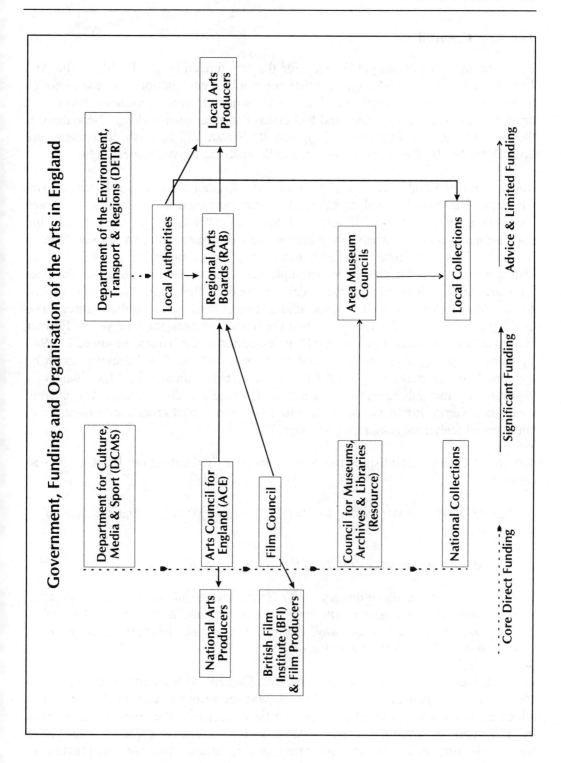

Government, Funding and Organisation of the Arts in England

The Arts Council

Much the most important public body for the arts funded by the DCMS is the Arts Council. Until April 1994 it had a rather complicated constitution, because although in theory the Arts Councils of Wales and Scotland were subsidiary bodies, in practice they were independent and had control of their own budgets. Now there is the Arts Council of England (ACE), and its Welsh and Scottish equivalents are directly funded by the devolved Welsh and Scottish executives respectively.

The composition and functions of the three Arts Councils are set out in their Royal Charters. The Arts Council of England is now governed by a Council of eleven members appointed by the Secretary of State for DCMS, who are part-time and unpaid (apart from expenses). They are all individual members and are not there as representatives of other organisations. Members normally include some distinguished artists (at present for example the sculptor Antony Gormley, the Poet Laureate Andrew Motion, the ballet dancer Deborah Bull, and the concert pianist Joanna MacGregor) as well as arts administrators and other public figures. The chairman is appointed for five years and the other members for four years. Former chairmen have included Lord Rees-Mogg, ex-editor of the Times, followed in 1989 by Lord Polumbo, a businessman and art patron and the first businessman to be appointed to the post, and Lord Gowrie, a former minister in Mrs Thatcher's government, and subsequently chairman of Christie's auction house. The current Chairman, Gerry Robinson, appointed in 1998, has a background in business and commercial television (Granada and BskyB).

The Royal Charter establishing the Arts Council of England set out its objectives as follows:

> *"(a) to develop and improve the knowledge, understanding and practice of the arts;*
>
> *(b)   to increase the accessibility of the arts to the public; and*
>
> *(b)   to advise and co-operate with Departments of Government, local authorities, the Arts Councils for Scotland, Wales and Northern Ireland and other bodies on any matters concerned, whether directly or indirectly, with the foregoing objects."*

To do this the government provided the Arts Council with an annual grant, which for 1993/94 was just over £221 million. It was the principal task of the council to allocate this money. To assist it in making these decisions the council was advised by a network of advisory panels, boards and committees. Some of these were responsible for particular arts, including dance, drama, literature and painting, while others encompassed all the arts and included regional touring boards. The system of councils, committees and panels was serviced by a full-time staff of approximately 145 permanent officials under the direction of a Secretary-General.

But in the late 1990s the Arts Council has undergone an internal cultural revolution. It now has as its 'mission statement':

Our mission

- Developing, sustaining and promoting the arts.

Our Aim

- To promote access, education and excellence in the arts through partnership.

Our Priorities

- bringing the arts to a wider audience

- encouraging individuality and experimentation

- nurturing creativity across the generations

- embracing the diversity of our culture

- exploring new forms of expression.

The structure was streamlined, with the number of Council members reduced, and many of the advisory committees and panels reduced in size or swept away. The permanent staff is reduced in size and headed by a chief executive. A number of activities are being increasingly devolved to the (English) Regional Arts Boards, and in April 2000 the Council transferred its responsibility for film to a new institution, the Film Council. The basic government grant-in-aid from DCMS in 1999 was £191 million, lower in real terms than the allocation for England six years before. For the three years 1999-2002 this has been raised successively to £227m, £237m and £252m, representing an extra £125m, in return for certain changes in orientation expressed in a funding agreement with DCMS which will be discussed below. But these grant sums are now rivalled by its annual share of National Lottery income at £211 million, and the fact that it also advises in the distribution of part of the Millennium Fund.

Distributing the Funding for the Arts

The Arts Council's task each year is to distribute the grant-aid provided by government. The way it does so has been changing. In 1999 it planned to distribute £188 million, of which it allocated £130m directly and £58m went to Regional Arts Boards to allocate in their areas. In 1999-2000, the amount going to the regional bodies who will make the allocation decisions will increase to nearly £83m. In 1999-2000 the Arts Council budget divides up its own grants into artistic categories, with music taking the largest slice at £37m and literature the smallest at £1.7m. It also targets funds at specific initiatives such as 'new audiences' (£4m), and 'education and employment' £1.1m.

Traditionally Arts Council spending was dominated by grants to the big institutions: the four national companies: Royal Opera House, English National Opera, Royal National Theatre and the Royal Shakespeare Company, the major London symphony orchestras, various key provincial companies (by-passing the RABs) such as the Sheffield Crucible Theatre, the Halle Orchestra (in Manchester) and the Bristol Old Vic Theatre. There were several hundred lesser clients up and down the country. Finally, there are general items such as touring, capital building projects and arts centres. In the last few years the Arts Council has been moving away from the big players, encouraging them to find other sources of income, and shifting responsibility for smaller groups to the RABs. But some of the traditional recipients have continued to receive alternative capital funding via the National Lottery route, with the Royal Opera House at Covent Garden winning £78m and the National Theatre over £31m.

The 'crafts' are deemed to have special problems of their own, and for a long period there was a small separate body funded by the DCMS, the Crafts Council, (founded as the Crafts Advisory Committee in 1971) to deal with the needs of artist-craftsmen. It had a small exhibition space of its own and has also encouraged and helped to fund the British Crafts Centre. In 1999 (having survived the Wilding Report) it was finally merged with the Arts Council, against the opposition of those who thought that although administratively tidy, it would inevitably mean crafts taking second place to the fine arts. It has kept its name, charitable status, and Royal Charter, but has lost its autonomy.

Film: Culture and Industry

The position of film within the arts system has always been complicated, partly because as a new artistic medium in the 20th century it was not easily accepted by traditionalists. Its separate needs on the cultural side have for a long time been largely catered for by the British Film Institute (BFI). But film is also an important commercial industry, and this aspect was the responsibility of the Department of Trade and Industry.

The British Film Institute (BFI)

Founded in 1933, the BFI is much the oldest of the government-aided bodies. It has a rather strange constitution, with a Royal Charter and charitable status, and was set up as a limited company run by a Board of Governors with members instead of shareholders. Annual membership of the BFI's National Film Theatre or National Library, or a subscription to *Sight and Sound* now confers membership status. In fact the Secretary of State for DCMS appoints the 15 strong board (although two places are reserved for elected Member Governors). Furthermore, the members can question the board at the AGM, and even dismiss them all, having studied the annual report and accounts.

The BFI was set up to:

(a)   encourage the development of the art of film

(b)   to promote its use as a record of contemporary life and manners

(c)   to foster public appreciation and study of it from these points of view.

It attempts to fulfil these aims in a number of ways. The BFI runs the National Film Theatre, showing classical films, holding lecture series, etc.; there is a national film archive where old film is preserved; there is an information and documentation service and an educational advice service. The Institute also publishes the journal *Sight and Sound* as well as books and pamphlets. .

In 1961 the aims of the Institute were amended to include television. That is, to:

(d)   foster study and appreciation of films for television and television programmes generally

(e)   encourage the best use of television.

The BFI now acquires copies of television programmes for its archive, organises lectures and publications and gives educational advice. But, for reasons of lack of funds, it has not developed the television side of its activities as it might have done. Indeed, the BFI is chronically under funded relative to its aims. Furthermore, it has no automatic rights to acquire copies of the films and television programmes it wishes to preserve. The BFI is also responsible for the Museum of the Moving Image on the London South Bank, and the new IMAX Cinema opened in June 1999, and also runs the London Film Festival. Much of its work will eventually relocate into a major new complex under construction on the South Bank site between Westminster and Waterloo bridges.

The British Film Institute employs some 450 staff, and used to receive direct government funding from DCMS, which covered about half its costs, and raised at least as much again through its own activities. Some of its grant was passed on to Regional Arts Boards for film activities. The BFI was also involved in the production of innovative and experimental films, and helped to launch the careers of a number of successful filmmakers including Ken Russell, Ridley Scott, Peter Greenaway and Derek Jarman. Unlike the Arts Council and the Crafts Council it had its own artistic projects, and particularly with the availability of quite substantial Lottery funding for film production (nearly £34 million in 1999-2000) there were some tensions about its role and that of the Arts Council (which had its own lottery film department), another production body known as the British Film Commission and the commercial film industry.

The Film Council

The DCMS has now made a major change in the film sector, by creating a new body, the Film Council, which started up on 1 April 2000. This has been established as a company (although it is intended to give it a statutory status) with a Board of 15 Directors. Its first Chairman is the film maker Alan Parker, and its Chief Executive was Director of the BFI. It is intended to be the lead organisation for the UK film industry and has thus taken over:

- all the direct government funding from DCMS for film (with the exception of the National Film & Television School)

- the Arts Council Lottery Film Department

- the BFI Production department

- responsibility for funding the BFI as a whole (although BFI stays independent with its cultural and educational remit)

- funding the British Film Commission, two other national production agencies and regional film production.

There appears to have been a decision to sort out the film sector by separating out the production activities from those of film appreciation, but while in principle maintaining a balance, in practice tending to give priority and overall control to the former. The rationale is the need to promote film production in the UK, through a wide variety of collaboration with other industry organisations and commercial partners.

Regional and Local Provision for the Arts

Regional Arts Boards

Below the national level, the main agency for promoting the arts is the Regional Arts Boards (RABs). RABs were first set up by local initiative, and then the Arts Council brought support with advice and funds. There were originally twelve Regional Arts Associations, but a reorganisation in 1991 (following the Wilding Report discussed earlier) reduced the number to ten and changed their names to Boards. (Merseyside disappeared into Northwest Arts, the Humberside and Lincolnshire Association was split and shared between Yorkshire and Eastern Arts; there were also some minor boundary changes).

The basic idea of a Regional Arts Board is of an organisation which is a focal point and clearing house for funding, co-ordination and advice. Money comes from several sources:

- The major provider of funds is the Arts Council passing on part of its DCMS grant (and which may also directly subsidise bodies and events in the region, such as orchestras and arts festivals quite separately from the RAB, although this system is changing).

- Much smaller grants have come from the Crafts Council and the British Film Institute.

- The second most important source of funds is from the local authorities in the area.

- There may be funding from a variety of other sources, including business sponsorship and local universities.

- There may also be money-raising activities by the association itself.

This money is then channelled to local arts organisations to help them develop their work. It is important to stress that other money may also be coming, often on a large scale from the Lottery funds, particularly at the moment the Millennium Fund, for capital projects and various other schemes. This is not income for the Regional Arts Boards themselves, but is paid for projects in their areas. They will often have advised in the initial application, and will be consulted before awards are made.

For example, in 1998-99 the following Lottery Arts capital awards were paid:

Regional Board	Under £100,000 £ total awards	Over £100,000 £ total awards
Eastern	433,000	....
East Midlands	474,000	2,473,000
London	1,217,000	21,246,000
Northern	510,000	4,320,000
North West	545,000	1,707,000
Southern	264,000	2,380,000
South East	228,000	16,401,000
South West	713,000	535,000
West Midlands	269,000	2,446,000
Yorkshire	371,000	4,779,000

Each RAB has a governing board made up of representatives from contributing organisations, plus arts bodies. A small group normally acts as an executive or management committee to deal with day-to-day problems. The Board appoints a small full-time staff of administrators and specialists in various fields who help local groups to set up arts projects, organise exhibitions and tours, advise on arts festivals, and generally plan the development of the arts in the region.

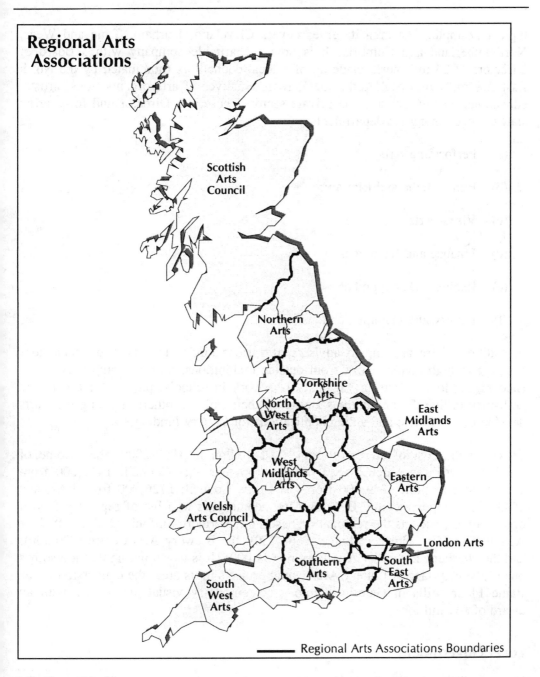

Regional Arts Associations

- Scottish Arts Council
- Northern Arts
- Yorkshire Arts
- North West Arts
- East Midlands Arts
- West Midlands Arts
- Eastern Arts
- Welsh Arts Council
- London Arts
- South East Arts
- Southern Arts
- South West Arts

—— Regional Arts Associations Boundaries

Northern Arts

RABs have been set up by local people to serve local needs, and not surprisingly each have their differences in how they organise themselves and operate. Some, for example, regard heritaas an important aspect of their work, while others do not regard it as their responsibility at all; some concentrate on professional artists, others do not; and so on. Yet they are broadly similar and Northern Arts is a fairly typical example. The area it serves covers Cleveland, Durham, Tyne and Wear, Northumberland and Cumbria. It is now a charitable company with a Board of Directors of 24 members, made up of 8 local councillors (nominated by the North East Assembly of Local Authorities), representatives of arts organisations, artists, educational institutions and the private sector. There is a Director and forty-seven staff divided among six departments:

(a)   Performing Arts

(b)   Film, Media and Literature

(c)   Visual Arts

(d)   Finance and Resources

(e)   Regional Development

(f)   Lottery and Communications.

In addition, there are unpaid advisers of various kinds. The work done includes bringing in high quality work from outside (exhibitions, touring companies, etc.); encouraging local artists in various ways; work in schools; paying for artists and craftsmen to live in communities and teach their skills to others; funding local arts development officers; and aiding applications for Lottery funding.

To cover the cost of all this - some £10 million in 1999-2000- the income of Northern Arts was roughly £8.3 million from the Arts Council; £417,000 from British Film Institute; £59,000 from the Crafts Council; £726,000 from LAs; and £543,000 of other income. Over half its income goes to a list of regularly funded organisations, such as the regional orchestra the Northern Sinfonia (£281,960), Jazz Action (£32,250), Northern Stage (£664,250), the Brewery Arts Centre (£70,500), and the Northern Disability Arts Forum (£54,000). It is worth noting that it also has one of the very largest Lottery Arts capital projects in its area, the conversion of the Baltic Flour Mills in Gateshead into a contemporary visual arts centre with an award of £41 million.

Local Government

The role of local government in relation to the arts is more complicated, and the variations from authority to authority far greater. Certain kinds of local authority were given optional powers to provide museums and galleries in the 19th Century, and compulsory powers to provide education and libraries came later. Beyond these, expenditure on the arts in the past was only possible under a private Act of Parliament allowing a particular LA to run a municipal theatre, or (as with Bournemouth in 1893 and Birmingham in 1919) an orchestra. It was not until the

1948 Local Government Act that LAs had an opportunity to do much more: it enabled LAs to charge a 6d rate for arts and entertainments in their area. It was the age when the experience of CEMA and the new Arts Council was fresh, and many thought the provision would lead to a flowering of locally subsidised arts. But more than half LAs ignored the provision altogether and many others made little use of it. It was mainly the big cities and seaside resorts that took advantage. There was little tradition of civic patronage (as existed in some continental countries) and arts were usually given a low priority.

However, by the 1960s support for the arts was becoming more acceptable in the world of local government, partly through joint projects with the Arts Council, such as to create a municipal theatre and repertory company. By the big reorganisation of local government, following the 1972 Local Government Act, there had been a general growth of the amount local authorities spent on the arts, although the situation was still very patchy. The 1972 Act (Clause 142) removed the restriction on the amounts LAs could spend. Since then there has been a growing awareness among local authorities of the importance of leisure in general and arts in particular to the life of their community. On the other hand, the economic difficulties of the 1970s and 1980s followed by the pressures to reduce spending and privatise, often meant arts were among the first to suffer. Some local authorities provide their own arts centres, support local arts associations and put a lot of resources into local arts festivals and other projects. It is estimated that LAs between them put some hundreds of millions into supporting the arts; although many authorities confine their support for the arts to subscribing to their local RAB.

However, there are some LAs that give very little support to their RAB. This may be simple meanness, but there is also a suspicion in some local government quarters that despite many LA members, RABs are not properly accountable for the ratepayer's money they spend; that there is unnecessary duplication of LA administration; and that local authorities, certainly in the big cities, could do, and should do, the job themselves. In many areas there is little co-operation between different authorities, such as between district and county, or between local authorities and RABs, to plan the development of arts in their region. Lord Redcliffe-Maude argued (in his report *Support for the Arts in England and Wales* of 1976 for the Calouste Gulbenkian Foundation) that in the long run:

> "We must look to local elected councils, at district and county level, to become the chief art patrons of the long-term future, developing a comprehensive service as part of the main fabric of local government."

In present circumstances this looks something of a vain hope.

On the other hand, there is certainly scope for greater co-ordination and planning in most areas. Where county and the districts all work with each other and with the RAB, and where local schools and libraries make their facilities available, local authority adult education classes, WEA and university adult and continuing education departments and local arts centres all co-ordinate their activities, much can be done with modest resources. In the longer term much might depend on how local government develops. Whereas the Conservative governments between 1979-97 have been diminishing the role of local government, the other parties are committed to expansion. In the arts field Labour's policy statement *Voices and Choices* promised a statutory duty on LAs to consult with local arts organisations and provide support for the arts according to local needs, for which there will be a special allocation in the rate support grant. Such a legal obligation on local government would be the first of its kind in Europe and is likely to result from the Local Government Bill currently before Parliament. The debate over the role of local government in the arts is also part of a wider discussion of the best way of funding the arts.

Issues in the Arts

After World War II there was all-party agreement on the need for state subsidy of the arts, and all subsequent Labour and Conservative governments followed this policy without hesitation. The arts were seen as something intrinsically good in themselves, an expression of the higher human aspirations and achievements. There was a general assumption that there was a common artistic tradition in Britain, especially in the fine arts such as painting, sculpture, literature, theatre, and classical music, that needed both to be preserved and also developed as a living and continuing enterprise. This broad consensus gradually came to be questioned and challenged from a number of different directions, from which some new approaches to the arts gradually began to emerge.

The Role of the State: the Thatcher Strategy

One of Mrs Thatcher's fundamental priorities since 1979 was to reverse post-war trends in government. These trends have included the steady increase in state responsibilities, particularly in the fields of welfare provision and control of the economy, with a consequent increase in the size of government (more and more civil servants, quangos, and other bodies) and increasing taxation to pay for it all. Mrs Thatcher believed these developments to be a mistake; that the growth of government has crushed free enterprise and initiative; and that what we need is to reduce the size of government, allow market forces to operate more freely and give private enterprise the opportunity to flourish. These ideas inspired some of what the Conservative government tried to do in broadcasting and the arts.

In the early 1980s arts subsidies suffered their due share of cuts along with other government expenditure. It was when the expansion of the economy and government income in the second half of the decade did not result in the expansion of subsidies that it was clear that the government was intent on a permanent change in arts policy. It resolutely ignored demands from many quarters, including some of its own MPs, for more money and sought a 'free-market approach'. The response of the Arts Council was to try to persuade the government in terms it thought it would understand. In 1985 the Council began using the language of business to make the case for more subsidy. In a document called *A Great British Success Story* it sought to promote the arts as a sound investment for government: creating jobs at low cost; a high return for a small investment; good for exports; good for tourism; and so on.

The basic aim of the government's arts policy has been to ease the subsidised arts away from a total dependence on state aid, making them more independent. In a speech to a conference of regional arts bodies in July 1988, the Arts Minister, Richard Luce, put the matter bluntly:

> "...*there are still too many in the arts world who have yet to be weaned away from the welfare state mentality - the attitude that the taxpayer owes them a living. Many have not yet accepted the challenge of developing plural sources of funding. They give the impression of thinking that all other sources of funds are either tainted or too difficult to get. They appear not to have grasped that the collectivist mentality of the 60s and 70s is out of date.*"

What he had in mind was arts organisations, like theatres and orchestras, just sitting around waiting for their state hand-outs instead of getting out and finding new forms of income. People in the arts should stop assuming that they have an automatic right to generous state support, presently being denied them by a mean and philistine government; and they should stop turning their noses up at things like business sponsorship and start learning to be more businesslike. The Minister went on to suggest that the majority of people in this country were highly sceptical about subsidising the arts, believing that if it is any good then people will be prepared to pay for it. He also insisted that, while experiment and freedom of expression are very important in the arts, nevertheless the first objective ought to be 'pleasing the customer'.

Business Sponsorship

In line with these attitudes, the government introduced business sponsorship schemes, and put part of the Arts Council grant in the form of 'incentive funding'. That is, government will put up money when the arts organisation has 'earned it' by having raised more money from other sources. In addition to this, the government wanted arts organisations to be more business-like and entrepreneurial. That is, being better organised; using more sophisticated marketing techniques; being more enterprising and making better use of assets and business opportunities (for example, by selling associated products such as posters and videos). Sponsorship and marketing have traditionally been anathema to the subsidised arts world, but they have been forced to learn to live with it. Both the Arts Council and the RABs were expected to play a major part in encouraging the development of these managerial and business skills among arts organisations. It was no accident that the next appointed chairman of the Arts Council was, for the first time, a businessman: Mr Peter Polumbo.

The Conservative government's DNH promoted and funded the Business Sponsorship Incentive Scheme (BSIS) to encourage sponsorship. For first time sponsors, the government would match £1 for £1 money from business of a minimum of £1,000 and a maximum of £35,000; for second time sponsors it is £1 for every £2 of sponsorship money, and £1 for £4 thereafter. However, the scheme was not run directly by government, but by the Association of Business Sponsorship for the Arts, a voluntary body, on behalf of DNH. Significantly, since 1997 the Labour government has continued to encourage sponsorship, the DCMS commending the efforts of the current Arts and Business (A&B) organisation which produced business support of £141 million for the arts in 1999.

Debates on the Market Approach

Many objections have been voiced against these attitudes and policies, which are often, in the arts world, characterised as philistine and as regarding the arts as no more than a branch of the entertainment industry. The arts, it is argued, are an essential part of civilised life which people need to be fully developed human beings. To treat it as just another industry is a vulgar mistake. It is good for tourism and exports, and can help to regenerate the inner cities, but only if it is of high quality. The government's error, so its critics argue, is to pursue policies that will diminish the quality of the arts. It might be said that some of the self-proclaimed defenders of the arts display an unworldly attitude to money which was hardly characteristic of many of the great creative artists. Shakespeare, Dickens, Turner, Tennyson, Elgar and many others quite clearly worked and created masterpieces with the intention of making a very good income.

Most fiercely attacked in this respect is policy on funding, especially the attempt to replace state subsidy with business sponsorship. Critics say that this cannot be an answer to the needs of the arts, which need secure funding so as to plan ahead. But business sponsors are fickle. They think in the short-term, perhaps one or two years, after which they may decide that sponsoring a sport for a while would be better for their image; or, if money is tight, just suddenly give up sponsorship altogether (business sponsorship did shrink in the early 1990s because of the recession). Furthermore, business sponsors, it is argued, are only interested in prestige projects and guaranteed successes. Experimental or unusual work, work aimed at working class or ethnic or other minority audiences, or work critical of the government or what the government believes in, are all unlikely to attract support. In consequence, new ideas and art that challenges people to think will tend to suffer and may wither for lack of support. And this may also be the consequence of the Minister's injunction to 'please the customer'. The final result of the government's policy could therefore be, it is claimed, the encouragement of 'safe', bland, unimaginative art, which is bad art; the only proper way to promote good quality is by adequate government subsidy.

One might reply that this may be rather overstated. The Arts and Business (A&B) organisation lists plenty of examples of continuity in funding from business, some in quite experimental and unusual arts projects, and with small business as well as large. The Norfolk Rural Life Museum received sponsorship from Anglia Funeral Services! But clearly one must also recognise that this is usually done with a certain hard headed attitude. A&B themselves sell the idea to business in these terms:

> *"Sponsoring the arts is a proven, cost effective and highly visible strategic marketing tool. It is one of the most powerful ways to reinforce your corporate image, allowing you to promote your company's name, logo, products or services to a wider but targeted audience, whilst strengthening your links with the community."*

Pressure Groups

Support for state funding is strongly advocated by various arts pressure groups. One of the most important of these is the National Campaign for the Arts. It was founded in 1984 to focus public and political attention on the needs of the arts. It does the standard pressure group activities of lobbying Parliament (circulating information to MP's, briefing sympathetic ones on particular issues, providing suggested questions, etc.), keeping the media informed and persuading public opinion. Most of the arts world supported its general aims, but one or two individual artists, including Kingsley Amis and John Osborne (both commercially successful writers), argued that state subsidy is inherently bad for artists; but these are a small minority.

Serious opposition to state-supported arts comes from right-wing think-tanks that believe in maximum scope for the free market and a drastic reduction of government responsibility generally. One such body is the Adam Smith Institute. In its *Expounding the Arts* (1987), it advocated the complete phasing out of government arts subsidies and greater encouragement for museums and galleries to exploit their assets commercially (and if this cannot cover costs, give them endowments with an independent income). While the recent Conservative government showed some sympathy for these sorts of ideas, at no stage did the government express an intention to eventually phase out arts subsidies altogether.

Indeed, allowing for inflation, there was not a great deal of difference between the overall level of subsidies in the early 1990s and what they were in the 1960s.

The Arts in the Economy and Society

Other parts of the debate have concentrated on different themes. One which is related to the business approach is to play up the potential for the arts as a positive force in the British economy. This has fitted well with the 'New Labour' approach to modernisation, in which economic development and growth have been related to improving the image of Britain and its international competitiveness. This is not 'art for art's sake' but art as a means of promoting economic growth. In October 1997 the DCMS established the Creative Industries Task Force (CITF), to draw all relevant parts of the government together with practitioners in the creative industries in order to achieve their full economic potential and remove obstacles to growth. CITF is chaired by the DCMS Secretary of State, has nine practitioner members from film making, recorded music, publishing, and fashion among others, and civil servants. It has so far produced a number of papers on different areas of the sector, and also promoted a sub-committee in the DfEE concerned with creativity and training in schools. The recent reorganisation of the provision for film and the creation of the Film Council seems to owe a lot to this approach.

In the late 1990s Labour has also heightened the debate about the arts and their relationship with social objectives, especially the notion of 'inclusiveness'. This has several aspects. Partly this is simply the use of the arts in economic regeneration projects, by providing employment in inner city areas, promoting community identity, and developing education and training projects. But it also relates to recognition of problems of diversity and access in the arts. In a multi-cultural Britain living with the consequences of its long colonial history there are different cultural traditions, some of them linked with ethnic groups from the Caribbean, the Indian sub-continent and elsewhere. The older tradition of the arts sponsored by the government did not relate very much to the interests of large sections of the population, especially youth with its own varieties of popular culture and much of the working class. So in this view, the arts needed to be liberated from the grip of the highly educated white middle classes and opened up. The current mission statement of the Arts Council (quoted earlier in this chapter) reflects these concerns and addresses them. It is keen to promote and spend money on access programmes, recognising different artistic forms of expression and the links between them and all forms of entertainment. Thus it has now developed an interest in popular street carnivals, artistic festivals for ethnic minorities, and highly visible public sculptures which are placed within communities and attempt to symbolise their values.

The Administration and Delivery of the Arts

Whatever the rights and wrongs of public subsidy for the arts, and the objectives it should serve, there is the separate question of whether the system distributing subsidies is as economical, efficient, effective, fair and accountable as it ought to be. Of particular concern to the government and some other critics since the 1980s has been the nature and workings of the Arts Council, which has variously been thought to be bureaucratic, overstaffed, neglecting the provinces and not making the best use of the public money it received.

Criticisms of National and Regional Arts Bodies

While for a long time it was widely accepted that the Arts Council had done a good job since its creation, and that the 'arm's length' principle ought to govern these matters, there have been dissenting voices, and a number of criticisms that have often reflected the general concerns which have just been discussed. It has been suggested that the Arts Council system:

- fudges some important issues about political choice and accountability

- is too inflexible and bureaucratic

- is not representative because its council and advisory panels are appointed and not elected, and often favour their own particular artistic circles and interests

- promotes an elitist view of art

- is far better at catering for its established clients, especially the big national companies which can be extravagant, and is not very good at encouraging new ideas and new art

- its grants tend to go to those with greatest skill at playing the bureaucratic game, filling the right forms and effective lobbying, or else make the most fuss (those who shout loudest get most), rather than those with greatest artistic merit

- puts too much emphasis on the national companies in or near London, and not enough is done for the regions, where the need is greatest, and where the Council has done little to encourage local government support.

Just how fair these criticisms are is a matter of dispute and might well depend on particular cases. But it must be remembered that they are made in a context where scarce resources have to be allocated and many are inevitably disappointed, so that there is bound to be strong criticism no matter what the Council does. But the basic structure has always had its weak points. While the 'arms-length' principle is claimed to insulate the arts from political control this has always been somewhat doubtful. It certainly allows the Secretary of State to disclaim responsibility, particularly over controversial artistic projects, saying that this is all a matter for the Arts Council. But the Arts Council members are DCMS appointees, and it is also the case that in practice it recognises that since the government holds the purse strings its wishes must be considered.

The involvement of practising artists in the Arts Council, while apparently highly desirable does have its potential problems. There are members of the Arts Council itself who apply to it for funding for their own work, or sit in judgement on applications from artists with rather different visions and links. So questions of conflicts of interests and favouritism, either for personalities or particular artistic movements surface from time to time. Last year columnists in the *Guardian* (29 September 1999) and *Independent* (11 December) drew attention to the spread of gigantic public sculptures with the implication that this might be connected to the fact that two such sculptors were members of the Arts Council.

Similar criticisms are also sometimes made against the RABs, or at least some of them ~ their procedures are long-winded and bureaucratic, that they tend to favour established clients, and so on. But there are also specific criticisms, that they do a job that could be more efficiently done by local government and their 'regions' are too big and do not mean much to local people. There is also something of a worry over accountability, with no adequate machinery for ensuring that the taxpayer's money, in the form of the Arts Council grant, is being spent in the best possible way.

The creation of the National Lottery has brought in substantial new funds for the arts. This has strengthened the case for effective administration allied to clear objectives. Rather paradoxically, the existing structures have found it difficult to spend the extra money which has been provided. Funds have piled up in the accounts, and interest earned, before expenditure can be agreed. There is also a continuing danger that money is not being spent in the most appropriate way. Enormous sums are being invested in the infrastructure, such as buildings and state of the art equipment for theatres, arts centres, opera houses and concert halls. Much less finds its way to the people who will occupy them and produce the art. The Arts Council has only slowly come to realise that it must find ways of dealing with the revenue deficits (often with substantial accumulations over several years) through its so-called stabilisation programmes of many artistic organisations. There is no point in contributing gleaming empty white elephants to the national heritage.

Chapter 6

The Countryside and Government

Historical Introduction

Concern about the countryside being threatened is very much a modern phenomenon which has followed upon the spread of industrialisation and urbanisation. To understand the nature of the threat we need only consider the growth of population in this country. In the thousand years up to the middle of the 18th Century the population grew from around three million to around five-and-a-half million; in the next half century it doubled to eleven million; it more than tripled to thirty-seven million by 1900; and by 1950 it had gone on to fifty-six million. Yet alongside this population explosion went a steady depopulation of rural areas, so that all the growth was concentrated in towns and cities. These grew and spread their houses and factories and swallowed up ever greater tracts of the countryside. Modern developments have exacerbated the problem. People today demand better living conditions, with more space and gardens, so that housing takes up a greater area than it used to. Developments in transport, particularly the motor car, have made it possible for suburbs to be built further and further out, from which people can still commute to work. There is now greater pressure than ever to build in the countryside, to the extent that much of it will disappear or be ruined in many parts of Britain if developers have their way. At the same time the more remote parts suffer from threats of a different kind.

Beginnings of the National Parks Idea

Thinking about the countryside as a place for physical and spiritual recreation, and of in some way preserving it for that purpose, begins in the 19th Century. As early as 1810 the poet Wordsworth was making a case for the Lake District becoming "a sort of national property" for the enjoyment of people of "pure taste". Although this apparently did not extend to factory workers and other coarse persons, who would ruin the area if allowed to swarm over it in large numbers. Later, the urban working class appeared to be deprived of access to nature by modern developments, and this became a theme of Victorian critics who railed against the growth of ugliness and squalor.

However, the idea of government stepping in to set aside whole areas for the enjoyment of the people in perpetuity comes from America; and it was here that the national park movement began in the late nineteenth century. Areas of untouched wilderness began to be protected in order to prevent their ruination by commercial development. In 1872 Yellowstone National Park in the state of California was the first such park to be established. Others soon followed. Initially they were the responsibility of the local state government, but in 1916 the federal government took over responsibility for all national parks. Since then, the American idea of government-protected wildernesses has spread throughout the world. It has influenced British thinking, although, as we shall see, the British idea of a national park is quite different from what the rest of the world understands by the term.

Progress Between the Wars

In this country, the organised movement to put pressure on the government to protect the countryside developed in the twentieth century, particularly after the First World War. There were growing worries about urban sprawl and ribbon development, especially in the area around London. At the same time, there was growing awareness of people's need for physical recreation and of the need for open spaces to satisfy it. The result was an increasing demand for powers to control development. Limited powers of control had existed in towns since 1909 and these were extended to the countryside in 1932, but they were not compulsory and had little effect.

It was in response to some of these concerns that the idea of a 'green belt' arose. The most urgent problem was the growth of London eating up more and more of the rural areas surrounding it. In 1935 the London County Council began to give grants to LAs in the Home Counties to purchase land and maintain it as countryside. There was also concern further north. Leeds, Birmingham and Sheffield also began a policy of purchasing land or making agreements with landowners to prevent development. In 1938 the Green Belt (London and Home Counties) Act was passed making it possible to acquire land and prevent development without first having the consent of the minister or local authority concerned.

Another development was the growth of a movement to have the most beautiful parts of Britain specially protected by the nation for the benefit of future generations, through the creation of national parks. This movement had a number of strands:

1.   There were organisations, such as the National Trust (founded 1895) and the Council for the Preservation of Rural England (1926), that were principally concerned with protecting beautiful countryside, and in which landowners had a strong influence.

2.   Other organisations were more concerned with outdoor activities and with public access, such as the Rambler's Association, the Youth Hostel Association and the Common Open Spaces and Footpaths Preservation Society, founded in 1865 and the oldest surviving pressure group in the country.

3.   Yet others were principally interested in the protection of wildlife and therefore its habitats. The best known of these is the Royal Society for the Protection of Birds.

Representatives of all these different groups came together in 1936 to form the Council for National Parks to press for legislation for their establishment.

The ideas for countryside preservation in the form of general planning powers, green belts and national parks all became increasingly accepted in the 1920s and 30s. However, there were strong vested interests in keeping things as they were and progress was slow. As with so many things, it was the catalyst of war that provided the stimulus for rapid change.

Statutory Protection of the Countryside

During the Second World War there was a widespread feeling that the nation must not go back to the poverty, unemployment and social injustice of the pre-war years, and that the nation could and should strive to build a better society. Consequently, during the war a great deal of effort was put into research and planning for the post-war world (resulting in the welfare state, support for the arts, and other policies). Various studies were made of planning and land use, the creation of national parks, and other possibilities. The outcome of all this effort was principally embodied in two major Acts of Parliament: the Town and Country Planning Act of 1947; and the National Parks and Access to the Countryside Act of 1949.

> *The Town and Country Planning Act* introduced a comprehensive system of planning. It established the counties and major cities as the principal planning authorities. They had to prepare structure plans, requiring ministerial approval, which set out their broad policies for land use in their areas, designating zones for housing development, industrial development, agriculture and amenity use. These plans would guide local authorities in their exercise of planning powers: that is, the granting or refusal of planning permission (although the Act gave applicants a final

right of appeal to the appropriate minister). It was this Act that made the Green Belt policy possible. It was no longer necessary to purchase land to keep it open; all that was needed was the refusal of planning permission in the appropriate areas.

The National Parks and Access to the Countryside Act did not itself create national parks. What it did was to define national parks, set out their objectives and set up the machinery for their creation and management. The Act created a National Parks Commission (which later became the Countryside Commission) to designate, subject to ministerial approval, certain areas as national parks and others as 'areas of outstanding natural beauty' (AONBs). Under this Act the first ten national parks were created between 1951 and 1959.

Since the passage of these two major Acts there have been a number of significant developments. But first we will examine the role of government and related bodies.

Government Bodies and the Countryside

Central Government Departments

The central government department mainly in charge of protecting the countryside was the Department of the Environment (DoE) which in 1997 was merged with Transport to create the Department of the Environment, Transport and the Regions (DETR.) This is a huge department with an enormous range of responsibilities, including the whole system of local government, housing, environmental pollution, road and rail transport, and umpteen other matters. Of crucial importance to the countryside is the fact that the Secretary of State is responsible for the planning system, and makes final decisions on all planning appeals. The department is also directly responsible for Green Belt policy, National Parks and AONBs. It appoints and supervises the work of the Countryside Agency, the Environment Agency, English Nature and a number of other bodies concerned with the countryside. There is usually a junior Minister of State with special responsibility for countryside matters.

The DETR has to co-ordinate with a number of other government departments on issues of countryside protection. These include:

- devolved Welsh, Scottish and Northern Ireland institutions on all issues

- Ministry of Agriculture, Forestry and Fisheries (MAFF) on land-use, agricultural chemicals, and a great many other matters

- Department of Trade and Industry (DTI) on industrial and commercial land-use, mining and quarrying, pollution control, siting of power stations, etc.

- Department for Education and Employment (DfEE) on rural unemployment and youth training schemes, rural schools, etc.

- Ministry of Defence (MOD) use of remote areas for military training, etc.

- the Department of Culture, Media and Sport (DCMS) on tourism, heritage protection, etc.

The Countryside Agency

This was created in April 1999 by the merger of the Countryside Commission and the Rural Development Commission in England. There were previously three Countryside Commissions, for England, Wales and Scotland. Now there are the separate Countryside Council for Wales and the Scottish Countryside Commission, each responsible to the devolved institutions for their respective areas.

Its broad objectives are to conserve and enhance the countryside, promoting social equity and economic opportunity for the people who live there, and to help everyone (wherever they live) to enjoy this national asset. Inherited from the Countryside Commission it has important statutory duties:

1. encouraging and promoting measures to conserve and enhance the natural beauty and amenity of the countryside

2. encouraging the development of facilities for open-air recreation in rural areas

3. providing expert advice on countryside matters to the government and other bodies

4. conducting research and publishing material on questions relating to the countryside

5. providing grants for suitable projects designed to enhance the countryside

6. designating areas of particular beauty requiring special protection.

It has the responsibility of designating, with DETR approval, national parks, AONBs, lengths of Heritage Coast, and long distance pathways (the most famous being the Pennine Way). Among recent initiatives is the decision to create a National Forest of 194 square miles (as big as the Isle of White) in the heart of England between Derby, Birmingham and Leicester, which will provide leisure and educational facilities, produce timber, and generally enhance the environment. Furthermore, twelve 'community forests' are being created (another 137 square miles) near major conurbations including the Great North Forest, near Tyne and Wear; the Forest of Mercia, north of Birmingham; and the Thames Chase, to the east of London. These projects, developed in partnership with the Forestry Commission, have been made possible partly by the large amounts of derelict land left by declining industries, and also by the fact that less agricultural land is now needed to grow food. Other initiatives have included the Countryside Premium scheme where farmers in particularly sensitive areas are helped to manage land set aside from agriculture for the benefit of wildlife and the landscape, and the Countryside Stewardship scheme, where farmers are given grants and help to restore traditional features, such as meadows and orchards. There is also the Hedgerow Incentive Scheme to preserve those we have and restore hundreds of miles of those that have been lost.

In addition, the Countryside Agency has helped to finance projects such as providing country walks, picnic sites, country parks, tree planting and other schemes in association with local authorities, other public bodies or with private owners. It has further helped to fund dozens of county conservation advisors, hundreds of park rangers and countryside management schemes, nine demonstration farms, plus a variety of other projects.

The other side of its work has been inherited from the Rural Development Commission (RDC). Its purpose was to promote the social and economic development of rural England in co-operation with local authorities and other bodies. This was done particularly through increasing employment opportunities, trying to diversify the local economy and improving local services. Its activities included:

- giving loans, grants and advice to small firms

- supporting the development of new rural transport facilities

- supporting the Rural Housing Trust

- providing grants for community projects

- building workshops in partnership with local government

- running partnership schemes with the private sector for training.

The merged Countryside Agency came as the culmination of a long period of discussion, and was the alternative to a merger of the Countryside Commission and the nature conservation bodies. The Commission had already seen its government grant cut back by nearly 25% in three years, down to just under £24 million in 1997-98. It raised small sums from commercial activity and sponsorship, and was starting to utilise Lottery funding for some projects. The Chairman and 14 members are appointed by the Secretary of State for the DETR. Its budget expenditure in 1999-2000 was £48.8 million (significantly less than the combined budget of its predecessor bodies), covered by its grant from DETR. It has a supporting staff of over 300, half based at the headquarters in Cheltenham and the other half at seven regional offices in London, Bristol, Cambridge, Birmingham, Manchester, Leeds and Newcastle. There has been a great deal of upheaval and difficulties in personnel in the aftermath of the merger.

Nature Conservation

In 1990 the Nature Conservancy Council was abolished and replaced by three national bodies: English Nature, Scottish Natural Heritage and the Countryside Council for Wales which are now accountable to their devolved institutions. English Nature has statutory functions under the Environmental Protection Act 1990, and is funded by and responsible to the DETR. Its prime duty is promoting nature conservation in England. The Scottish and Welsh bodies, along with an equivalent in Northern Ireland, have similar functions and share in the work of a joint committee.

To achieve these aims English Nature:

- advises government and other bodies

- publishes literature and scientific data

- commissions ecological research

- gives grants to voluntary conservation bodies

- promotes public awareness

- establishes and runs National Nature Reserves (200) and Marine Nature Reserves (1)

- designates and monitors over 4,000 Sites of Special Scientific Interest (SSSI), which are mostly privately owned and makes management agreements with farmers and other owners for the protection of these

- implements, on behalf of the government, international conventions and EU directives on conservation and biodiversity.

English Nature has a governing Council consisting of a Chair and twelve members, appointed by the Secretary of State for DETR. It currently employs over 660 permanent and about 80 temporary staff. Its budget for 1999-2000 is just over £49 million, of which £44.7 million came from a DETR grant and £4.4 million from other sources. It is worth noting that, in addition to the national reserves, there are also 635 local nature reserves owned or controlled by LAs.

The Forestry Commission

Another major public body concerned with the countryside is the Forestry Commission, which is a statutory body under the Forestry Acts 1967 and 1979. It does not come under DETR but is the responsibility of the Ministry of Agriculture, Fisheries and Food, which appoints the Commission's eleven members in conjunction with the Welsh and Scottish devolved institutions. The Chairman and six of the commissioners (two of whom are Scottish and two Welsh) are part-time. The four full-time members are all senior executive officers, headed by the Director General who is also Deputy Chairman. The Commission has a staff of some thousands, working on the land, in its regional offices and the headquarters in Edinburgh.

The Forestry Commission was created in 1919 following concern over supplies of timber during the First World War. Its first priority was to guarantee a strategic supply of timber in case of future war. But at least since the 1950s this has been replaced by a series of other priorities, which sometimes conflict with each other. The Commission now has multiple roles.

Its objectives are to:

- protect Britain's forests and woodlands

- expand Britain's forest area

- enhance the economic value of forest resources

- conserve and improve the biodiversity, landscape and cultural heritage of forests and woodland

- develop opportunities for woodland recreation

- increase public understanding and community participation in forestry.

Among other things it advises government and other bodies, conducts research and promotes forestry generally, manages its own estate, advises on private forestry projects, and provides public access and recreational facilities. As a business organisation it operates through an executive agency, Forest Enterprise (launched in 1996), managing more than three million acres of land and producing timber and timber products for the commercial market. Its research is carried out by another agency, Forest Research. The Commission has to reconcile the competing demands of profit, preserving the landscape and its wildlife, and recreation. In recent years there has been pressure on the Forestry Commission to be more commercial and less dependent on public money, with Forest Enterprise generating more income through revenue and sales of parts of the estate. In 1998-99 the Commission's government grant was £62 million, down from £97 million six years earlier, with most of the balance coming from timber sales and other commercial enterprise.

Forestry plays an important part in the rural economy in some parts of Wales, Northern England and Scotland. While some aspects of commercial forestry are resented by tourists and conservationists, the Forestry Commission does also contribute to leisure activities. It runs the famous Westonbirt Arboretum in the Cotswolds, and many of its forests, such as Kielder in Northumberland and the Scottish Borders, provide important facilities for visitors.

The Environment Agency

This is a large agency primarily responsible to the DETR, but with links to MAFF and the devolved institutions in Wales and Scotland. It was established by the 1995 Environment Act and came into operation in 1996. In particular it has taken over the functions of several other bodies including the National Rivers Authority, Her Majesty's Inspectorate of Pollution, and waste regulation functions from LAs. As such it has many functions which impact on quality of life and leisure issues, including improving air, land and water quality, conservation, protection from river and sea flooding, river navigation for recreational purposes and freshwater fisheries. It has a board of 15 members appointed by the Secretaries of State at DETR and MAFF, and controlled a budget in 1998-99 of £594 million and 9,500 staff mostly working in seven regional offices.

Pressure Groups

All these government bodies, as well as others such as British Waterways (running most of the canal system), have a bearing on countryside and recreation policies. They are primarily instruments of government policy. But they also argue the case for their area of policy to the government and to that extent act as pressure groups. Beyond them is, of course, a whole range of pure pressure groups. Some are interest groups, protecting their members, such as the National Farmers Union (NFU) or the Country Landowners Association, while others are cause groups intent on preserving wildlife, such as the Royal Society for the Protection of Birds (RSPB), the countryside and the general public's access to it. The latter involves the National Trust, the Council for the Preservation of Rural England and a great many more. There are national groups, regional, county and local groups. Some are old and permanent, while others are short-lived and concentrate on a single issue. Some, like the three just mentioned, are national institutions, significant landowners, and conduct their activities in a dignified way. Indeed the National Trust cares for over 600,000 acres of countryside and nearly 600 miles of coastline, and the RSPB has 150 nature reserves covering about 250,000 acres.

However, the last twenty years have seen the flourishing of more aggressive environmental groups, such as Greenpeace and Friends of the Earth, who prefer to campaign in a more unorthodox, dramatic and disruptive way. These various groups are an expression of increased public awareness of and concern for the countryside and the environment in general. This popular concern has given rise to an entire political movement, which has had sensational successes in European politics and has enjoyed, at various times, a good deal of support in this country. This is the Green movement, which if it has little hope of forming a government or even winning parliamentary seats at Westminster at present, has won British seats in the European Parliament in 1999. It has helped to jolt the other political parties into paying more attention to the countryside and related matters.

There has also been more acute awareness of the problems of rural economic and social decline, which have been dramatised by the mass demonstrations and agitation of the Countryside Alliance. This is a hybrid movement, defending country sports (especially fox-hunting) from threatened legislative bans, but also protesting against threats to the rural way of life. These have been fuelled by the significant recent decline in farming incomes in some sectors, and thus brought together the NFU with the Masters of Fox-hounds and local protestors against the closing of village schools, post offices, banks, shops, and pubs.

Policies dealing specifically with the countryside (rather than the environment generally) tend to fall into three main areas. These are the planning system, the Green Belt policy, and the national parks and other protected areas. Each needs to be looked at in turn.

Planning and the Green Belts

The Planning System

Planning is essentially the control of change in the interests of the community. Although the need was recognised a good deal earlier, it was only after the Second World War that this country developed a comprehensive planning system. The Town and Country Planning Act of 1947 for the first time:

1.   made planning compulsory for the countryside

2.   created planning authorities for the whole country (basically the counties and the big towns)

3.   laid down the planning system which, with some modifications, we still have today.

The planning authorities were required to draw up 'development plans' for their area which would show intended land-use for the next twenty years. Once approved by the minister, these plans would be the basis of development control, through planning permission. As a result of the Act virtually all new building, mineral extraction or any significant change in the use of land or buildings had to have planning permission from the planning authority; and in deciding whether or not to grant permission, the authority would be guided by its development plan. The 1947 Act also gave planning authorities powers to deal with particular amenity problems, such as the protection of buildings of historic or architectural interest, the preservation of trees and woodland and the control of advertisements.

This system worked well for a long time; but in the 1960s it was felt that it needed more flexibility. Development plans evolved into two kinds: broad strategic documents covering the whole county, called 'structure plans', and 'local plans' covering a smaller area in more detail. After reorganisation of local government in 1974 planning was split between counties and districts. The county is now responsible for compulsory structure plans and some development control. This provides a framework for the bulk of development control for which the district is responsible, and for local plans where it was felt they were needed. These local plans may be comprehensive, or be concerned with one aspect of planning (such as mineral extraction) or focus on some particular development scheme. In Scotland there is a similar system, except that here comprehensive local plans are required in all areas. After the abolition of the GLC and Metropolitan Counties in 1985 the London Boroughs and Metropolitan Districts have to produce plans that combine features of structure and local plans, and the same now applies in the other unitary LAs.

Planning Permission

Although LAs make the plans, which are then approved by central government, it is still central government that ultimately controls the system through the appeals procedure. Any rejection of planning permission can be appealed against to the minister, the Secretary of State for the DETR, who may then find against the local authority. Likelihood of successful appeal is made apparent from DETR circulars, which provide guidelines for planners.

Applying for planning permission involves an elaborate procedure in which plans must be publicised, various parties consulted and objections considered. Objectors to development must be heard, if necessary in a planning inquiry. These are normally held as the result of a developer appealing against being refused planning permission. In such cases the Minister appoints an inspector who hears both sides and then makes a report, although it is the Secretary of State who takes the final decision which may ignore the inspectors recommendation. The subject of these inquiries may range from cutting down a tree to building a nuclear power station, such as the Sizewell B nuclear power station inquiry which took two years and generated tons of documents. (A fuller account of planning application procedure can be found in Chapter 2.)

The Conservative governments of 1979-97 tended at times to be suspicious of some aspects of planning and were more inclined to let the free market have its way. Consequently it allowed more appeals than previous governments. It speeded up the plan-preparation and planning application procedures, and this tended to diminish public participation. The government also insisted on greater participation by the private sector, and in some respects (enterprise zones, urban development corporations, etc.) by-passed the established planning system altogether. Finally, the government required local authorities to sell off land to the private sector which was not needed for statutory purposes.

In 1985 the government issued a White Paper entitled *Lifting the Burden* (Cmd. 9571), which proposed a great deal of deregulation of business, including the reduction of planning controls. But in a DoE circular of the same year the government also reaffirmed its commitment to other things, in addition to helping business:

> *"Development proposals are not always acceptable. There are other*
> *important objectives to which the government is firmly committed: the*
> *need to preserve our heritage, to improve the quality of the environment,*
> *to protect the green belts and conserve good agricultural land."*
> (DoE 1985a)

Nonetheless, the government was criticised, and by its own supporters as much as anybody, for not protecting the countryside as much as it ought to by allowing developments in country areas. Some decisions caused great controversy, especially in respect of the Green Belt.

The Green Belt Policy

Green belts are areas of countryside near towns which are set aside to prevent development that would detract from their rural character. They are regarded as necessary areas of recreation for those who live in the towns, although the designation of an area as green belt does not carry with it any special rights of access for the public. In the 1950s the government defined the purposes of green belts as follows:

1.   to check the further growth of large built-up areas

2.   to prevent neighbouring towns from merging into one another

3.   to preserve the special character of a town.

In 1984 the government added a fourth objective for the policy, which was

4.   to assist in urban regeneration.

That is, by restricting opportunities for developers on the outskirts of towns, to encourage them to turn their attention to redeveloping derelict and other unused sites within the existing urban area. These aims may also be furthered by planning policies that simply restrict development in any countryside near towns. The only real difference between countryside designated as green belt and countryside that is not, is the assumption that the green belt land will remain so for ever, while other land near a town might be built on eventually.

The idea of Green Belts gained currency before World War II and a start was made to try to establish them then. But the policy was only fully developed after the war, as part of the reconstruction programme. Britain had problems of unhealthy slums and overcrowded, congested Victorian cities before 1939; but extensive wartime destruction made the problems many times worse. A massive clearance and rebuilding programme was essential. But this implied more building in the suburbs, more urban sprawl and more destruction of the countryside. A combination of policies was designed to deal with these problems. Some towns were allowed to expand to a strict limit and attempts made to house large numbers of people in the suburbs in a compact way with large council estates and high-rise blocks. Beyond the limits towns would be surrounded by countryside, i.e. green belt. Where excess population could not be adequately housed within the town limits, new towns were built. For example, Stevenage, Crawley, Hemel Hempstead, Harlow, Hatfield, Welwyn Garden City, Basildon and Bracknell were all built to take 'overspill' from London. In these various ways the disappearance of huge tracts of countryside around the big towns was avoided.

The creation of new towns was made possible by the New Towns Act of 1946, but the green belt policy did not need legislation once the new planning system was in operation. Appropriate councils, backed up by the minister on appeal, simply refused planning permission for new developments of an inappropriate kind in the green belt areas. Green belts are broadly defined in county structure plans and in more detail in local plans, although not all the green areas are covered by local plans, creating a degree of uncertainty over precisely where development is and is not possible. The process of designating areas of countryside as green belt is still going on. For example, the Tyne and Wear Green Belt Local Plan, which consolidated and greatly extended previous green belt schemes, was adopted in 1985. In recent years many of the controversial issues have arisen in the home counties in the south and south-east of England. Here, in the most prosperous part of the country, the pressure of population growth, the increase in the number of households and the desire to live in more spacious accommodation has led to government projections of very large expansions in housing provision. Much of this cannot be located in 'brown field sites' and will almost inevitably result in private sector building in once small towns and villages in Kent, Sussex, Hampshire etc.

National Parks and other Specially Protected Areas

Protected Landscapes

The National Parks and Access to the Countryside Act of 1949 created a system whereby the government, on the advice of the National Parks Commission (later the Countryside Commission and now the Countryside Agency), could designate certain areas as National Parks or Areas of Outstanding Natural Beauty (AONBs), to be protected from some types of development for the benefit of the nation in perpetuity. The difference between them was that the status of National Park was slightly higher, with a little more protection afforded. While the AONB was simply the responsibility of the LAs within whose area it came, the National Park was supposed to have its own independent authority to run it. At least, this was the theory.

It is important to note that the idea of a national park did not involve the nation actually owning the land, and the bulk of land is still in private hands. Nor are National Parks about preserving an untouched wilderness, even though this is what most of the rest of the world (following the Americans) understands by the term 'national park'. The National Park areas of Britain have been occupied and exploited by man for a thousand years or more. Indeed, man's shaping of the landscape is often an important part of what is being preserved. For example, much of the beauty of the Yorkshire Dales comes from the ordered cultivation of the valleys with the dry stone walls and stone barns (dating not from time immemorial, but mostly from the 18th Century), and their contrast with the wilder moors above (which also owe a good deal of their nature to man's use of them). Thus, the British idea of a national park is of a protected landscape, and to a large extent a protected way of life, rather than a wilderness.

All of the National Parks in Britain are in England and Wales. There are none in Scotland where it might be thought there was even greater scope for them. In fact, during the Second World War, while the feasibility of national parks in England and Wales was being studied, a parallel study of national parks in Scotland was undertaken. It too reported in 1945 and recommended the setting up of ten Scottish national parks, mostly in the wilder areas; that is, more like wildernesses of the American model. However, the opposition of Scottish landowners sank the plan. The Scottish Office did continue to recognise the designated areas as requiring stricter planning controls, but planning was in the hands of local councils who were generally more interested in economic development than in protecting the wilderness. There are currently proposals to establish two National Parks to cover Loch Lomond and the Trossachs and the Cairngorms, but this is a matter for the Scottish Parliament and Executive.

There were originally seven National Parks created between 1951 and 1959 in England: Peak District, Lake District, Dartmoor, Exmoor, Yorkshire Dales, North York Moors and Northumberland; and three in Wales - Snowdonia, Brecon Beacons, and Pembrokeshire Coast. Other areas had been proposed, such as Central Wales, but these were turned down, and for a long time it seemed there would never be any new ones. However, in 1988 the Norfolk Broads, by special Act of Parliament, was given a status virtually the same as a national park. Since then there have been very slow discussions about two areas. In September 1999 the DETR Secretary of State publicly announced that he was asking the Countryside Agency to consider designating the New Forest and the South Downs as new national parks. This will take several years at least, because the Countryside Agency moves slowly, there are many consultation required and possibly public enquiries will be held. In addition, forty one AONBs have been created under the 1949 Act (37 in England, 4 in Wales). These started with the Gower in 1956, included the North Pennines (which many felt should have been designated a National Park) and the latest was the Tamar Valley in 1995.

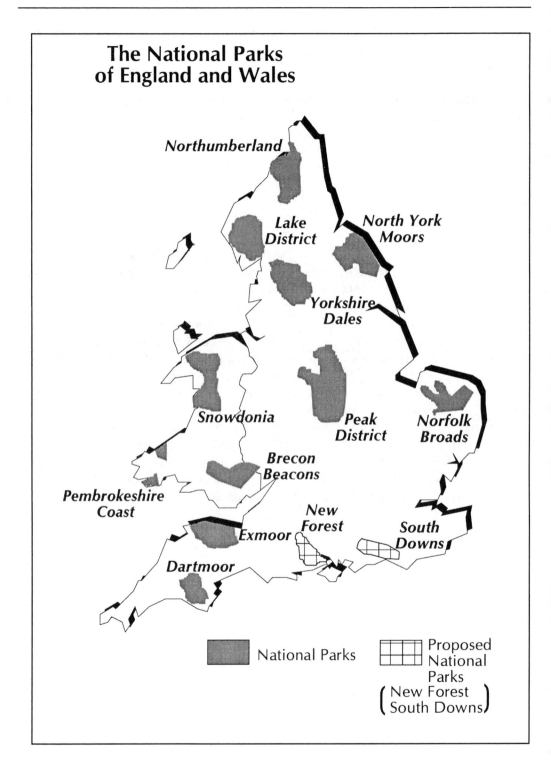

The National Parks
of England and Wales

Northumberland

Lake
District

North York
Moors

Yorkshire
Dales

Snowdonia

Peak
District

Norfolk
Broads

Brecon
Beacons

Pembrokeshire
Coast

New
Forest

South
Downs

Exmoor

Dartmoor

National Parks

Proposed
National
Parks
(New Forest
South Downs)

Criticisms of the System

Although the 1949 Act made possible all these National Parks and AONBs, it was not an entirely satisfactory piece of legislation and supporters of the national parks idea were disappointed for a number of reasons.

1. It failed to create an adequate management and planning system for the parks with adequate powers.

2. Partly as a consequence of this, it failed to protect the park areas as it was supposed to be designed specifically to do.

3. It failed to guarantee public access in the way it ought to have done.

These are serious weaknesses, which subsequent legislation has partially overcome.

Management of the Parks

The 1949 Act failed to ensure adequate provision for the proper running of the parks. The earlier 1947 Town and Country Planning Act had made the counties the planning authorities in the countryside generally, and each national park fell within the area of a county or group of counties. The National Parks Act left these counties as the ultimate planning authorities for the parks, yet envisaged each park being planned and managed as a single entity. The first National Park was the Peak District, which covered parts of six counties; and here a joint board was created to run the park, with its own staff and with a great deal of independence. But this was an ideal that was not followed elsewhere. The Lake District (covering parts of three counties) got a similar joint board, but with no staff of its own. Subsequent national parks did not even have this.

No attempt was made to give them their own management authority; and in cases where a park covered part of several counties, each county planned for its own bit of park and there was no co-ordination. Consequently, only the Peak District was effectively run as a national park from the beginning, and indeed became a pioneer in developing park facilities and other ideas for improvement. What happened with the rest was that the counties jealously guarded their planning powers and would not have them exercised by any independent or semi-independent body.

The authorities governing the parks, such as they were, were not given adequate powers to do their job. They could not buy land by compulsory purchase in order to protect it; could not prevent farmers or other owners abusing the land in various ways; and could not compel public access where it was being unnecessarily denied. Even where it was possible to buy land to protect it there were no funds. (There was in fact a National Land Fund created in 1946 for this kind of purpose, but it was shamelessly used by successive governments for their own purposes, and money was not made available until 1979 when it was reconstituted as the National Heritage Memorial Fund. (See Chapter nine.) Lack of proper management and powers meant that the parks were not protected from damage as they ought to have been.

Failure to Protect

Lack of an effective management system was at least part of the reason why the National Parks have failed to protect the countryside against a variety of developments considered detrimental by conservationists. That is, a failure to provide the protection for which the parks were set up in the first place. There have been failures in respect of developments by government departments and government agencies; by commercial developments; and by farmers and foresters.

Government Bodies

In many ways the worst offenders have been the government and its agencies. It allowed the building of a nuclear power station at Trawsfynnydd in the Snowdonia National Park in 1959 and soon after approved Hinkley B on the edge of Exmoor. It has allowed the building of reservoirs by the water authorities, the erection of huge radio and television masts, the stringing of electricity power lines across the landscape, and so on. It has also allowed large areas of the Pembrokeshire Coast, Brecon Beacons, Dartmoor and Northumberland National Parks to be used as military training grounds, denying those areas to public access and often rendering them unfit for future public use. It allowed the building of the Okehampton bypass through part of the Dartmoor National Park. Against the government's argument of 'national interest' there is little that anyone can do.

Commercial Developments

Of detrimental commercial developments perhaps the most spectacular has been the massive oil terminal at Milford Haven, which, though not in the Pembrokeshire National Park, is surrounded by it. Another threat has been mineral extraction. Huge mining and quarrying works deface the landscape in parts of Dartmoor and the Yorkshire Dales National Parks. More recently, a different and insidious kind of commercial threat has come from leisure developments, but this will be discussed later.

Farming and Forestry

That farming and forestry could be any kind of threat was not originally envisaged. In all the war-time studies of national parks and landscape conservation, and the White Papers and legislation that followed, it was always assumed that there could be no conflict between countryside conservation on the one hand, and farming and forestry on the other. It became clear only later that this was simply not the case. But park authorities had no powers of control in this respect. To take the case of forestry, the Forestry Commission is under pressure, especially recently, to earn the quickest possible return on investment; which usually means planting fast-growing conifers in straight rows close together. The resultant fenced-off patch on a bare hillside where such trees would never normally grow, looks artificial and unattractive, though a common enough sight in the national parks. It is, however, farming which poses the most problems.

Farmers can diminish the protected landscape in a number of ways. Traditional stone walls and hedgerows may be torn out and replaced by barbed wire. It is estimated that since 1945 more than 140,000 miles of hedgerow have been lost in Britain. Old barns and other buildings can be pulled down and replaced by ugly, modern, concrete and plastic structures; fertilisers and pesticides can pollute rivers and streams; traditional meadows, with their wealth of flowers, may be destroyed to grow a more profitable crop; valuable heath land (a special problem on Exmoor) or woodland may be destroyed to provide more land to cultivate; public access may be denied and footpaths and stiles may be destroyed; and so on. Modern farming methods are now recognised as the most destructive force in the countryside. However, only a limited amount can be done without large grants to induce the farmer to behave differently and such funds are not at the disposal of the parks authorities.

Public Access

Another disappointment has been with problems of public access. Although the national parks are supposed to be for the benefit of the public, the public were given no more rights of access in these protected areas than in any other part of Britain. The war-time studies that led to the creation of the parks did recommend that the public should have such rights (subject to certain conditions and exceptions) to walk over all open and uncultivated land. This was ignored. Instead, the 1949 Act gave local planning authorities some powers, where a landowner refused access, to issue access orders giving people rights. The law, however, is exceedingly complex and, apart from the Peak District Park, such access orders have rarely been used to extend the public's rights. The Rambler's Association campaigned for years, with little success in many areas.

Later developments have produced slow improvement. There were hopes of progress when the National Parks Commission became the Countryside Commission in 1968 with a much wider brief for countryside conservation as a whole; and again when the Department of the Environment was created in 1970 as a response to greater public concern with environmental issues.

New National Park Management

An important change did come with local government reorganisation. In 1974 (when the Act took effect) a new management system was introduced in most of the parks. The Peak District and to some extent the Lake District Parks already had an effective system, while the rest tended to be administered as part of the counties in which they were located, with no authority for the park as a whole. The Local Government Act required that where parks had no independent committee, one should be appointed (with members from the different counties) and would be required to appoint a National Parks Officer charged with preparing management plans for their park as a single entity. This meant a considerable improvement in the running of the parks concerned.

A further important stage came in 1991 with the publication of a major report on the National Parks commissioned from Professor Ron Edwards by the Countryside Commission. It was called *Fit for the Future* (although it is often referred to as the 'Edwards Report') and it contained a host of detailed recommendations. These included a redefinition of what a national park was for. Their purpose as defined by the National Parks and Access to the Countryside Act of 1949 was:

(i)   preserving and enhancing the natural beauty of the areas

(ii)   promoting their enjoyment by the public.

The report argued that this was too narrow, that it did not recognise how the beauty of these areas was dependent on the communities that live there. It suggested instead the following aims for a national park:

1.   to protect, maintain and enhance the scenic beauty, natural systems and land forms, and the wildlife and cultural heritage of the area

2.   to promote the quiet enjoyment and understanding of the area, insofar as it is not in conflict with the primary purpose of conservation

3.   to support the appropriate agencies in fostering the social and economic well-being of communities within the national park, in ways which are compatible with the purposes of conservation.

In order to fulfil these wider aims, the report argued, the parks must have a more effective management system. Each must be run by an independent authority, with its own budget and its own staff; and each be the planning authority for its area, with wide powers and a duty to prepare a local plan. The government eventually accepted the main recommendations and tackled most of them in the Environment Act 1995. Section 61 now lays down as the objectives of national parks:

1.   to conserve and enhance the natural beauty, wildlife and cultural heritage of their areas

2.   to promote opportunities for the public understanding and enjoyment of the special qualities of their areas.

If there is a conflict between the two, then conservation takes precedence. The National Park Authority should also seek to foster the economic and social-well-being of local communities, but without incurring significant expenditure. This proviso is hardly necessary since money is still in short supply.

The National Park Authority

Each park is now managed by its own National Park Authority (NPA), which in some respects represents an extra layer in the local government system in their areas. They are the sole local and mineral planning authority for the area, prepare their own local plans and deal with all aspects of development control. The NPA board membership is made up of 50% + 1 from the constituent LAs, with the rest being appointed by the DETR (just over half to represent the wider national interest and the balance on the nomination of local Parish Councils.) Core public funding comes 75% from central government and 25% from a levy on LAs (for which they receive an item in their own annual Revenue Support Grant from the government.)

For the financial year 2000/01 the total central and local government grant to the English NPAs is set at £25.7 million. This is not a lot to cover functions over 7.6% of the land area of the country. NPAs do in fact supplement their finances for specific projects through EU schemes, National Lottery funding, grants from the landfill tax administered by the Environment Agency, and also make modest amounts through income from car parking, sale of publications, running accommodation and study courses etc. The distribution of core government funding between NPAs follows a pattern set in the 1970s, and leads to some complaints. Thus Northumberland (the poorest) is twice the area of Exmoor and has the same number of visitors, but received 35% less core funding in 2000. The Countryside Agency has been examining the problem and it is possible that the formula used may be amended in the future.

The Peak District NPA (the largest, oldest and best established) in 1999-2000 had core funding of just under £6 million, and generated over £3.5 million of other income (including other grants of just over £1 million). Northumberland NPA budget for 2000/01 totals £3.3 million. This is based upon £1.7 million core funding, supplemented by £1.3 million from other external grants and just over £200,000 other income generation. It employs the equivalent of 53 staff, and, like many National Parks, enjoys the support of 95 volunteer workers.

Issues in the Protection of the Countryside

The Future of the National Parks

There has been progress of a modest kind in the extension of areas protected and improvements in their management. While the proposed new Cambrian Mountains National Park in central Wales was turned down by the government in 1973 without even a public inquiry, the Countryside Commission did have more success with the Norfolk Broads (the Norfolk and Suffolk Broads to be precise). In the mid-70s the Broads were facing an ecological disaster through pollution by sewage, agricultural waste and unlimited recreational use. Pressure from the Countryside Commission, Nature Conservancy Council and popular opinion led the LAs in the area to set up a semi-independent Broads Authority. This proved to be a success, and was made permanent with a government-backed private Act of Parliament of 1988, which gave the authority special powers over water control and navigation, plus powers similar to those which exist in the parks. In other words, since 1986 the Norfolk Broads has been a national park in all but name. There is the possibility of the eventual creation of the New Forest and the South Downs National Parks. Meanwhile, the Scottish authorities are examining again the possibility of national parks in Scotland.

The designation of AONBs has also continued and there are now 41 of them, the 37 in England covering 15.6% of the land area. AONBs represent a compromise, often for obvious reasons. They tend to be more densely populated than national parks, and thus do not have the wide open spaces and recreational possibilities. Politically one has to observe that there are more vested interests in these areas which are hostile to stringent planning controls. So in some cases AONB status may seem the best solution, but may also be represented as a failure. This is a common view on the North Pennines AONB designated in 1988. In this area with a low population density and much wild landscape, what the Countryside Commission really wanted was national park status; but it did not press for this knowing it had no chance of succeeding. Even achieving AONB status was a struggle. Had it become a national park, a unified body could have managed the area more effectively, affording better protection against commercial forestry and inappropriate tourism development. As an AONB, the nine local authorities and two tourist boards responsible for this area are unlikely to do these things as effectively. The Countryside Agency receives a small grant from the government (£5.5 million in 2000/01) to spend on AONB projects.

Another area of some success is the coastline. From 1966 to 1970, building on work done in the voluntary sector by the National Trust, the Countryside Commission carried out a detailed survey of the entire British coastline. On the basis of this survey it began a process of designating sections of beautiful, unspoilt coast as 'heritage coast'. This was done in collaboration with local authorities concerned and aimed at preventing unsightly development. The task was completed in the early 1990s with some 37 sections having been designated, protecting nearly 640 miles. Meanwhile the National Trust, through its Enterprise Neptune campaign, has purchased 600 miles in England and Wales alone and hopes to increase this to 1000 miles in the foreseeable future.

Despite some progress in the national parks idea and countryside conservation generally, however, the future of the national parks is far from certain. The threats and problems discussed above are all still there; progress is very slow; and new threats now exist. Apart from old types of threats to the actual countryside (sometimes in new guises, such as gigantic wind farms), there are now a number of more recent challenges to the way of life that ultimately supports the landscape. Problems of hill farmers who have difficulty in surviving; the reduction of public transport and the closing of the village schools and post offices which make small communities viable; as well as the problem of newcomers, all contribute to the destruction of that way of life.

National parks are fine places to live, though often less so to work. Thus, there is a strong demand for housing from people from outside who contribute little to the economy in the area: visitors, second-homers, the retired, etc. Second homes force up prices so that locals cannot afford to live in their own villages. In some cases people are living in national parks and commuting to work (for example, parts of the Yorkshire Dales are within commuting distance from the West Yorkshire conurbation) putting further pressure on house prices and undermining the local community. There are some villages in national parks which are virtually deserted during winter, a situation which cannot sustain local shops or other services. In Snowdonia 60% of houses belong to outsiders, and it is because these are mainly English that Welsh Nationalists are angry that local Welsh people are unable to live in their own villages. But the national park authorities have no powers to restrict such developments and no powers to build houses for local people, while the right-to-buy legislation has reduced the stock of council housing.

Leisure and Tourism

Leisure and tourism also have their impact, which is sometimes a boon and sometimes a curse, and sometimes both at the same time. They undoubtedly help the economy of the park areas and in a sense are what national parks are there for. But they are no panacea or unmixed blessing. Large numbers of visitors at popular sights can do a great deal of damage, can ruin the peace and tranquillity, can induce ugly commercialisation, and can choke country roads with cars and caravans.

Managing access through the control of motor traffic is a particularly difficult issue, but one which is being slowly tackled in some areas. Encouraging visitors to get out of their cars and walk or cycle to enjoy the health benefits of physical exercise and the beauty and tranquillity of the landscape is also necessary. This is connected to improving legal rights of access to the countryside while maintaining necessary safeguards. The Labour Manifesto in 1997 had a commitment to give people greater freedom to explore open countryside, the so-called 'right to roam'. This is a complicated area, and is now being dealt with in the Countryside and Rights of Way Bill, published in March 2000 and in July 2000 still under parliamentary scrutiny. It is intended to confer rights of public access to mountain, moor, heath, down and registered common land, about one ninth of the land area. It includes safeguards for landowners, especially farmers, and to protect wildlife and Sites of Special Scientific Interests (SSSI). There are also moves to modernise, clarify and improve existing rights of way such as footpaths and bridleways, and to make sure that enforcement against those who obstruct them is more effective. While more public access generally appears highly desirable, it must be recognised that those who own land and earn their livings in the countryside have legitimate interests to protect. And the countryside itself is fragile; even large numbers of walkers can erode footpaths, cyclists do more damage on unsurfaced paths, and the invasion of bridleways, so called green roads, and the open countryside by maniacs indulging their desire to take their 4-wheel drive vehicles is extremely destructive.

Leisure developments can produce employment but can have other drawbacks. Jobs in tourism are often seasonal and low paid, and many go to outsiders. When leisure developments are by outsiders the profits usually go elsewhere. Developments are usually best when initiated internally, such as farmers providing accommodation and facilities for visitors. But it is often only the outside leisure company that has the capital to make a substantial investment. Furthermore, it may be that development is of a kind that is out of keeping with the area or the idea of a national park. A controversial example is the Langdale centre in the Lake District. This is a time-share development and leisure complex with 'Scandinavian lodges', sauna, tropical pool, hydro-spa and beauty salon, squash courts, tropical bar, etc., providing a 'Caribbean holiday'. It is entirely artificial, it monopolises a particular view, it excludes the general public, and so on. It can be argued that such developments bring jobs and prosperity to the area, but others argue that they are so out of keeping with their environment that they detract from what is being preserved.

National parks and AONBs are neither wildernesses nor museums, but are living landscapes. They are landscapes that sustain and are sustained by a way of life. If that way of life is undermined then so is the landscape, and the whole point of having national parks and AONBs is frustrated and lost. As we have seen, there are many forces of change at work that are detrimental to the landscape and to the way of life associated with it, while the means of resisting such changes are relatively weak. Nevertheless, the future is not entirely bleak. The example of the Broads Authority shows what can be done when enough people are interested and determined. There are also significant changes in agriculture. The EU Common

Agricultural Policy, which subsidised ever greater productivity whether the food was needed or not, has been modified. The farming lobby is becoming less powerful in Whitehall, while more and more farmers are accepting a responsibility for countryside conservation. Furthermore, the general growth of leisure prompts popular recognition of the greater need for conserving the countryside. This, combined with a growing popular concern for environmental issues, may be the best hope for the future of the existing protected areas and the future development of the national parks idea.

Chapter 7

Sport and Government

History of Government Concern for Sport

Central government has had an indirect interest in sport and recreation for more than a hundred years. From the nineteenth century to the present time it has been recognised as a desirable aim of government to maintain and improve the nation's health and fitness, and this has been the most important impulse behind the encouragement of sport and recreation generally. Early developments flowed from a concern over public health, and was expressed in encouragement to local authorities to provide public baths, parks and open spaces, as well as the introduction of physical education in schools (until very recently one of the very few compulsory subjects). Recent campaigns by the Sports Council to encourage various groups, such as women and the old, to engage in some kind of physical recreation, are another expression of this general policy.

However, central and local government involvement in sport and recreation has, from time to time, been inspired by other reasons than simply the health of the nation. In the 19th Century, there were concerns about public order, drunkenness and rowdy behaviour. Hence the repression of violent spectacles like bear- and bull-bating, bare-knuckle fighting and loose ball games like football, and even public executions (there are even echoes of this today in the football hooligan controversy). Another concern has been war. The poor quality of recruits for the Boer War in the closing years of the 19th Century was widely regarded as a scandal, and in the late 1930s government support for sporting bodies was at least partly inspired by the prospect of conflict with Nazi Germany. In the 20th Century national prestige has increasingly had a part to play. If we win Olympic gold medals or international football tournaments this is thought to be good for national prestige and morale. Some countries go to great, and in one or two cases dishonest, lengths to promote sport for just this reason.

Nineteenth Century Developments

The public provision of sport and recreation facilities in the 19th Century was exclusively a matter for local government, with greater or lesser encouragement from Whitehall according to the issue. Thus, the Baths and Washhouses Act of 1846 and the Recreation Grounds Act of 1852 allowed for the municipal provision of these facilities, although parks in particular were being provided already in more progressive towns through private legislation. For example, the first public park was laid out in Birkenhead almost a decade earlier in 1843. Such provision became a matter of civic pride. Joseph Chamberlain, the famous leader of Birmingham City Council, was a strong advocate of enhancing towns with parks ('social lungs' he called them) and other civic amenities.

In this way a concern for public health broadened into a wider concern for general well-being of the citizens with provision of libraries and museums and, from 1870, schools. The 1870 Education Act introduced universal elementary education. Until 1906 physical drill could be provided, though not games. Thereafter, greater emphasis was put on the physical education of pupils, and successive Education Acts up to 1944 encouraged this. A final aspect of development of local services in relation to sport and recreation in the 19th Century developed in the latter part of the century. This was the development of municipal trading, including the building and running of sport facilities. Much of this was done through private legislation, which was used particularly by resort towns wanting to provide recreational facilities for visitors. This is why a number of professional football teams play at municipally owned grounds. The town of Brighton even took over a racecourse when its financial backers withdrew.

Twentieth Century Developments

Local government provision of sport and recreational facilities has grown in the 20th century with demand. In addition to educational provision, local authorities began to provide football and cricket pitches and athletics tracks. Later came swimming pools, bowling greens, tennis courts and golf courses, while the more recent developments have included ice rinks, squash courts and ski runs. The major trend of the last twenty years has been towards the provision of indoor sports centres. In 1970 there were 20 of these around the country, but by 1990 there were about 1,700. Today, sport and recreation are part of a growing demand for leisure facilities of all kinds.

In the meanwhile, central government has shown an increasing interest in sport and recreation. This has been accompanied by a change of attitude beyond provision for the good of country (a healthy and fit workforce and potential army) to recognising that sport and recreation are good for their own sake. Initially, central government merely encouraged local authorities to provide facilities if they wished. More direct involvement began with the requiring of authorities to make educational provision. Beyond education, government interest in sports and recreational provision began to develop in the years between the World Wars.

In the 1930's fresh air and fitness became a national preoccupation. The Rambler's Association, Youth Hostel Association, and other organisations were founded at this time. In 1935 a number of people and organisations interested in physical training joined together to create the Central Council for Recreative Physical Training (which later became the Central Council of Physical Recreation, CCPR), which was set up to promote physical training and co-ordinate the organisations already in the field. Central government became involved two years later (undoubtedly influenced by the prospect of war), when it passed the Physical Training and Recreation Act of 1937 enabling it to aid local voluntary organisations that were providing sport and recreation. Two million pounds were earmarked for the purpose and the government was intending to set up its own body to do this, but in the end the Central Council was given the job of allocating the funds on the government's behalf.

After the War great encouragement was given to the provision of recreational facilities. Apart from the 1944 Education Act (which required education authorities to provide facilities for all levels of education, including youth and adult education), there was the National Parks and Access to the Countryside Act of 1949, and through the new planning legislation local authorities were encouraged to designate areas of the county for recreational purposes, and even acquire some land. Later the Countryside Act of 1968 encouraged local authorities generally to provide country parks, picnic sites and camping grounds and various outdoor sporting facilities.

Creation of the Sports Council

Meanwhile the CCPR continued its duel role as a sort of parliament of sporting organisations, while at the same time continuing to administer government subsidies to sporting organisations, establish and run national centres and generally promote the cause of sport in the community. In 1960 it published a report it had commissioned on the development of sport (the Wolfenden Report) which stressed the need for a great expansion of sporting facilities, both outdoor and indoor, and advocated a smaller body to advise government on the development of sport. This resulted in the setting up of a Sports Council in 1965 as an advisory body, while the CCPR continued to administer government monies. Finally in 1972 the Sports Council was given a Royal Charter and made into an executive body (rather like the Arts Council), taking over the CCPR's staff and assets and its role of dispensing government grants to client bodies and running national centres. The CCPR remained as a forum for sporting bodies (rather like the TUC or CBI) which provides various services for its member organisations and acts as a consultant to, and is partially funded by, the Sports Council.

A Minister for Sport

In 1974 Dennis Howell was appointed as Minister of State for Sport and Recreation within the Department of the Environment, with responsibility for the government's dealings with these bodies and to be responsible for sporting issues generally. His appointment gave sport a much higher profile in government. All subsequent governments have appointed a Minister for Sport. When John Major became Prime Minister in 1990 he transferred sport to the Department of Education, but later created the Department of National Heritage (now the Department for Culture, Media and Sport) where sport now has its permanent governmental home.

Government Policy for Sport

Central government does not itself provide any sporting facilities, but has a policy of positive encouragement which it promotes in various ways. It sets up bodies like the Sports Council; it can provide funds for the development of facilities and assistance of bodies whose aims it approves; it can co-ordinate the work of public and voluntary, and in some cases commercial bodies in the interests of sport; it can encourage and make possible, legally and financially, local government provision of facilities; and it can deal with particular questions as they arise, whether to do with foreign relations (e.g. the Gleneagles Agreement which forbade sporting links with South Africa until it abandoned apartheid in the early 1990s) or domestic policy (e.g. the football hooligan issue).

But the main object of policy has been the encouragement of more and more people to participate in sporting activity. There has been a general encouragement but also a series of special campaigns targeted at particular groups: the young, the old, women, the disabled, etc. All parties in government have subscribed to these policies. But the advent of the Conservative government in 1979 introduced a new emphasis. In line with its overall aims of reducing government expenditure and encouraging private enterprise, it introduced more businessmen on to bodies like the Sports Council, encouraged private sponsorship and voluntary sports bodies to be more commercial and entrepreneurial, and sought to make public subsidy play, as far as possible, a double role of helping sport and also helping with inner-city problems (all of which is very similar to what was happening with the Arts Council).

On the local government front, the policy of privatisation, especially in the form of contracting out, had an impact. It fitted in with the government's aim of the better management of resources, and of consumers of services paying when they are well able to do so. Finally, the Conservative government refused for a time to grant substantial aid for major events like international games (although this policy was modified under John Major, and further changed under Tony Blair as we shall see.)

Central Government and other National Bodies

The Department for Culture, Media and Sport (DCMS)

Sport and recreation covers a variety of subjects and touches on the work of a number of central government departments besides its main home in the DCMS:

- Education (DfEE) - sport in schools and other institutions

- Agriculture (MAFF) - countryside

- Environment and Transport (DETR) - countryside, local government, access to sporting events

- Foreign Office (FCO) - international events

- Home Office - hooliganism, betting

- Health - promotion of healthy life styles.

In addition, the devolved Scottish, Welsh and Northern Ireland institutions have responsibilities for sport within their own countries. Because of the high publicity profile of some sports issues, the Prime Minister and other senior colleagues take a more direct interest from time to time. In certain areas, such as the securing of major international events for Britain, there have been concerns that government strategy was not sufficiently 'joined up'. The House of Commons Select Committee on CMS published a report in May 1999 proposing among other things a 'Minister for Events'. In the summer of 1999 a Minister of State at the Cabinet Office, Ian McCartney MP, was given special responsibility for co-ordinating government policy on the 2002 Commonwealth Games in Manchester.

The Minister of State for Sport is a junior minister in the DCMS, which is responsible for the co-ordination of sport and recreation policy with all these other departmental interests. The current Minister is Kate Hoey, the first woman to hold the position, and also unusual in that she was once an active athlete (Northern Ireland high jump champion) and sports administrator before becoming an MP. This makes a change from her male predecessors who were mostly football fans and social golfers. Like the other junior Ministers she is subject to the Secretary of State (Chris Smith) who will tend to take responsibility for big issues. The DCMS appoints the Sports Council of England and various other advisory bodies, sets their objectives, provides their funds and speaks for them and other bodies in Parliament and generally oversees their work. It also deals with general sporting issues such as the use of drugs in sport.

But it must be stressed that its power to direct events in sport and recreation is limited. This is a sector which has many hundreds of individual governing bodies for diverse sports, which are themselves made up of vast numbers of local clubs firmly situated in the voluntary and private sector, and are also connected with international federations. Some sectors of sport are run as highly profitable businesses plugged into international TV network revenues with millionaire income players, while others are part time and genuinely amateur. There is the complication that for some purposes participation in the international sporting arena is organised through UK institutions and teams (e.g. the Olympic games) while in others (football) England, Scotland, Wales and Northern Ireland are separate entities. The distinction cuts through sports, so that for example there is a British (UK) track and field team at the Olympics but four separate national athletics teams at the Commonwealth Games. Much of the work of the DCMS is done through an 'arms length' relationship channelled through the Sports Council system. But the involvement of the DCMS and the Sports Council in the saga over Wembley Stadium (discussed later) is an illustration of the difficulties in providing a clear steer in a major flagship sporting facility.

The Sports Council (Sport England)

The main vehicles of central government policy on sport are the Sports Councils. In 1972 the Great Britain Sports Council had a dual role, responsible for English sport, but also co-ordinating some matters (such as international affairs and anti-doping measures) for the separate Councils for Wales, Scotland and Northern Ireland. Like the Arts Council, the Sports Councils were set up by a Royal Charter. In 1995, following the publication of a consultative paper *Sport: Raising the Game*, the government overhauled the structure. The old GB body was replaced by two councils: the English Sports Council, now rebranded as 'Sport England' while the UK Sports Council 'UKSport' was established to carry out international and co-ordinating activities for the four national councils.

The English Sports Council has nineteen members, who are appointed by the Secretary of State. There is a Chairman, at present Trevor Brooking (broadcaster and former member of the England football team), two vice-chairs and members who include distinguished former sportsmen and women (among them the athlete Tessa Sanderson, footballer Garth Crooks, and the yachtsman Robin Knox-Johnston), a PE teacher, three businessmen (two with leisure companies) and sporting administrators with national and local government experience. It has a series of advisory panels dealing with different areas such as lottery, local authorities, women and sport, disability, racial equality, and grant applications. The Council has a permanent staff of about 400 in its London HQ and the regional offices. Its work is partly funded through a government grant agreed with the DCMS. In the post 1979 period it was increasingly encouraged to find other sources of income and cut costs. This led to business sponsorship for some of its activities;

its own commercial/ entrepreneurial activities, including publishing materials, endorsement of certain commercial products, and also running its centres of excellence along more businesslike lines and charging more realistically for some of its services. But even more important in the 1990s has become its role as the distributor of Lottery funding for the sporting good cause. Traditionally the core grant was used to maintain the infrastructure of sport in England, while the proceeds of what is now called the Sport England Lottery Fund is earmarked for the development of sport. This distinction is hard to establish in practice and one of the central concerns of the Council today is to try to co-ordinate and integrate all these areas of activity.

Its range of commitments and activities include:

- acting as an adviser to government on all sporting issues

- drawing up an overall strategic framework for sport in England

- assisting the national governing bodies of various sports to draw strategic plans for the provision of facilities

- providing grants to introduce or improve sporting facilities, by local councils and other bodies

- providing grants for specific programmes of sporting activity in schools and the community

- helping finance the training of coaches in various sports; and for sporting bodies to develop their own coaching programmes

- running publicity campaigns to encourage more people to participate in sport and recreation

- funding development staff to help sporting organisations encourage more people to take up their sports

- conducting research into design of sporting facilities

- identifying and promoting best practice in provision and management of sporting facilities

- running national sporting centres.

The UK/English Institutes of Sport

One long running commitment of the Sports Council is the running of national sports centres, whose task is to promote excellence in the various sporting areas to which they are devoted. These are currently:

- Crystal Palace (athletics, swimming, boxing, etc.)

- Lilleshall (association football, cricket, gymnastics, etc.)

- Holme Pierrepont (water sports)

- Bisham Abbey (tennis, rugby, hockey, etc.)

These are now in the process of being incorporated into an ambitious project, the English Institute of Sport. This originated under the Conservative government in the mid 1990s, following criticisms of disappointing performances by English and British national teams in international competitions. This was originally a scheme to set up a single UK 'Academy of Sport' (in Sheffield) to promote excellence in the development of an elite group of sports men and women across a range of activities. This was partly modelled on some examples from elsewhere, notably Australia, and would involve sports science staff, sports medicine experts, dieticians, coaches, and training facilities. There was much debate and criticism about whether a single centre could adequately provide for a wide range of sports, and doubts about the attractiveness of the scheme to athletes who would have to detach themselves from home areas and suffer substantial personal inconvenience.

After some thought, the 1997 Labour government decided to establish a UK Sports Institute, which would in effect be a looser federal structure within which each of the four home countries would develop its own national institute. The English Sports Council came to the conclusion by 1999 that there was no need to create a single national centre in England for the English Institute of Sport. Instead there would be a network of ten specialist centres sharing some staff and facilities. These would incorporate four existing establishments: London/Crystal Palace, East Midlands/Holme Pierrepont-Loughborough University, South/Bisham Abbey, and West Midlands/Lilleshall. To these will be added: North West/Manchester Sports City (site of the 2002 Commonwealth Games), Yorkshire/Sheffield, South West/Bath University, and somewhat later probably North/Gateshead, South Coast/Southampton, and East/not yet determined. A total of £120 million will come from the Sport England Lottery Fund. Steve Cram has been appointed to the Chair of the Institute, with effect from October 2000 and it is expected to become operational over the following two years.

Many 'grassroots' policies are implemented in the regions through the ten regional offices, which are able to take into account local conditions and needs. They provide advice, information and technical expertise for local authorities, local sports organisations and other bodies. They also provide some direct grants and loans for projects which meet the Council's objectives of encouraging participation, according to the Council's priorities for facility provision. Advice to sporting organisations about the submission of bids for lottery funding, either under the Sports Lottery Fund, or the New Opportunities Fund, or the Millennium Fund are now probably even more important because of the large sums of money potentially available.

The Central Council of Physical Recreation (CCPR)

Although it is a national body, the Central Council for Physical Recreation is not a government body. It did act as the government's agent for many years and is still today funded by central government through the Sports Council, but strictly speaking it belongs to the voluntary sector. However, its close ties with the Sports Council make it convenient to deal with it here.

When the Central Council of Physical Recreation handed over its assets and funds to the newly created Sports Council in 1972, it had to decide whether to wind itself up or find itself a new role. It decided to carry on and revert to its earlier status as an independent voluntary body for promoting sport, its newly defined objectives being:

1. to constitute a standing forum where all national governing and representative bodies of sport and physical recreation may be represented and may collectively or through special groups, where appropriate, formulate and promote measures to improve and develop sport and physical recreation

2. to support the work of specialist sports bodies and to bring them together with other interested organisations

3. to act as a consultative body to the Sports Council and other representative or public bodies concerned with sport and physical recreation.

The CCPR has a membership of 250 governing and other bodies which together represent over 87,000 local sports clubs. Because much of the Council's work relates to particular sectors of sport, the CCPR conducts the bulk of its activity within six divisions:

(a) Games and Sports

(b) Movement and Dance

(c)   Outdoor Pursuits

(d)   Water Recreation

(e)   Interested Organisations

(f)   Major Spectator Sports.

In addition to being a forum, the CCPR provides various services for its members to do with such matters as legal advice, raising sponsorship, press services, and fund raising. To finance its operations the CCPR has an income from the Sports Council, with which it has a contract as official consultant. This covers about two-thirds of income, the rest coming from subscriptions, events and other sources.

Children's Play and The National Playing Fields Association

Two further voluntary bodies of national importance are the National Playing Fields Association (NPFA) and the Association for Children's Play and Recreation (Play Board). The NPFA was founded in 1925 to campaign for and help in the provision of playing fields. This is for everyone, but especially the young and disabled. It campaigns, puts pressure on central and local government and gives advice and sometimes money to bodies to extend their facilities. In recent years it has campaigned vigorously to reverse the trend in which school playing fields were being sold off for building development in order to raise money for local education budgets. It receives a small grant from the Sports Council, but most money comes from voluntary contributions; although in recent years its work has been limited for lack of funds. It has the status of a national charity.

In 1984 the children's play section of the NPFA was taken over by a new body that has come to be called Playboard. This has a network of regional advisors to give practical advice to LAs and other bodies on playground equipment, adventure playgrounds, holiday play schemes, etc. In addition, it conducts and commissions research into play, and campaigns for more facilities and to raise public and political awareness of the importance of play for children's development. From May 1996 NPFA carried out programmes for the DCMS to improve playwork education and training, play safety, and the dissemination of knowledge. In the summer of 2000 these arrangements are being changed with a transfer of functions to the National Training Organisation for Sport Recreation and Allied Occupations (SPRITO), the Children's Play Council (CPC) and the Children's Play Policy Forum (CPPF), along with a new National Play Information Centre (NPIC). No doubt this new array of acronyms will provide great pleasure to young people.

Other national government agencies which have an important role in relation to Sport and Recreation include the Countryside Agency, the Environment Agency (particularly with regard to rivers and angling), the Forestry Commission, the Nature Conservancy Council, and British Waterways, some of which were discussed in Chapter 6. Many other agencies have a less direct role.

Regional Organisations and Local Government

Regional Bodies

English Sports Council policies are implemented in the regions through ten regional offices, who are able to take into account local conditions and needs. They provide advice, information and technical expertise for local authorities, local sports organisations and other bodies. Regional councils for sport and recreation were set up by the Sports Minister in 1976 (replacing earlier councils devoted to sport alone that had been set up a dozen years before). These were to provide a consultative forum for discussion among local authorities and various sports organisations, and with bodies concerned with promoting sport and recreation regionally. They produce strategy plans for the development of sport and recreation in their areas. The Northern Council for Sport and Recreation covers Cleveland, Cumbria, Durham, Northumberland and Tyne and Wear.

Local Government

Local authorities are by far the biggest providers and operators of sports facilities in the country, not only for educational purposes but for general community use. This has been true for most of the 20th Century, although there has been a major expansion in the number and variety of facilities since the 1960s. The Durham City (District) Council is probably fairly typical. It provides 5 indoor sports and leisure centres, a public swimming pool, 5 fitness clubs, 27 football and 1 rugby field, 6 cricket pitches, 10 bowling greens, 2 putting greens, and 11 public parks. It has a leisure development team which organises a variety of events including coaching sessions for young people (especially) in the school holidays, road runs, and an annual international cricket festival for amateur club teams. It also promotes its own Sports Forum (a sort of local CCPR), which brings together representatives of local sports clubs such as rowing, rugby, tennis, cricket, athletics, martial arts, football etc.

Local authorities in general like to extend their sport and recreation facilities where they can for the same reasons as for leisure as a whole (as discussed in Chapter Two). They help to create a better environment for the people of the area, foster a sense of community, improve health and fitness, and make the area more attractive to visitors or to commercial investment. However, whereas in the past the desirability of extending facilities could be taken for granted, the role of local government in the provision of services became much more open to question during the Thatcher period. While there are some who would argue that the role of authorities should be greatly extended, there are others who would see it reduced to no more than an enabling and supervisory role.

A House of Lords report of 1973 (the 'Cobham Report') recommended a statutory duty be imposed on local authorities in Britain (as is the case in Northern Ireland) to provide facilities:

> *"as necessary in their area in adequate quantity and distribution for the recreational, physical, social and cultural needs of the community."*

It was suggested that county councils should have this responsibility in collaboration with district councils and other interested bodies. Successive governments have rejected this idea of a statutory duty and merely encourage local authorities to make use of permissive legislation to provide facilities which the authority thinks are needed and it can afford. The only statutory duty as regards provision is the education authorities have to provide facilities for physical education.

However, the local government picture was clouded by the effects of financial constraints, pressure to sell assets and by privatisation. There was considerable variation among local authorities in the response to these pressures; for example, some authorities continued to build new sports centres, some moved rapidly to contract out their management, and some were selling them off.

Effective Management

One common feature which has continued is that all local authorities are being encouraged to manage their facilities more effectively. An Audit Commission report, entitled *Sport for Whom?: Clarifying the Local Authority Role in Sport and Recreation* (1989), argued that although it would not question a local authority's decision to provide facilities in order to fulfil social objectives and not seek profit, it was nevertheless necessary that those facilities be managed in the best possible way. The report diagnosed the faults to which local authorities are particularly prone as follows:

- Investment decisions are sometimes poorly thought out: authorities do not always consider the full range of options, concentrating on direct provisions and overlooking co-operation with the private and voluntary sectors and with other authorities.

- Revenue consequences are not always considered in enough detail. Buildings with high running costs may be preferred with little thought of the long-term financial commitment. Revenue predictions are usually based on expected income and cost in the second year of operation;

upgrades to meet increased customer expectations and renovation and reinvestment cycles are rarely considered.

- Authorities assume that low prices and blanket subsidies encourage use and help ensure social objectives are met; but sports participation is biased towards people with a professional and managerial background who benefit disproportionately from low prices.

- Objectives are rarely quantified and success or failure in meeting objectives rarely measured or monitored. It is easy to 'move the goalposts' and explain away an unexpectedly high deficit by invoking social objectives.

The Commission insisted that these deficiencies had to be put right quickly in view of increasing financial pressure on authorities, growing competition from the private sector and a more volatile market generally, and the need to prepare for compulsory competitive tendering (CCT). The report went on to suggest a number of ways in which management of facilities could be improved. Among its recommendations the commission proposed that authorities should:

1. review the sport and recreation strategies at least every five years, taking into account the whole of the sport and recreation market, and setting specific targets to meet identified needs

2. define financial and social objectives and create mechanisms for monitoring their achievement

3. monitor pricing particularly closely, avoiding across the board subsidies

4. take care to avoid CCT contracts where the authority bears the losses if the contractor performs badly

5. seek to co-operate with each other, and avoid situations where authorities build rival facilities where the market cannot fully support more than one.

Many LAs followed the Audit Commission's advice in order to prepare for CCT which has helped to make them considerably more efficient and businesslike. Under the 1997 Labour government, while compulsory competitive tendering (CCT) has been abandoned, the legal requirement to define and seek 'best value' methods and practices has maintained the drive to scrutinise plans to set up or operate sports and recreation facilities.

Issues and Developments in Sport and Recreation

Sport is such a widespread and diverse activity that it inevitably generates a wide range of issues and controversies. Some are international and touch on many sports, as is the case with racism and with drugs; others are more domestic, such as whether tobacco companies should be allowed to participate in sports sponsorship. The issues discussed here all concern the proper and realistic role of government. There are a series of questions about whether and how far government ought to take a more active role, or if its role is of the wrong sort; or if government may perhaps be able to achieve rather less than it claims.

Government Support for Attracting Major Competitions

One of the most controversial policies in relation to sport during Mrs Thatcher's time as Prime Minister was its persistent refusal to subsidise international sporting events. In 1986 the Commonwealth Games in Edinburgh nearly went bankrupt. Despite considerable pressure, the government would not bail out the organisation, and a highly embarrassing closure of the games was only averted by the proprietor of the *Daily Mirror*, Robert Maxwell, stepping in with private money. Later, the government refused any financial backing for the bids of Birmingham and Manchester to stage the 1992 and 1996 Olympic Games respectively. The question again became topical when Sheffield successfully bid to stage the World Student Games (the world's biggest sporting event outside the Olympics) in 1991. Unfortunately, Sheffield's ambitious building programme soon ran into funding problems, the games were a financial failure, and the city is still paying off the debt. After John Major, a keen sports enthusiast, succeeded Mrs Thatcher in 1990, the hard line was softened a little, to the extent of guaranteeing part of the (unsuccessful) Manchester bid for the 2000 Olympics (£7 million to be called upon only in case of losses). The government stuck to its policy that such events must not receive any special government support. This is still a controversial policy, raising the question of what the proper role of central government should be.

Against Government Support

The roots of the Conservative government's initial attitude can be found in its general belief that it is not the business of government to go round doing everything for everybody (the 'nanny state' as Mrs Thatcher called it). Apart from certain essential services which only the government can provide, most other things can and should be provided by business enterprise operating in a free market. If the government starts paying out for one non-essential thing, then it will very soon find itself paying for a great many other things of the same kind. This just leads to ever more bureaucracy and taxation, followed by a steady decline in our prosperity. Sport is just one of many areas of policy which this argument is applied to.

More specifically, the government could point, on the one hand, to examples like the Montreal Olympics of 1976 which left the city and the Canadian government with massive debts from which they are still recovering. On the other hand, there is the example of the Los Angeles Olympics of 1984 which involved no government support and had to be self-financing. The result was a financial success for the city, while substantial sums went to benefit American sport. These Olympics should therefore be the model for organising such events. Finally, the government insists that it does provide money for sport through the Sports Council. If the Council wishes to fund international games it is free to do so, but must do it out of its existing budget (i.e. take money from other projects and clients). The government will provide no extra funds.

For Government Support

However, there are arguments on the other side. Many point out the close involvement of governments in other countries. The successful Seoul Olympics, for example, was based on a partnership between the private sector and the South Korean government. A major games brings prestige to the host country. It will encourage the development of the nation's sport. It will leave new facilities and other assets built for the games (e.g. athletes 'villages' become desirable housing estates). It can improve a country's image and attract tourists and long term inward investment. In other words, government backing for a major event is a good investment for the public, if otherwise it would not be possible to hold such games at all.

It can be argued that although the Los Angeles Olympics was financially successful, it was not a very good precedent. It used mainly pre-existing facilities, while the commercialisation of the games offended many. It could also be said to have encouraged cities around the world to forget the lessons of Montreal and believe that with a combination of good marketing, the sale of television rights, sponsorship and other forms of commercialisation, the hosting of a major games is a financially attractive project.

The Brazilian city of Sao Paulo was delighted to win the bid to stage the 1989 World Student Games, which they hoped would at least break even and prove a great boost to the city. But as costs mounted and commercial sponsorship and media interest was not forthcoming, the city realised that it was facing a financial disaster and had to make a humiliating withdrawal. The Games were hastily rearranged and took place in a scaled-down form in the West German City of Duisburg. Similarly, the 1990 Commonwealth Games in Auckland, New Zealand, while in many ways a great success, has left the city of Auckland with millions of pounds worth of debt, from which it will take years to recover.

Despite confident predictions of the organisers, the 1991 World Student Games in Sheffield faced problems very like those of the Sao Paulo games - lack of television and commercial interest. The Council and business interests in the city set up a company to run the games, called 'Universiad', with a staff of 40. It was supposed to raise £12 million in sponsorship money, but by June 1990 it had raised only £2 million when the company collapsed with a million pound's worth of debt. The City Council had to step in to rescue the project, leaving itself heavily in debt.

A leading consultant on international sporting events has said:

> "They're dazzled by the light of Los Angeles. Cities flutter round possible events like moths round a lamp. .... There are probably only three international events attractive enough to earn back their total costs - operating costs not capital costs. They are the Olympics, the soccer World Cup and the America's Cup. Everything else, however worthwhile, needs government help." (Quoted in The Sunday Times 28.1.90)

The Labour government since 1997 has taken a much more positive approach to gaining and running such competitions. The 2002 Commonwealth Games in Manchester is receiving grants of £80 million for two major projects. It gave its full backing to the Football Association in its bid to FIFA to stage the 2006 World Cup. Some £10 million was provided to back the campaign to convince FIFA delegates up to the Zurich meeting in July 2000. Sport England helped to prepare the case and provide finance for guaranteeing the facilities, especially the stadiums. The Prime Minister provided an introduction to the promotional video. In this he was in good company, since the South Africans deployed Nelson Mandela and Germany its Chancellor. The fact that the bid failed also demonstrated the political danger of a high governmental profile. Winning might indeed enhance prestige, but losing has the opposite effect.

On the way, ministers became embroiled in annoying controversy over the rebuilding of Wembley Stadium. Since the early 1990s it had been widely recognised that the stadium, despite its great history and unofficial status as the 'national stadium' for sports such as football and rugby league, was obsolete. In 1995-96 (under the John Major Conservative government) the Sports Council decided to support a plan for a total rebuild with a lottery grant of £120 million. Driving the proposal was football (the FA, Premier League and Football League), as the major sport likely to require such a large stadium regularly for fixtures, and with the desire to bid for the World Cup in the foreseeable future. Rugby League played a minor supporting role. Athletics did not play a big part in the formulation of the plans, partly because there are no domestic and only two international competitions (Olympics and the World Championships) which can fill a large stadium. In addition the British Athletic Federation had just gone bankrupt. The possibility of using the new stadium as part of a London bid for the Olympic Games lurked in the background, but never became clearly articulated in terms of the technical specifications which would be required. The British Olympic Association (BOA) would not commit itself on the question of making a bid for the Olympics and seemed ineffective in communicating with either Sport England, or the DCMS. It was only very late in the day, when the newly recreated body UK Athletics and the BOA suddenly saw and objected to the architectural specifications and plans that conflicts came into the open. The stadium had been designed primarily as a football arena, but was intended to be capable of being fully adaptable for big athletics meetings. The athletics groups did not find this satisfactory and persuaded the Secretary of State to get an alternative consultants report in the very short timeframe of three weeks. This appeared to confirm their criticisms, which were then supported by the Secretary of State in a statement to the House of Commons on 1 December 1999. In a flurry of press coverage the footballers, athletes, architects, and the stadium company refuted each others points and the government ended up having offended almost everyone concerned. Athletics is likely to look elsewhere, and some public funding will follow. The House of Commons CMS Select Committee (4th Report 1 March 2000) was not impressed.

Football: Safety, Hooligans, and Fans

The safety of the public attending football matches has become a national issue. The problem has two dimensions. On the one hand, there have been a series of disasters in which large numbers of people have been killed and injured. There was the Bradford fire of 1986, which killed fifty-three and badly burned many more, and the Hillsborough disaster of April 15th 1989, where ninety-six were crushed to death as a result of too many people being forced into too small a space. On the other hand, there is the problem of football hooliganism. In 1985 Liverpool fans rioted in the Heysel Stadium in Brussels, resulting in the deaths of thirty-nine fans, while at home the violence associated with some groups of fans meant that there was often violence and destruction at many matches. On the face of it, these two problems are quite separate, but in fact they are closely intertwined. In the case of the Hillsborough disaster, for example, there was no hooliganism. Yet there would have been no deaths if the fans on the overcrowded terrace had been able to spill out onto the pitch. They were prevented from doing this by fencing erected to keep hooligans in check.

The prime duty of any government is to ensure the safety of its citizens, and the British government is therefore necessarily involved in making sure football grounds are safe from accidents like fire and overcrowding, and in dealing with the public order problems of hooliganism. No one could dispute that government has a responsibility in this areas. What has been questioned are the measures the government introduced which many within the sport considered to be excessive. In the case of ground safety, new regulations were so expensive to comply with that clubs faced bankruptcy, but the government resolutely refused to help with public funds. On the question of hooliganism, the government's favoured policy was for a time a national identity card scheme which was strongly opposed by virtually everyone concerned.

Football Hooliganism

How to stop the persistent violence associated with football in this country and English fans travelling is the longer running and more contentious of the two issues. English fans have acquired an international reputation for violence. After the Heysel Stadium disaster of 1985 when 39 Juventus fans died because Liverpool fans rioted, English clubs were banned from all European competitions for several years (Liverpool FC for longer). They were not allowed back before the European authorities were confident that the hooligan problem was under control. This did not have the shock effect that some hoped. The problem continued at home, while the violent behaviour of British fans in the 1988 European Nations Cup tournament in West Germany proved that the situation was not getting any better. Other countries also have a problem with football hooliganism, but it was British fans who had the worst reputation and whose behaviour constituted a national disgrace.

It was the violence in West Germany that finally provoked the government into taking drastic action. The result was the Football Supporters Bill. This contained important measures relating to ground safety (following Lord Chief Justice Popplewell's public inquiry into the Bradford fire disaster and other events). There would be new regulations and a new body with authority to monitor and enforce the safety of football grounds. But it was the measures dealing with football hooliganism that caught everybody's attention. This was a national identity card scheme administered by a second new authority, the Football Membership Authority. All fans would have to have valid identity cards in order to see a game, and by depriving hooligans of their cards they could be prevented from attending matches and causing trouble.

The opposition to the scheme was massive: football authorities, the Football Supporters Association, the Police Federation and many others all voiced powerful objections. The two most important arguments were that it would put very large numbers of casual fans off coming at all, and the belief that the technology upon which the scheme relied would create immense and insoluble difficulties. It would have to work under intense pressure, seeing through vast numbers of fans very quickly, be reliable in all conditions, and be immune to fan sabotage. Furthermore, the scheme was to a large extent based on the experience of Luton Football Club, whose chairman, David Evans the Conservative MP for Welwyn and Hatfield, was personally advising the Prime Minister, Mrs Thatcher. Luton had a membership scheme that prevented away supporters coming to Luton, and this, so it is argued, had eliminated hooliganism and turned Luton into a family club. However, it has been pointed out that banning away fans is a quite different idea to the national scheme, and that Luton is a relatively small club and knows little of the problems of a big city club. Nevertheless, Mrs Thatcher personally backed the scheme and all objections were brushed aside.

However, the Football Supporters Bill was overtaken by events. In April 1989 there was a disaster at Hillsborough, regarded as one of the best and safest football grounds in Britain, in which 95 Liverpool fans died (and a 96th a year later when his life-support machine was finally switched off); after which the government immediately set up a public inquiry conducted by Lord Justice Taylor. The Bill was nearing completion in the House of Lords, and initially the government refused to halt it, arguing that violence was a separate issue; but later, after the Act was passed, it agreed to suspend its working until Lord Justice Taylor had reported. An interim report was published in August 1989 making forty-three safety recommendations, of which twenty-eight were to be implemented immediately, ready for the new season. The full report followed later in January 1990. The final report expressed 'grave doubts' about the national identity scheme, suggesting that it could be dangerous if it did not work efficiently. The government immediately announced that it would not implement the scheme although it would remain on the books as a reserve measure in case clubs did not co-operate in tackling the problems of safety and hooliganism.

The second part of the Taylor Report criticised the football authorities and those who ran the clubs. It talked of massive complacency, of inadequate facilities and squalid conditions, of drunkenness and violence, of bad leadership and the poor example set by players. The Report went on to make seventy-six recommendations, which included all-seater stadiums for Premier League and First Division clubs, and their Scottish equivalents, by August 1994 and the rest of the lower divisions by 1999, a Football Licensing Authority with statutory powers, and a host of lesser measures. Other recommendations dealt with the making of certain activities, such as pitch invasions and shouting racial abuse, illegal. It was clear that Lord Justice Taylor hoped that by following his recommendations football would treat its fans in a more civilised way and this should result in more civilised behaviour.

Whether or not the implementation of the Taylor recommendations would be a cure for hooliganism, it was certainly likely to be a long term process. Much discussion followed over the merits of a multitude of ideas for dealing with the problem: banning open terraces altogether, banning the sale of alcohol in or near grounds, depriving convicted hooligans of their passports, different methods of segregating fans, expelling clubs with violent supporters, various kinds of fences and moats, and clubs being more involved in their local communities.

After a massive police effort to control English fans during the 1990 World Cup in Italy was reasonably successful, English clubs were allowed to compete again in European competitions. And the problem seem to subside for a while. The England team was not in the 1990 World Cup in America, but England had been chosen to host the 1996 European Championship tournament and this worked very satisfactorily. Unfortunately the behaviour of some British fans in the 1998 World Cup in France was again disgraceful, and in spite of major attempts to take preventive action there was serious violence in Belgium in the Euro2000 competition. This prompted a rapid response from the government, with the Home Secretary introducing the Football (Disorder) Bill into Parliament. But this in turn has produced much criticism because of the draconian powers it gives to the police to prevent travel, and an apparent reversal of the fundamental presumption of innocence.

Financial Problems

The most immediate problem facing most clubs was the cost of implementing the Taylor Report proposals. The football authorities promised to follow them up vigorously, but was aware that without government help many clubs faced financial ruin if the recommendations had to be followed to the letter. Most of them in the lower divisions do not make any profit, and the main proposal of replacing all terraces with seating was not only expensive in itself, but would also reduce the number of fans that could be accommodated, thereby reducing the means of paying for it. The estimated cost of the Taylor proposals was some £600 million by 1999, but the government insisted that it would not provide any of it. The Football Trust, a body devoted to improving football in various ways and funded by the pools companies, offered some financial assistance. Nevertheless many of the smaller clubs faced bankruptcy. In 1992 the new Secretary of State for National Heritage, David Mellor, relented and dropped the governments requirement that lower division clubs have all-seater stadia by 1999. This meant that with a few temporary exceptions the clubs in the top two divisions were able to comply.

A Beneficial Football Revolution?

By 1994 some £300 million had been spent and new stands and gleaming new facilities were appearing everywhere; some new stadia had been built, with more planned. But not all fans were happy. Many argued that all-seating destroys the old atmosphere, as do new rules in some grounds where waving banners and standing up and singing are banned. The game was being sanitised; and this was part of a process in which the commercialisation of the top football clubs was proceeding at an amazing rate. During the 1990s the old BBC-ITV duopoly on coverage of football broke down. The satellite channel Sky effectively put £1 billion pounds into British football, 95% of this concentrated in the Premier League. Major clubs such as Manchester United have become national and international brands, and their companies have floated on the stock exchange. They have exploited merchandising rights for club products and started signing contracts for coverage of their matches on the internet (Liverpool making £20 million from their deal in July 2000). The income of players has risen sharply, but so have the costs to fans. Admission prices have risen by 350-400%, TV viewing increasingly comes at the expense of a satellite or cable subscription or pay-per-view on an individual match basis, and the scheduling of fixtures has been placed in the hands of the TV moguls. In much of this the government has been powerless to exercise much influence to answer the grumbles of traditional football supporters. The DTI, on competition grounds, has prevented TV companies from actually taking over football clubs, but has kept their stake in any particular club below 10%. But Sky now has shareholdings in Manchester United, Leeds, Sunderland and Chelsea, while the cable operator NTL has shares in Newcastle, Aston Villa, and Middlesbrough, and Granada has a stake in Liverpool. In 1997 the Labour government established a Football Taskforce, with the former Conservative Minister for Sport David Mellor in the Chair, to bring together football authorities and clubs, fans, media and other interests to consider these problems. But there was little evidence of any meeting of minds and it was disbanded in December 1999 with little achieved.

A Sporting Future for All?

One of the problems with a sports policy is the fact that it deals with so many issues. Not only are there many different sports, but they operate at different levels. The concerns about sport of the public, and thus the electorate to which democratic politicians are rightly sensitive, are very varied. Is it the failure of the England football team to advance beyond the first round of the European Championships? Why are there so few successful female British tennis players? Why is the swimming pool in our town not open for longer? Are there too many unhealthy and unfit children who fail to take regular exercise? Should schools concentrate on team sports rather than individualistic physical activities? Should the proceeds of TV sports revenues simply stay in the professional sectors of highly prosperous commercial sport?

In April 2000 the Government launched an ambitious programme on sport described in the title of its paper as *A Sporting Future for All*. With an introduction by the Prime Minister to mark its importance, it is an attempt to relate many of the sorts of issues raised above and attempt to deal with them in an integrated way. So it argues that one of the keys to achieving greater international success in sport is to increase the pool of younger players from which talent can be drawn and developed through coaching schemes and facilities which can achieve the highest levels of excellence. Youth participation must be increased through improving the situation in schools, providing more facilities and giving a higher priority to sports. So Sport England will devote 20% of its lottery funds to youth sport, there will be an extra £150 million for facilities in primary schools, there will be 110 specialist sports colleges at the secondary level, money to run after-school sports clubs, 600 schools sports co-ordinators, and a network of specialist coaches to bring on young talent.

Similarly there are programmes to promote life-long sports participation in the community, including an audit of local government provision, in order to promote the widest availability and use of facilities. At the highest level it is hoped that the system of UK and National Sports Institutes (UKSI/ESI etc) will be linked to the specialist sports colleges and a more developed national coaching system. The government is hoping to persuade all the professional sports which have significant broadcasting revenues to devote between 5-10% to grassroots activities. On July 25th Tony Blair was able to appear with the England football coach Kevin Keegan to announce the launch of a scheme by which the FA and Premier League would provide their 5% to fund a Football Foundation to invest in local authority, school, and voluntary facilities.

Will such initiatives reverse the decline in school sport? It is possible. But one should note the enormous pressure that the government (wearing its DfEE educational hat) places upon schools, teachers, and pupils to raise academic standards through a very full national curriculum, regular testing of pupils at many levels, and rigorous and time-consuming external inspections. The necessary time, energy and enthusiasm for sports activity may be in shorter supply than the government might wish.

Chapter 8

Tourism and Government

Tourism is now one of Britain's major industries, and an expanding one. However, compared to some other countries, and to other leisure fields, like heritage and countryside, the government's involvement in tourism is very modest. It is only relatively recently in the history of tourism that it has been considered an appropriate field for any government intervention at all.

The Development of Modern Tourism

Beginnings of a Tourist Industry

Travelling for purposes of leisure is at least as old as the Roman Empire. But it was an activity largely confined to the rich until the 19th Century. The Industrial Revolution provided, among many other things, the essential conditions for the development of a large-scale tourist industry. In the first place, it created a huge urban, industrial population in need of recreation. Secondly, it created widespread prosperity; initially a prosperous and rapidly growing middle class, but steadily some of that prosperity filtered down to large sections of the working class. Thirdly, there was the development of cheap and efficient mass transport, above all the railways. Together these created a large market for leisure travel of various kinds. On the one hand, there was Thomas Cook who was catering for the taste of the newly well-off middle class for foreign travel, while at the other end of the spectrum seaside resorts were increasingly catering for a mass market, with, for example, Blackpool serving the industrial workers of the Lancashire cotton industry and beyond.

In the last half of the nineteenth century tourism developed into a significant business (although it was not to become an industry of national economic importance until the second half of the 20th Century). There was the development of bulk travel, travel agencies, package tour operators - in each of which Thomas Cook was a pioneer - an enormous growth of domestic spas and resorts catering for different groups, a hotel industry, a wealth of maps and guides being produced, increasing foreign travel by train and ship, and a growth of foreign tourists coming to Britain, especially rich Americans. By the end of the century resorts all over Europe were catering particularly for British tourists, while at home among the working population the annual holiday was becoming an established feature in some industries, for example, Wakes Week in the northern textile mills.

The Coming of the Railways

The railways not only provided the means to travel, with cheap and efficient mass transport, but also played a major role in promoting the idea of travelling for leisure. The competing railway companies, in their desire to increase their volume of passengers, promoted all kinds of excursions, cheap returns, etc. And this also applied to foreign travel. From the 1860s the railway companies increasingly dominated the cross-Channel ferry services, as well as the ferry routes to Ireland. The railways were a major factor in the growth of resorts. Some, like Brighton or Scarborough, were greatly expanded by the influx of rail-borne travellers. Blackpool had a population of 2,000 in 1841 which soared to 47,000 by 1901 and to nearly one hundred thousand in 1921. Some resorts, like Bournemouth, were actually created by the railways and might never have existed without them.

Urbanisation and industrialisation gave people confined to factories and tightly packed terraces a desire for the refreshment of the countryside, and the railways catered for this market, with special excursions to places like the Yorkshire Dales and Lake District. The process was aided by the introduction of bank holidays by Act of Parliament. The first was on August 7th 1871, and the MP who had promoted the Act that made it possible wrote that the day was:

> *"...a great success - the day was splendid and the holiday was very generally kept. Every seaside place near London, every railway and place of amusement was chock full. Eight excursion trains went to Margate alone. The South Western Railway had only prepared for two. Indeed the railways and hotel keepers were altogether taken by surprise."*
> (*The Times*, 28.8.1871)

The growth of the hotel industry in the late nineteenth century also owes much to the railways, particularly in the provinces. Many railway companies built their own, and the proximity of the railways stimulated the building of others, while some of the old coaching inns adapted to the new age by providing feeder services to the railway stations.

Early Twentieth Century Developments

These developments, and the prosperity that encouraged them, continued up until the First World War. But after that war was over, there was a different atmosphere. The decades between the two great wars were marked by depression and, particularly in some parts of the country such as the north-east, economic decline. Nevertheless, there were important developments in the field of leisure and tourism. Annual holidays became more common, and there was a general interest in health, fitness and the enjoyment of the countryside. However, the most important developments were in transport.

Before the Great War, the motor car had been largely the plaything of the rich, but in the post-war world it steadily became more commonplace, thanks largely to mass-production bringing down the price. By the Second World War it was a common sight in the middle class suburbs. For the rest of the community there was the steady expansion of bus services. As a result of these developments the railways began their long slow decline, and by 1939 they were in financial difficulties. As well as the motor car, the Edwardian Age had also seen the development of the fast ocean liner, which served Britain's empire, as well as the trans-Atlantic trade, on which it was possible to travel in great luxury (the most famous liner being the ill-fated Titanic). Great liners were also built in the inter-war years, although by the end of the 1930s long-distance air travel had developed sufficiently to threaten this trade in the future.

Mass-Market Tourism

The post-war world witnessed a period of prolonged economic prosperity. During the 1950s and 1960s there was full employment, continuous economic growth and a rise in living standards. Even with the occasional recessions since the 1970s, the prosperity and opportunity of the majority in work still continues to grow. This has involved a vast growth in leisure in general, and travel for leisure in particular. In the 1950s millions of people began to enjoy a lifestyle unthinkable a generation earlier, with decent housing, consumer goods and spare money for leisure. Holidays at home (resorts, holiday camps, caravanning, etc.), and even abroad, became possible for many people for the first time.

People travelled as never before, although not all forms of transport flourished as a result. More prosperity meant more motor cars and bus travel, which hit the railways, and they continued to decline despite nationalisation in 1947. Secondly, the development of aircraft, especially the passenger jet, destroyed sea travel, apart from car ferries and a small cruise business. Big jets made much cheaper air travel possible, and their use in package holidays at much cheaper rates than scheduled services led to an explosive growth of overseas holidays that became increasingly possible for more and more sections of the population. Eventually, such was the cheapness of Mediterranean holidays that British resorts increasingly declined. However, in recent years some British resorts have been making a comeback, as there has been a growing trend towards second holidays, weekend holidays and short breaks of various kinds. Although in this area resorts are having to update their appeal as well as compete with all kinds of places which have developed a tourist potential that would have been unthinkable a generation earlier.

Since the 1960s the importance of the industry catering for foreign tourists in Britain has been recognised as making a significant contribution to the economy. We could not guarantee good weather, but the attractions of our heritage and the speed and lowering cost of air travel made Britain a major attraction for Americans and others. The importance of foreign tourists has grown over the last thirty years in terms of making a contribution to the national income. This is apparent from the growth in numbers. In 1948 about half a million visitors came; by 1955 it was one million; by 1962 two million; by 1967 four million; by 1971 seven million; by 1977 eleven and a half million; by 1987 it was 15.4 million; in 1990 it was 18.2 million, and in 1999 it was nearly 26 million who spent almost £13 billion. It was this growth that stimulated significant government intervention in the industry to improve its organisation and potential.

The Role of Government

Government involvement in the tourist industry has been a comparatively recent development. Local authorities in resort towns have, since the late nineteenth century, provided facilities and amusements for visitors, often by means of private legislation. But it took longer for central government to concern itself with such matters. It was in the depression of the inter-war years that national government realised that tourism could make a contribution to the economy and began to give a small subsidy for promoting Britain abroad, which continued after the war. This was paid to a voluntary association of commercial groups with an interest in encouraging tourism, which came to be called the British Travel Association. By the 1960s there were similar bodies promoting Wales and Scotland, together with local association in one or two parts of England (only Northern Ireland, with its own regional government at that time, had a statutory body created in 1948). The system was rather ramshackle. It did not cover the whole country, the associations had no powers to oblige members to work together, they had no means of promoting tourist facilities, and, despite the grant, were seriously under funded. Government for its part had no policy or strategy for tourism beyond helping to fund the voluntary bodies.

It was in the late 1960s, when the country was running into economic difficulties, that tourism began to be taken more seriously by central government. The result was the Development of Tourism Act of 1969, which was the first Act of Parliament ever to be specifically devoted to tourism. The Act's main provision was the setting up of the British Tourist Authority (BTA) and three national Tourist Boards for England, Scotland and Wales. The BTA was responsible for attracting foreign visitors and for co-ordinating the national bodies; while the national boards would promote their particular areas and stimulate the provision of facilities. These new bodies became a source of information and advice for government on tourism policy, and, under Section 4 of the Act, a channel whereby government funds, known as 'Section 4 grants', could be directed to tourism related projects. A further aspect of the 1969 Act was the aid it offered to the hotel industry to build new hotels and extend and improve old ones. Virtually no new hotels had been built for forty years, and those that existed were often old-fashioned and lagging behind international standards (although this was only a short term scheme to quickly boost provision). The Act also provided for a system of notification of accommodation. In this way, the government created a framework for the future development of tourism in Britain.

Recent Development of the Industry

The importance of tourism for our national prosperity has been particularly recognised since the late 1970s as our economy has been moving from one based on heavy industry and manufacturing to one based more on service industries; a process accelerated by the severe recession of the early 1980s. As a result, not only are the earnings from visitors important, but catering for those visitors and for Britons taking holidays at home, and the foreign travel business, are all seen as making an important contribution to employment. Furthermore, this not only applies to London and traditional areas of physical beauty and cultural interest, but can be extended to run-down industrial areas with high unemployment. It is the job-creation and regional development side of tourism that government has been anxious to promote in recent years. For this reason the responsibility for tourism was transferred from the Department of Trade and Industry to the Department of Employment in 1985 (before its later transferred to the Department of National Heritage, now renamed Department for Culture, Media and Sport).

Although domestic resorts are trying to fight back, the picture is patchy. Too many have not made enough effort to market themselves or improve their competitiveness in terms of quality and price (although the government squeeze on local authority expenditure since the 1980s has not helped). Spas have also failed to recapture lost business; unlike their continental counterparts which are flourishing. On the other hand, other parts of the country, not hitherto associated with holidays and tourist attractions, have developed their attractions - Glasgow, Liverpool and Bradford are examples - and moved into new sectors, such as industrial history and conference centres.

In recent years the number of tourist attractions has enormously increased. There is no agreed definition or means of counting because there is such an enormous variety: theme parks (Alton Towers which has 3 million visitors a year, and the Millennium Dome which is likely to have at least 6 million in 2000), historic houses, museums, art galleries, historic and heritage sites, seaside piers, zoos, nature reserves, golf courses, and many others. While there has been a long-term decline of domestic holidays in the UK relative to foreign holidays, the tourism sector in the UK is large and growing. About 1.75 million people are employed in tourism related industries (attractions, hotels, restaurants and cafes, bars, pubs and clubs, travel agencies and tour operators, sporting and recreational activities) and the numbers are increasing. Between 1979 and 1999 employment in this sector increased by 40%. There are about 125,00 businesses, most of them small, with 80% having an annual turnover of less than £250,00. This fragmentation of the sector is a sign of vitality but also indicates that much can be done to increase the attractiveness of holidays in Britain by joint action. Although the government has cut back expenditure by the statutory bodies in recent years and tried to increase the industry's own expenditure on promotion, government policy does have a major role to play.

Tourism and Central, Regional and Local Government

The Central Departments

Until 1985 direct responsibility for tourism belonged to the Department of Trade and Industry (DTI), where there was a junior minister specially assigned to the subject. But in December of that year responsibility was transferred, together with responsibility for encouraging small firms and complete with junior minister, to the Department of Employment. These moves show that the government saw tourism chiefly in terms of generating new businesses and jobs. It is still viewed by government in this light, even though it now has a permanent base in the Department for Culture, Media and Sport (formerly DNH) to which it was transferred in 1992. Certain other aspects of the DCMS fit in well with its tourism portfolio, such as its responsibilities for the arts and heritage. But it is not surprising, given the fragmented and ill-defined tourism sector, that many other government departments retain important interests, so that the DCMS at times appears to have a more limited co-ordinating role.

The work of a number of central departments have a bearing on tourism, either directly or indirectly.

- The Foreign Office (FCO) deals with our relations with other countries to which we send, or from which we receive, tourists.

- The Home Office deals with control at ports etc., with licensing laws, shop hours, regulation of entertainment and a variety of other matters.

- The Department of the Environment, Transport and Regions (DETR) deals with road, rail, air, and public transport, and countryside questions.

- The Ministry of Agriculture (MAFF) also deals with countryside questions.

- The Department of Trade and Industry (DTI) is responsible for the hotel, catering and entertainment industries, travel agencies, etc.

- The Department for Education and Employment (DfEE) is important in terms of educational visits and exchanges, the use of universities and colleges for conferences and accommodation, training people for the tourist industry, stimulating job creation, regulation of working conditions etc.

Finally, the three devolved national sets of institutions in Scotland, Wales and Northern Ireland are responsible for tourism in their respective areas and must co-ordinate with the relevant UK functional departments where appropriate.

The Department for Culture, Media and Sport is responsible for overall tourism policy and co-ordinates the work of all departments in this area. In addition, it appoints and partly funds the statutory bodies, the British Tourist Authority and the English Tourism Council (the Welsh, Scottish and Northern Ireland Tourist Boards are appointed and funded by their respective institutions.)

The British Tourist Authority (BTA)

The British Tourist Authority is a small body consisting of a chair and four other members who include representatives of the separate national boards. The basic aim of the BTA is to maximise the benefit to the economy of tourism to Britain from abroad, working world-wide in partnership with the private and public sector organisations involved in the industry and the English, Scottish and Wales tourist bodies. It employs professional staff in its London head office and in its overseas centres.

The most basic task of the BTA is to sell Britain (excluding Northern Ireland) abroad as a tourist destination. It has overseas offices and information services in 36 countries around the world (four in the USA) and a London base to support them. It promotes Britain both to individual potential tourists, but also to the overseas tourist trade, particularly travel agents and tour operators. It has to work closely with the British public and private sectors in identifying opportunities, creating links and running campaigns. So it is both a consumer marketing body and also a business-to-business organisation. It is now vigorously exploiting internet technology, establishing sites in 36 countries, based upon its very successful 'visitbritain.com' web site. The aim is not only to provide promotional material and information, but also to build in links to allow on-line booking.

The BTA pursues its objectives in conjunction with the national and regional tourist boards, and in close co-operation with other public bodies and commercial interests. It has had to do so under conditions of declining real resource from the government. For 1999-2000 it was originally due to receive £36 million in grant, but this has been increased by an extra £5 million, spread over three years, so that it should be around £38 million in 2001/02. This is less than in the mid 1980s in real terms, allowing for inflation, because government has required the BTA to find more of its income from other sources: selling its services, selling its publications, etc. The majority of its marketing expenditure comes from outside sources. Many of its advertising campaigns are done in conjunction with commercial partners, such as British Airways, tour operators and hotel chains.

The English Tourism Council

Originally there were four National Tourist Boards, for England, Wales, and Scotland (established by the Development of Tourism Act 1969) and for Northern Ireland (established by the old Northern Ireland Parliament). These were broadly similar in functions, and in addition to advising government on tourism issues, included such activities as:

- advertising and promotional campaigns to consumers and operators and the publication of literature for visitors

- working with the BTA and regional boards in their campaigns and provision of information to consumers and operators

- helping in the development of tourist information centres

- running schemes of hotel and accommodation classification and organising competitions for best hotels and other facilities

- working for the improvement of training for the industry

- helping to co-ordinate public and private sectors on joint schemes

- helping to fund and co-ordinate the regional tourist boards

- distributing grants for various schemes

- engaging in research into new markets and the tourism implications of new developments, such as the Channel Tunnel.

In the late 1980s the English Tourist Board (ETB) had an expenditure of over £31 million, of which approximately £26 million came from central government. A substantial part of this expenditure went on Tourism Development Grants (so-called 'Section 4 grants') to encourage investment and job creation. These grants were normally dependent upon further investment coming from other sources, and in fact generated nearly ten times as much investment. They were thus a most cost-effective job creation scheme. However, in January 1989 the Secretary of State for Employment announced the ending of these grants. By 1993 government financial support for ETB had fallen to approximately £16 million. After further cuts were announced for the following financial year, William Davis, chairman of both the ETB and the BTA, resigned in January 1993. Some months earlier, government cuts had been partly responsible for the bankruptcy of one of the Regional Tourist Boards, the Thames and Chilterns, which the ETB helped to finance. Further cuts in expenditure during the 1990s brought the grant down to about £10 million and forced the ETB to reduce its activities and make many staff redundant. At the same time some of its expenditure and activities were devolved to the regions, so that there came to be increasing doubt about its role and how it fitted with the BTA and the regional agencies.

In July 1998 the DCMS grasped the nettle and began a review of the whole system. After consultations, it announced in December 1998 that the ETB would be transformed into a new national body. This is the English Tourism Council (ETC), which was officially launched in July 1999, and which is charged with helping deliver the government's strategy for tourism which was published in *Tomorrow's Tourism* (February 1999.) This is supplemented by the DCMS convening an annual 'Tourism Summit' (the first one held in March 2000) to involve Ministers from key departments and industry representatives, and a Tourism Forum which is an advisory body linking the industry, ETC, and the DCMS.

The radical transformation into the new ETC has not resulted in extra funding (which stays at £10 million), but in changing its role and divesting it of some old ETB functions. The ETC becomes a strategic body for English tourism, concerned with quality, competitiveness, and sustainable growth. It no longer has responsibility for running marketing campaigns or direct links with tourists - these are the concerns of the BTA and the Regional Tourist Boards. The ETC becomes a 'business-to-business' organisation working to enhance the work of other agencies and the industry. A number of operational activities, such as training and the support of the Tourist Information Centre (TIC) network are passed on to the regional boards along with extra funding. While the ETC will not take part in tourism marketing, it will support it through researching advances in marketing techniques and spreading information about best practice throughout the industry. It will oversee (but not operate itself) standards and quality classification systems for accommodation and tourist attractions. In order to carry out these strategic research and advisory roles there are substantial staff changes in train.

Regional Tourist Boards

In 1969 when the national boards were created, there were only a few regions with tourist boards. The national boards helped to set them up in the early 1970s, and now the whole country is covered. These boards are not statutory. They represent a voluntary coming together of interested parties (something like the regional arts associations) to co-ordinate work, prevent duplication and develop a common strategy.

There are now ten regional boards in England (down from the original twelve following a bankruptcy and some rationalisation) and their job is to promote and develop tourism in their regions. They are essentially public-private partnerships which formulate and encourage the implementation of regional strategies for tourist development. Their main task is the promotion and marketing of their own region both within the UK and, in association with the BTA, abroad. They should work closely with the new ETC and run in their regions, accommodation grading, training and other national schemes.

The ETC provides an annual grant to each of the regional boards, which they now bid for on an annual basis. In 2000-01 the total amount is £5.5 million, but this was far lower in real terms than the £6.7 million available in 1993. Local authority contributions, commercial membership subscriptions, and other income from sales, booking fees, grants from the EU etc. will typically increase the central grant by about 400%.

The regions are not the same as the usual government regions. Thus, the Northern region has two tourist boards: the Cumbrian and Northumbrian. This does mean that while the RTBs will want to work with the new Regional Development Agencies (RDA) described in Chapter 2, there will not be an exact fit in a number of cases. The Northumbria Tourist Board (NTB) covers the counties of Durham, Tyne and Wear, Northumberland and the territory of the former county of Cleveland. All the counties and the district and unitary councils are represented on its Board as well as representatives of trade associations and interests. There are currently 1400 members, including a wide range of commercial interests such as hotels, caravan parks, guest houses, attractions, pubs, tourist guides, restaurants, and transport firms. These pay a subscription, starting at £80 (+VAT) per year. There is an executive committee and a small staff.

Apart from the general work of promoting their areas and providing information for visitors, regional boards are involved in training, research and advice for businesses, and development. A whole network of local partnerships exist between the public and private sectors, with the tourist board often playing an initiating role. However, within the national and regional framework, local government authorities are free to develop their own tourist programmes as they see fit. Thus, within the Northumbria region in recent years Durham County has put more effort into tourism with its 'Land of the Prince-Bishops' programme. South Tyneside Council has rebranded itself as 'Catherine Cookson Country', after the best selling popular novelist from the area, as it is featured in her books and in the televised adaptations of them. LAs in England alone are estimated to spend £75 million on tourist promotion. They play a particularly important role in providing local Tourist Information Centres, often in collaboration with a local chamber of commerce or trade, which are vital high street sources of local information and usually run accommodation booking services.

Other Government Agencies

Apart from the British Tourist Authority and the national tourist boards, there are a number of other government agencies with an interest in tourism. Most of these, including the Countryside Agency, Forestry Commission, English Nature, the Environment Agency, English Heritage, the Arts Council, British Waterways, and various others, are dealt with elsewhere. However, there are one or two more that are worthy of mention. First of all, there are a number of bodies concerned with the promotion of economic development in various areas.

The former Urban Development Corporations were concerned with inner city regeneration, and their work (as on Merseyside and Teesside) were partly designed to establish Liverpool and Hartlepool as tourist centres. To varying degrees, tourism is an important industry which all these economic development agencies seek to attract to their areas. They have the advantage of being able to offer benefits of one kind or another - grants or infrastructural provision, (some from the EU) - to attract private investment.

Another area of quasi-government vitally connected with the tourist industry is public transport. Potentially this has a major role in planning the development of tourism in Britain. However, the Conservative government showed little interest in this role. On the contrary, it sought to divest itself of the means to influence the development of transport by a consistent policy of privatisation and deregulation, with the ultimate aim of leaving everything to the commercial judgement of the private sector. To this end, it:

- privatised British Airways in 1986

- privatised the British Airports Authority in 1987, which put the national airports, such as Heathrow and Gatwick, into private hands. However, some other airports remained in the public sector since they belong to local authorities

- privatised the National Bus Company and deregulated local bus services through the 1986 Transport Act

- obliged British Rail to sell off Sealink Ferries and British Transport Hotels

- privatised the railway infrastructure into one company (Railtrack) and the passenger rail services into a series of other private operating companies (GNER, Virgin, Connex etc)

- refused to assist in the building of a high speed rail link between the Channel Tunnel and London.

These, and other policies, reflected a determination to allow market forces to have maximum play in the field of transport. In practice this could not be sustained if certain objectives were to be achieved. The high speed Channel-London link project has required the promise of over £2 billion from the government to slowly get under way. And the present Labour Secretary of State for the DETR, John Prescott, has had to try (with limited success) to put together some sort of integrated approach to transport.

Issues Relating to Government and Tourism

During the 1980s and early 90s the Conservative governments steadily scaled down the commitment to tourism. However, the government was prepared to invest resources in tourism where such investment was thought to assist in the solution of other problems, most notably unemployment and inner city decay.

Tourism and Urban Renewal

The policy of using tourism as a means to solving social problems was apparent in ETB programmes designed to develop tourism in run-down urban areas. Inner city problems were highlighted by inner city riots in many parts of the country in 1981, and many government initiatives followed in the 1980s and 90s. Throughout this period the encouragement of tourism was seen as making a contribution to solving these problems. Although where substantial funds have been involved, they have not been channelled through specific tourism agencies such as the ETB, nor through conventional local government, but through other government departments and agencies. Thus, Urban Development Corporations were used, or the Department of Environment's "City Challenge" initiative, introduced under John Major, where run-down urban areas could put in bids for substantial funds for imaginative urban renewal programmes, which often had a tourism element.

It was Merseyside, where in many ways the encouragement of tourism in derelict areas was first attempted on a large scale in this country, that showed what could be done. The first step was the creation of the Merseyside Development Corporation (MDC) by the government in 1982, following severe riots in the city. The MDC took over the City Council's planning powers in the derelict docklands area and was charged with the task of redeveloping it in association with private business. The Liverpool Garden Festival was one of the two projects in particular that helped to regenerate a derelict area and develop a significant tourist industry. The second was the Albert Dock complex, which was a longer term project. As with the festival, the MDC had to spend a great deal of initial money (£35 million in this case) to clear and prepare the site in order to attract private sector cash. The private sector initially put up £8 million, which steadily increased later. Albert Dock is now a thriving tourist centre, where, apart from the magnificent docks and buildings (which had been long derelict and almost demolished some years ago), there is now a host of shops and restaurants, a maritime museum and a modern art gallery (the Tate in the North), as well as television studios and a variety of small businesses. There are now many million visitors each year. A somewhat similar strategy on a smaller scale was followed by the Teesside Development Corporation in the derelict Hartlepool Docks. A (newly built) Historic Quay complex has been created, several ancient ships have been moored as additional visitor attractions, and a recreational yacht marina established.

Garden Festivals

The other major development of the MDC was to run the first garden festival in Britain. The idea of a garden festival came from continental Europe, especially from West Germany where they are held most frequently. Such festivals are an obvious boost to the whole gardening industry and in particular the landscape gardening profession. However, their chief importance lies in what they can do for the area in which they are held, for example:

- large areas of derelict land can be cleared and put to good use

- the surrounding district can be given new life and hope, including a boost to local business

- a festival can leave behind new facilities and other assets (a park, exhibition halls, sites attractive for housing and/or business, etc.)

- the host city gains prestige and good publicity, which raises morale and can attract future investment

- a festival helps to develop a city's tourist potential.

Festivals last for six months but their benefits can last a long time and may even be permanent.

The first garden festival in Britain was held in Liverpool in 1984, on a 125 acre site on the banks of the Mersey. It was all organised by the Merseyside Development Corporation, with little or no help from Liverpool City Council. Large areas of derelict dockland were cleared, filled in and landscaped. Millions of visitors attended the festival, a profit was made and Liverpool was left with a variety of amenities it did not have before. It was a considerable success and was followed in 1986 by another in Stoke-on-Trent, another in Glasgow in 1988, one in Gateshead in 1990, and finally one in Ebbw Vale in 1992. After the success of the Liverpool Festival, local authorities were competing to have future festivals in their city.

There are three main areas of expenditure for a garden festival:

- clearing of the site and making it fit for general use

- specialist landscaping, building of exhibition halls and other facilities

- administration, publicity, etc.

The land clearing attracted government Derelict Land Grants to cover up to 50% of this cost (although the government can claim some of this back if the land is subsequently sold for a profit). The second and third areas of expenditure were expected to be self-financing, through admission charges; franchises for catering and internal transport; commercial sponsoring, etc. However, the government also gave one-off grants to the local authorities concerned (and the Development Corporation in the case of Liverpool) to help with part of these expenses.

Planning garden festivals was a huge undertaking that required massive investment and years of planning, and the government (and increasingly most other observers) concluded that it was not worth all the expense of public money. Consequently, Ebbw Vale in South Wales in 1992 was the last one in Britain.

Single Regeneration Budget Projects

Some direct aid to tourism development (directed by the ETC/ETB and regional boards) comes in the form of assistance for projects financed under Single Budget Regeneration (which used to be called Local Area Initiatives, and before that Tourism Development Action Programmes.) This has funds of some £2.3 billion for the three years to March 2002. Recipients have included many coastal resorts, as well as industrial and maritime areas. The basic idea is of a partnership between public and private sector to achieve specific goals in a specific area. Thus, local authorities get together with local businessmen, voluntary bodies and other public bodies to jointly develop some tourism project to enhance the potential of their area.

The Government's Approach to Tourism

It is generally true of countries around the world that the more important tourism is for their economy, the greater is the extent of government involvement. Since 1979 Britain became a marked exception to this generalisation. As tourism has developed in importance, government involvement (especially financial) has reduced. This turned out not to be a purely Conservative phenomenon; Labour in government has (so far) not been very much more prepared to spend public money directly on tourism.

The Conservative government's general approach to tourism was well expressed in May 1985 by Norman Lamont, then a junior minister. He said that the government was aware of the great economic importance of tourism for the country. He went on:

> *"As with other sectors of industry and commerce, however, we consider that the successful expansion of tourism in the UK must depend primarily on the industry's own efforts and on increased investment by the private sector. The Government's main role lies in supporting the Tourist Boards, emphasising the importance of tourism, and removing the obstacles to its development."*

This rather negative approach reflected the Thatcherite belief in the free market and the minimum of government interference. Since tourism was a successful industry then it needed less government attention and not more. The attitude was subsequently criticised by the report of the all-party House of Commons Trade and Industry Committee of 1986, entitled *Tourism in the UK* (which quotes Norman Lamont's statement in para.72). The Committee felt that government ought to be doing more to encourage the industry. They argued that government guidance and investment, at both national and local level, could have great benefits for the industry and for Britain.

Later government statements of its general policy for tourism - *Pleasure, Leisure and Jobs: the business of tourism* (HMSO 1985) and *Tourism in the UK: realising the potential* (1992) - did not contain any new initiatives or changes. What they did was to confirm the government's belief in the importance and future growth of the industry. But they went on to insist that, in line with its general policies, the best way to help any sector of business to flourish is not by direct intervention (with new government bodies, investment, etc.) but by providing a general economic climate which encourages growth, and at the same time removing unnecessary restrictions or burdens.

> *"The government's job is to provide a framework in which enterprise can flourish, in tourism as in other industries. The main thrust of the government economic policy is to make markets work better. Restrictions*

have been lifted. Businesses have been given new freedoms. It is no coincidence that the tourism industry has grown so rapidly."
(Tourism in the UK, p.5)

By this it meant such things as keeping inflation down, lowering taxes and reducing government regulation which unnecessarily hampered the operation of businesses.

The approach of the Labour government, indicated in the substance of *Tomorrow's Tourism* (1999), *Focus on the English Tourism Council* (July 1999), and the *DCMS Report to the Tourism Summit* (March 2000), shows a substantial degree of continuity. There is only a marginal increase in government subsidy to the main organisations, leaving them well below the level (often in cash as well as real terms) of the 1980s. There is continued talk of government help taking the form of relevant deregulation, particularly in the form of removing obsolete restrictions on alcohol licensing law, casinos, and entertainment activities on Sundays. But there is also a greater leadership role for government set out, co-ordinating the efforts of a fragmented industry, helping to define strategy, to define quality standards, and provide a positive environment in which co-operation between the agencies of the state (central and local) and the private sector can flourish.

Whether the tourist industry is better off in the long run from less state involvement, and whether leadership can act as a substitute for hard cash, will no doubt continue to be a matter of controversy.

Tourism and the European Union

The European Union has an important influence on tourism, both directly and indirectly. It is an influence that is bound to grow in the future. Even such a relatively symbolic gesture as the EU designating certain cities as a 'European City of Culture' has very beneficial effects in promoting tourism, as Glasgow recently discovered.

Assistance for Tourism Projects

One of the principal ways in which the Union has a direct influence on tourism development is in the provision of grants and loans for tourism projects in various parts of Britain, many of which would not have been possible without EU help. The money comes from the Social and Regional Funds, as well as the European Investment Bank, and is mainly designed to boost jobs in areas of high unemployment or relatively low prosperity. In areas which are eligible all kinds of tourism related projects have received grants. These include tourist attractions, such as Beamish Open Air Museum in Durham, and restoration work on Bolsover Castle in Derbyshire. New or improved roads, the upgrading of railway stations, improvements to provincial airports, and tourist information centres have all been beneficiaries in Britain of EU funding. The excellent Northumbria Tourist Board web-site was developed with the aid of an EU grant to promote high technology in certain regions. Under the common agricultural policy, in order to reduce surplus production, grants have been available to encourage farmers into diversification into rural tourism.

Easier Travel

The EU has a more indirect, although vital, role in tourism in the more general sphere of facilitating easier travel around the member states. Certainly travel for the tourist, as well as for business and other purposes, has been made progressively easier as a result of EU action on matters such as passports and other documentation, frontier checks and the like. One of the major aims of the Single Market was to do away with all frontier controls by the beginning of 1993. This was largely achieved, although the British government did insist upon some frontier controls because of such problems as drug smuggling and terrorism. However, what is more difficult and more controversial is the question of a European transport policy.

Transport Policy

Transport was one of those subjects, like agriculture, for which the Treaty of Rome of 1957 required the Council of Ministers to create an integrated European policy. This has happened only slowly, and transport remained for a long time the EU's greatest policy failure. Different countries have different and often contradictory policies that serve their own national interests with little regard for the Community as a whole. In 1984 the European Parliament (with the encouragement of the Commission) brought proceedings against the Council of Ministers in the European Court of Justice for failing to implement the Treaty of Rome's requirement to create a common transport policy. The Court found against the Council of Ministers, rejecting its excuse that a common policy in this field was simply too difficult to achieve. The Council is now obliged to work towards a common policy. The Court's judgement, combined with the impulse of the Single Market programme, has led to some movement in this direction.

One of the major developments in the 1990s has been a move to establish what are called Trans-European Networks (TENs). Many national rail and road systems were (very naturally) designed in the past to fit within the particular country, but do not join up in a rational way with the neighbouring countries to create a proper long distance transnational system. The TEN programmes are attempting to identify the major transport routes and links which should exist in the EU, crossing frontiers and connecting major centres of population, and then encourage governments (sometimes using various financial incentives) to construct or complete them.

Road, rail and sea transport all raise large and difficult issues, but it is air transport that is the most controversial and to which most attention is paid. It is notorious that scheduled air travel within Europe has been extremely expensive and effectively confined to business travel. This is not true elsewhere. In the USA internal air travel has always been cheaper than Europe, and since their system was deregulated in the early 1980s it has been cheaper still. The reason for the high cost of European air travel is its tight regulation through which national governments protect their own airlines. What tends to happen is that national airlines swap routes with other national airlines, making it difficult for independent carriers, especially new ones, to break into the market. The result is effectively a cartel in which established airlines conspire to prevent competition and keep up prices.

Moves towards deregulation have been difficult and slow but progress is now being made. Moves are also being made to establish a Europe-wide air traffic control system, that is now partly operational. The result should eventually be cheaper prices and fewer delays. However, a fully integrated European transport policy, let alone an integrated transport system, is a long way off.

Tourism Policy

There is now increasing recognition of the need for European policies on tourism itself, and a number of moves have been made in this direction. European tourism ministers met for the first time in December 1988 to begin the task of working out common policies. A further move was the declaring of 1990 as European Tourism Year. This attempted to promote a number of themes, including the encouragement of:

- off-peak tourism and travel

- spreading tourism out to new destinations

- youth travel

- cultural tourism

- co-operative ventures across Europe

- improving customer care.

The year involved a number of competitions and projects across Europe, but events were more a series of national affairs than a genuinely European programme. It rather reflects the fact that European tourism policy is still in its infancy.

So far policies tend to be concerned with relatively detailed matters concerned with documentation, common forms of classification of hotels, access to foreign health care, standardised contracts in the industry, and computerised reservation systems, rather than with wider strategy. But the effects are cumulative, and more EU standard consumer protection standards, for example on package holidays offered by tour operators, are starting to have an effect on the industry. And there are moves to consolidate through mergers among some of the big tour operators. The Single Market is inevitably bringing about major changes for tourists, including the end of 'duty free' goods but allowing travellers within the EU to bring with them substantial quantities of alcoholic drinks and tobacco for their own consumption into more highly taxed countries. When a single currency, the 'Euro' is fully introduced into most of the countries of the EU, this will be a great convenience to tourists who will not have to bother converting currencies to take on holiday, and will be able to compare and understand prices far more easily. Even if Britain does not join the Eurozone, the domestic tourism industry will feel the effects and many businesses in practice will have to learn to use the Euro, because their customers will expect it.

Tourism is now the world's biggest industry and Europe has a major share of it. But such is the growing competition that Europeans may have to co-operate much more closely in the future if they are to maintain that share. Tourism could well develop into a major area of EU policy-making in the future. The European Commission now produces reports showing the effect of EU measures on tourism, and the results are likely to become more significant with time.

Chapter 9

Heritage and Government

The term 'heritage' covers a wide range of topics. These include museums and galleries, ancient buildings, great country houses and their treasures, townscape and architecture, archaeology, industrial archaeology, libraries and rare books, as well as preserving beautiful landscape, seashore, wildlife, old crafts and ways of life. Preserving the natural environment is dealt with elsewhere. Here we will concentrate on museums and galleries, together with sites and buildings of historic interest.

Museums and Galleries

The History of Government Involvement

The first involvement by government in this area was in the eighteenth century. In 1753 Parliament authorised the purchase of Sir Hans Sloane's private collection for the nation. The collection was a great miscellany of paintings and sculpture, coins and medals, books and manuscripts, natural history specimens and various curios from around the world. This collection, together with two earlier bequests to the nation of books and manuscripts, became the basis of the British Museum (BM). It was the first museum of a non-religious kind in the world that was a national, public museum. But the government did little to house it, and the present BM building was raised from the profits of a private lottery (surrounding which there was much scandal). Very occasionally a grant was made for a special purchase, the most famous being in 1816 when the Elgin Marbles were acquired for reasons of national prestige, preventing them going to France. Later the Angerstein collection of paintings was purchased in 1824, which became the National Gallery, although it was not properly housed for more than a decade.

All these decisions were isolated ones, depending on the mood of the House of Commons at the time. There was no continuing policy of acquisition, nor for housing what had been acquired. It was all random. Other great collections were not purchased; the outlays were tiny relative to the worth of what had been acquired; and there was never the provision of adequate funds for the upkeep of what had been bought for the nation. The whole exercise was widely unpopular, while many MP's were loudly hostile. (One Chancellor of the Exchequer in the early 1830s, Lord Althorp, privately expressed his opinion that the best thing to do with the National Gallery was to sell it all off. This is perhaps the earliest of all privatisation proposals.)

A more consistent government policy began to develop in the 1840s, mainly in respect of art education. Some attempt was made to establish schools of art with the express purpose of improving industrial design; although the system had little success until after the Great Exhibition of 1851 had focused attention on the fact that Britain was suffering commercially because of the superior design of many foreign products. In consequence, art and design training was overhauled by Henry Cole, who had played a major role in creating the Great Exhibition and in using the profits to create the South Kensington museum area. Cole was an outsider, a businessman brought into the government and given charge of a small new department, the Department of Art and Science, with headquarters in South Kensington. This small department was attached, significantly, to the Board of Trade, which was then the central department that dealt with commerce and manufacturing, and which is now called the Department of Trade and Industry.

The Victoria and Albert Museum was Cole's idea, and was conceived specifically as a museum of good design, which would inspire industrial designers and educate the general public into demanding well-designed products (although what Cole and most of his contemporaries thought of as good design was decoration that was added on, rather than being an integral part of the whole product). Apart from the V & A, the profits of the Great Exhibition also financed the other South Kensington Museums: the Science Museum, the Geological Museum and the great Natural History Museum (along with the Royal College of Music, Imperial College of Science and Technology and the Albert Hall).

Such practical considerations were behind the growth of civic provision of museums and galleries in the middle of the century (although there was also much talk of civilising the working class by bringing it into contact with beautiful and morally uplifting objects). Thus, the Libraries, Museums and Gymnasiums Act of 1845 enabled town councils to set up local museums on the rates. Within five years there were 50 museums in Britain. Later in the century the great Victorian cities created great museums and galleries as symbols of civic wealth and pride. By 1889, when the Museums Association was formed (a professional association of museum staff) there were 200 museums in the country.

The latter part of the nineteenth century saw the addition of Scottish National Museums (the Welsh National Museum was created much later). The oldest was the National Museum of Antiquities of Scotland belonging to Scottish Society of Antiquaries: founded in 1781, but not open to the public until 1858. In addition there was the creation of two further art galleries of national stature: the National Portrait Gallery and the Tate Gallery (devoted to British art and also to modern art). Since neither of these were devoted to arts and sciences of a 'useful' kind there was a great deal of delay and foot-dragging on the part of the government. The National Portrait Gallery was created in 1856 but was not properly housed until forty years later, mainly through privately raised money. In the case of the Tate a great opportunity to acquire the great collection of Henry Tate (the sugar magnate) at no cost was nearly lost. It was a gift to the nation, and Tate offered to build a gallery for it, if the government would only give him a site. Negotiations dragged on for years and Tate nearly gave up before the Millbank site was reluctantly made available. The Tate Gallery opened in 1897. However, by this time the general public was taking pride in our national museums, and government funds for the maintenance and enlargement of their collections were provided on a regular and fairly adequate basis. The Imperial War Museum and the National Maritime Museum were created after the First World War.

The considerable growth of museums in the late nineteenth and early twentieth centuries was on a rather haphazard and uncoordinated basis: there was no co-operation and a good deal of competition. In 1931 the government set up the Standing Commission on Museums and Galleries, charged with advising on the development of national museums and galleries in the United Kingdom; fostering co-operation between them and with the provincial museums; and encouraging those who might support museums and galleries with gifts and money. Although only an advisory body, the Standing Commission has helped to develop the national collections in a more rational way.

However, apart from encouraging national museums to lend them exhibits from time to time, the Standing Commission had little to do with provincial museums and galleries until in 1960 the government asked it to survey non-national museums and galleries and make recommendations for their development. The subsequent report led to the creation of a network of regional bodies called Area Museum Councils to foster regional co-operation and to channel the very first central government grants to local museums and galleries. These new developments preoccupied the Standing Commission during the late 1960s, but the new decade brought a fresh issue that focused attention on the national institutions. This was the government's decision, without consultation, to introduce entrance charges at the national museums and galleries. There was fierce opposition and the policy was dropped with a change of government in 1974, only to be revived again a decade later.

During the 1980s the Standing Commission was transformed from an advisory body to an executive body similar to the Arts Council. Its name also changed to the Museums and Galleries Commission, and its legal status changed along with its new responsibilities.

Recent Growth

In the meanwhile, the number of museums grew and grew. There were more than 500 by 1929. Steady progress followed in the post-war years, so that by 1963 there were 876, and by 1985 over 1,000. But since then there has been an explosive growth so that now there are around 2,500 employing more than 80,000 staff. There are still many general museums, with archaeology, natural history, geology, painting, crafts and other thing all in the same building; many run by local authorities. There are also university museums and regimental museums. But most of the recent growth has been in private sector specialist museums covering an amazing range of subjects:

> *"from advertising to artificial limbs, from lawnmowers to lifeboats, from tomatoes to trams, from wine to whales"* (The Times Museum Year Guide, 1989)

A new museum opens on an average of one every two weeks. Among those being planned in the 1990s were museums of hot metal type, cartoons and medical surgery.

In addition to new specialised museums there have been major changes in the way museums present their material. Lighting and display techniques have become more sophisticated. Glass cases are not entirely a thing of the past, but determined efforts are now being made to give visitors more direct contact with exhibits. Where these are valuable or fragile, replicas can be used. More and more museums are using working models that visitors can handle (e.g. in the National Film, TV and Photography Museum in Bradford and the Science Museum in London). In some cases visitors can walk about in a recreated world (e.g. the Beamish Folk Museum); or they can see an industrial process at work (e.g. Killhope Wheel Lead Mining Centre, Durham). Sometimes life-size models of people are used (as at Jorvik in York), and even live actors (e.g. Ironbridge), to convey a stronger impression of the lost world being illustrated. Then there are videos and diaramas (e.g. the Geological Museum, London), and a host of increasingly interactive computer-based devices, to set the exhibits in context and make them more exciting.

Preserving Sites of Historic and Architectural Interest

Our ancient monuments and buildings of historic interest are highly vulnerable to damage and destruction. We live in a crowded island where there are strong pressures to put land to new uses and redevelop urban sites. Preservation is often inconvenient and costly, bringing little benefit to those who own such sites. However, there is a system of legal control, without which much of our heritage would be rapidly destroyed. Although many would argue that our present controls are not firm enough and that too much is still being lost.

The Nineteenth Century Conservation Movement

Concern for preserving our ancient remains and historic buildings developed in the nineteenth century. It grew at the same time as the concern for preserving the countryside, and partly for the same reasons: as a reaction to the destructive effects of industrialisation and urbanisation. Perhaps a further factor was the romantic passion of the Victorians for the Middle Ages, which led them to restore so many mediaeval churches (often very badly). The pressure for preservation and restoration expressed itself in the founding of a number of preservation societies. The first was in 1877 when the Society for the Protection of Ancient Buildings was founded by the great artist-craftsman William Morris. This was followed in 1895 by the National Trust. These and other bodies helped to raise public awareness and put pressure on government to pass protective legislation.

At that time a landowner had every right to destroy an ancient monument on his property, and there were many who were outraged by the suggestion that an Englishman's right to do exactly what he liked with his own property should be limited. The breakthrough came in 1882 with the passing of Sir John Lubbock's Ancient Monuments Act of 1882. It involved no compulsion and its working depended on the voluntary co-operation of landowners, but it did establish the principle of the government having a duty to identify and protect monuments of national importance.

Early Twentieth Century Developments

It was not until 1913 that there was any legal compulsion to prevent damage or destruction, but in the meanwhile, it had been recognised that if protection of monuments was to be seriously undertaken then it was essential to compile a comprehensive register of exactly what there was in need of protection. To further this end in 1908 the Government created the Royal Commission on the Historical Monuments of England, charged with making:

> *"...an inventory of the Ancient and Historical Monuments and Constructions connected with or illustrative of the contemporary culture, civilisation and conditions of life of the people in England ...from the earliest times to the year 1700, and to specify those which seem most worthy of preservation."*

Similar Royal Commissions were created for Scotland and Wales. It was not realised at the time just how massive the task that had been set. Over eighty years later it is still nowhere near complete. Although it is worth noting that the task has been extended in various ways, including a photographic record and an extension of the time span covered by some 150 years.

By the time of the First World War in 1914 there was, therefore, a measure of protection for ancient monuments; but as yet there was still no protection for habitable historic buildings. Owners were free to alter or demolish their buildings, whatever their historic or architectural value. After the First World War there was a further growth of voluntary societies - including the Ancient Monuments Society (1921), the Council for the Care of Churches (1922), the Council for the Protection of Rural England (1926), the National Trust for Scotland (1931) and the Georgian Group (1937) - which helped to persuade the government to extend its protection to buildings of architectural or historic value. This began with an Act of 1932. The present system of protection, however, began in 1947.

The setting up of a comprehensive planning system after World War II created a framework into which the means of protecting monuments and buildings could be integrated. Since the Town and Country Planning Act of 1947 central government has been charged with 'scheduling' ancient monuments and 'listing' historic buildings so as to guide local authorities in the exercise of their planning powers.

Until recently the task was assigned to the Department of the Environment, the department responsible for the planning system, but in 1992 it was transferred to the Department of National Heritage, now the Department for Culture, Media and Sport. However, neither scheduling nor listing in themselves prevent alteration or destruction. They merely mean that special permission is required, and access given to the appropriate Royal Commission on Historic Monuments so that the building may be recorded before it is altered or destroyed. The system did not prevent a great deal of permitted destruction in the years after it was set up.

Post War Reconstruction

The Second World War inevitably involved considerable destruction and neglect of ancient monuments and buildings (Coventry Cathedral was the most famous building destroyed in the Blitz). Unfortunately the period of reconstruction and new development that followed the war was in many ways just as destructive. The post-war generation was intent upon building a better society, and this was thought to include the rebuilding of large parts of our towns and cities. The period was seen as an historic opportunity to finally rid ourselves of slum areas that disfigured many cities, and to redesign our overcrowded city centres, created in Victorian times for smaller populations and volumes of traffic. The general policy was to disperse people and industry away from the crowded central areas of cities and relocate them in a planned way on the outskirts or, in the case of big cities, in new towns beyond the Green Belt. Local councils were encouraged to use modern building methods and high rise blocks, built of pre-fabricated sections, appeared around many of our cities, with industries confined to industrial estates. In the meanwhile, the old city centres were redeveloped, with new shopping centres, office blocks and urban motorways.

Objections to these developments were brushed aside as old-fashioned and standing in the way of social progress. However, by the late 1960s popular protest was becoming too great to be ignored. People disliked living away from the centre in high rise blocks and there was increasing protest against the tearing down of old housing and traditional city centres in favour of ugly modern buildings which were making every city centre look the same. By the late 1960s resistance had come to a head and some redevelopment schemes began to be shelved or abandoned. In 1967 Parliament passed the Civic Amenities Act which allowed local planning authorities to establish conservation areas as:

> *"areas of special architectural or historic interest, the character or appearance of which it is desirable to preserve or enhance"*

This allowed for the protection of groups of buildings which are not necessarily listed, but which together have a special character. By the mid-1970s major redevelopment schemes had virtually ceased and national policy had shifted towards schemes of renovation and conservation, and towards persuading people back to live and work in the inner cities.

The Failure of Post War Planning

Looking back, the post-war push towards comprehensive planning and redevelopment can be seen as a massive mistake. Dispersing people from city centres into suburban estates broke up communities, induced crime and vandalism, turned city centres into derelict areas characterised by poverty and crime, and destroyed much of the character of our major cities. The centre of Birmingham is generally agreed to have been ruined by redevelopment, along with parts of Liverpool, Manchester and many others. In the process, many fine buildings were lost despite the post-war planning system.

A leading part in the opposition to the destruction of the post-war planning boom was played by conservation societies. In this the older organisations were joined by a crop of new ones, such as the Vernacular Architecture Group (1952), the Civic Trust (1957), the Victorian Society (1958), the Landmark Trust (1963) and SAVE Britain's Heritage (1975), together with numerous local groups. During the 1980s the conservation organisations became increasingly accepted and a widespread reaction against modern architecture had clearly set in. Despite this, the present system of protection is still needed, and many feel it ought to be strengthened.

The Present System of Protection

The Ancient Monuments Act of 1882 had attached to it a 'schedule' specifying which sites were to be protected. There were just sixty-eight of them. The number is now 18,000 (covering 30,000 monuments), with perhaps still more than half a million more that could be considered. These range from 6,000 year-old Stone Age settlements to remains of the Industrial Revolution. Since the passing of the Ancient Monuments and Archaeological Areas Act in 1979 whole cities can be designated 'areas of archaeological importance', and this has been done for Canterbury, Chester, Exeter, Hereford and York.

However, neither scheduling nor being in an archaeologically important area necessarily prevents sites being damaged or destroyed altogether. All these things do, in most instances, is to make the acquisition of planning a little more difficult, and if permission is granted, to allow archaeologists a little time to investigate the site as best they can before the development destroys it. On the other hand, landowners can be, and are, prosecuted for destruction without permission. In 1987 Lord Hertford was fined £10,000 for having valuable archaeological remains on his estates ploughed up.

The listing of buildings is a similar system. Listing began in 1947. As with scheduling of monuments, it is the responsibility of the Department of National Heritage, although the actual work is done by English Heritage (and similar bodies in Scotland and Wales) on its behalf. By 1970 there were some 120,000 buildings on the Statutory List. Today there are 500,000 listed buildings; which means that more than one in every forty buildings in this country is listed. As with ancient monuments, some are owned by the government and its agencies, some by voluntary bodies like the National Trust, while the vast majority are in private hands.

There are different degrees of listing: Grades I, II* and II, with Grade I as the most important. Listing provides a guide for local planning authorities. It does not mean that a building cannot be altered or even demolished, but the consent of the planning authority must be obtained and a much stronger case than usual will have to be made for permission to be granted. There are in fact several thousand successful applications to demolish or part-demolish listed buildings every year.

Again, there are penalties for unpermitted destruction. In 1981 Sir Bruno Welby demolished a 17th Century almshouse, much admired by experts on English architecture, rather than sell it or pay for its repair. The prosecution left him £3,000 out of pocket, although this was considerably less than the cost of repairs.

However, in 1981 there was a case where the prospect of listing led directly to demolition. The Trafalgar House company had recently acquired the Firestone Building on the outskirts of London, a magnificent Art Deco factory of the 1930s. Hearing that the building was going to be listed in a few days time, Trafalgar House promptly had the building demolished overnight. The decision was subsequently described in the Guardian as "the most brutal and despicable act of vandalism".

Finally, there are Conservation Areas. These are chosen and designated by local authorities, which can now treat all buildings in such areas as though they were listed, even though they have not been listed individually. Local authorities have so far declared over 8,000 Conservation Areas, and around seventy percent of English towns have one or more such areas in their centres.

The Future of Conservation

As the work of investigation and study continues the number of protected properties goes on growing. It also grows as a result of changing perceptions of what is valuable and worth preserving. Again, the growth of preservation societies has helped to make the public and government aware of an ignored part of our built heritage under threat. These have included the Vernacular Architecture Group and Victorian Society already mentioned, but also the Thirties Society (1979), the National Piers Society (1980), the Railway Heritage Trust (1985) and the Fountain Society (1985) together with various societies devoted to industrial archaeology. As a result the Royal Commissions on Historical Monuments have extended its task of recording to include the eighteenth and nineteenth centuries, while listed buildings now include, somewhat controversially, modern architecture as late as the 1970s.

It can be seen that our physical heritage of ancient sites and historic building is afforded some degree of protection. There is protective legislation, a series of government departments and agencies charged with protection, as well as a formidable number of voluntary bodies devoted to the same end. Nevertheless, many would insist that the system is still far from strong enough to be adequate to the task. Furthermore, it is argued by some that the Conservative government since 1979 did not fulfill its duty of conservation as fully as it ought to have done. It was a government that disliked planning, and tended to favour developers more than conservationists. The boom in the late 1980s, in which retailing played a major role, led to a revival of city centre redevelopment (though with a less brutal style of architecture), threatening old centres once again. It was also accused of making the heritage under its direct control less secure than before because of the application of market principles where they were not appropriate.

One aspect of this is the creation of English Heritage. Before 1984 the great monuments which the government owned, such as Stonehenge and many of our great ruined castles and abbeys, were run directly by the Department of the

Environment and its predecessor ministries. But in 1984 these were hived off into a semi-independent agency officially called the Historic Buildings and Monuments Commission, but which has come to be called English Heritage. Its first task was to manage 404 buildings and monuments, as well as providing advice and grants for buildings and monuments not in its care. But it was seriously under funded, and its grant reduced in real terms. It was encouraged to be more commercial and entrepreneurial and raise more of its own funds, which led to charges of vulgarising our heritage and putting aspects at risk which cannot be sufficiently commercial. Furthermore, the management of the government's own properties has been substantially privatised, which could have implications for some of the thousand or more listed buildings the government has under its control.

In the end it is not so much what legislation or public bodies exist as the state of public opinion. At the present time it is generally favourable to conservation. It is up to those who believe in preserving the heritage to keep it so.

Government Bodies and Heritage

Central Departments

A number of government department have a concern with heritage. There are the devolved Welsh, Scottish and Northern Ireland institutions which have their own national responsibilities. The Department for Education and Employment (DfEE) has an obvious educational interest, while the Department for the Environment, Transport and the Regions (DETR) is concerned to preserve the heritage through the planning system and local government (planning and museums). However, the leading central department in this field is the Department for Culture, Media and Sport (DCMS) formerly the Department of National Heritage (DNH).

The DCMS is responsible for government policy on libraries, museums and galleries. It has direct responsibility for national collections: the National Library, British Museum, Victoria & Albert Museum, Natural History Museum, Imperial War Museum, National Maritime Museum, Science Museum, the National and Tate Galleries and National Portrait Gallery, the Wallace Collection and the Royal Armouries, as well as any outposts these may have in the provinces (e.g. the Tate on Merseyside). For all of these it appoints their governing bodies and provides funds organised through grants and a series of funding agreements. For public libraries and for local museums and galleries the DCMS sets policy and provides advice through Resource: the Council for Museums, Archives and Libraries (formerly the Museums and Galleries Commission) which it also appoints. But being provided by local government these local institutions are the direct responsibility of the DETR. Finally the DCMS jointly appoints the members and supervises the National Heritage Memorial Fund (including the Heritage Lottery

Fund), which saves objects, buildings and the environment for the nation. Many of these responsibilities had previously been held by the small Office of Arts and Libraries until 1992.

The DCMS is also responsible for the preserving of historic buildings and ancient monuments which it took over from the Department of the Environment. This field includes the listing of buildings and scheduling of monuments. It is also responsible for the key heritage agencies: Historic Buildings and Monuments Commission (English Heritage), the Royal Commission on Historical Monuments (recently merged with English Heritage), the Churches Conservation Trust, the Royal Armories, the Royal Palaces, and the Royal Parks. The DCMS appoints the managing bodies and provides the core funding grants for all of these.

Resource: The Council for Museums, Archives and Libraries (MLAC)

The original Standing Commission on Museums and Galleries, created in 1931, was essentially an advisory body that met only a few times a year and had a staff of only five. In 1981 it was renamed the Museums and Galleries Commission (MGC) and given much wider responsibilities, particularly for the development of local collections. In 1987 the Commission was incorporated under a Royal Charter; as a registered charity it assumed complete control over its own financial affairs. With its new responsibilities, the Commission's staff increased from 5 to 22 and its budget from £70,000 to over £6 million within a few years. In 1998-99 it had a budget of £14 million with a full time staff of 46. This was mostly spent on grants to Area Museum Councils in England, the national museums and galleries being funded directly by the DNH. The Commission provides a series of other grant schemes to help with security, conservation, etc. It has also taken on a number of special tasks, such as directing extra funds provided by government to compensate certain collections for local funding losses caused by various local government reforms, which abolished or reduced the size of LAs which had previously supported museums and galleries. In many ways the Commission became to the world of museums and galleries what the Arts Council and Sports Council are to their respective spheres.

In 1998 the DCMS conducted a major spending review, after which it decided to reshuffle some of the pack of quangos (or non-departmental public bodies in official terminology) for which it is the sponsoring department. One of the outcomes was a decision to merge the Museums and Galleries Commission with a smaller body, the Library and Information Commission, under the new title of Resource: the Council for Museums, Archives and Libraries. This came into effect in April 2000. It is run by a Board of 15 members, and will have an income of about £22 million (£17 million directly from DCMS) for 2000/01.

At a regional level the Area Museum Councils (AMCs) are similar to Regional Arts Associations: distributing funds, co-ordinating, providing publicity, giving advice on such matters as security and conservation of exhibits, etc. There are seven AMCs for England, funded mainly by Resource (just over £4 million in 2000/01) and by local authorities; and one each for Scotland and Wales, funded by the Scottish and Welsh devolved institutions respectively. There is only a tenuous link with Northern Ireland which has no AMC and where museums and galleries are the responsibility of the Northern Ireland institutions.

The Historic Buildings and Monuments Commission (English Heritage)

English Heritage is by far the largest of the heritage quangos. It was created by the 1983 National Heritage Act and began work on the 1st April 1984. Its duties under the Act are:

1. to secure the preservation of ancient monuments and buildings situated in England

2. to promote the preservation and enhancement of the character and appearance of conservation areas situated in England

3. to promote the public's enjoyment of, and advance their knowledge of, ancient monuments and historic buildings situated in England and their preservation.

In its first Annual Report of 1985 the Commission set out its functions in more detail as follows:

- managing and presenting some 400 monuments and buildings previously managed by the Secretary of State for the Environment

- making grants to individuals and other bodies in respect of historic buildings, conservation areas, town schemes, ancient monuments and archaeological investigation (rescue archaeology)

- acquiring, or becoming guardian of, ancient monuments and historic buildings

- advising the Secretary of State for the Environment on the selection of buildings for inclusion in the list of buildings of special architectural or historic interest, on the monuments to be added to the schedule of monuments and on the designation of areas of archaeological importance

- advising the Secretary of State on applications for permission to carry out works to listed buildings and scheduled monuments

- carrying out research and helping others to do so

- undertaking archaeological investigation and publishing the results

- providing educational facilities and services

- advising any person in relation to ancient monuments, historic buildings and conservation areas.

Although perhaps best known for maintaining great monuments like Hadrian's Wall and Dover Castle, English Heritage is in fact responsible for all ancient monuments and historic buildings in England, no matter who owns them. They amount to some half a million historic buildings and 60,000 ancient monuments, ranging from Neolithic stone circles to twentieth century telephone boxes, and including, in some cases, gardens, machinery and even ships. It does all the work of scheduling monuments and listing buildings and special archaeological areas on behalf of the DCMS. It also administers a substantial budget to help in preservation projects of various kinds.

English Heritage provides various kinds of grants to help with conservation work. (The total of £35 million in 1999 is lower than a few years previously, reflecting the fact that an increasing amount of this work is now funded by Lottery money.) The conditions of such grants include very high quality of workmanship and the right of the public to reasonable access. The main grants are for:

- individual listed buildings

- ancient monuments

- rescue archaeology

- improving a conservation area

- the conservation of listed churches (although it is the Church of England and other denominations who are principally responsible for the upkeep of their buildings.) There is a separate body for dealing with redundant churches.

The Commission is directly responsible for over 400 properties of major importance, which it maintains and makes accessible to the public. Many of these housed military and administrative establishments of the Crown in previous centuries but are now no longer used (those still in use are under the care of the Property Services Agency). Other properties have been bequeathed to the nation by private owners. These properties attract some four million visitors each year. It is mainly through opening monuments to the public that the Commission's role of enhancing public knowledge and enjoyment of our heritage is pursued. In addition, there is a membership scheme with over 300,000 members, who enjoy benefits such as free access, a magazine, special events, etc.

In April 1999, as part of the DCMS spending review, English Heritage was merged administratively with the Royal Commission on Historical Monuments of England, described below. The English Heritage name will be used, and at some time in the future the necessary legislation may be passed to transfer responsibilities and activities into the merged body and to give the name changes official status.

The English Heritage Board of Commissioners now consists of fifteen members. The budget in 2000/01 is £146 million, of which £114 is the DCMS grant and £32 million generated from other sources: entrance fees, publication, merchandise, and other external grants. It employs more than a thousand staff, including archaeologists, curators, craftsmen and conservation specialists of all kinds.

Similar bodies exist for Scotland and Wales. These are the Historic Buildings Council (Scotland) and the Historic Buildings Council (Wales). These are appointed by, and are responsible to, the Scottish and Welsh devolved institutions respectively.

Royal Commission on Historical Monuments (RCHME)

In 1908 three Royal Commissions on Historical Monuments were set up, one each for England, Scotland and Wales. The tasks of the Commissions are:

- the recording, analysing and assessing of ancient monuments and buildings

- recommending which monuments and buildings are most worthy of preservation

- the compiling and preserving of this information as national archives

- making this information available to the public through access to the archives and through publication.

The original intention was to restrict the work to structures built before 1700, but this was extended to 1714 and then to:

> "...such further Monuments and Constructions subsequent to that year as may seem...to be worthy of mention."

Effectively this has meant the aim is now to record all building dated to before the middle of the 19th Century.

The work of the Commissions has been extended in other ways. They became responsible for the Industrial Monuments Survey of England (since 1981), the archaeological survey work of the Ordnance Survey (1983), the air photographic library of the DoE and other projects.

Under Section 55 of the 1971 Town and Country Planning Act, the RCHME has a right to record listed buildings for which consent has been granted for demolition or alteration. The owner must inform the RCHME, giving a month's notice and adequate access. Although only a small proportion of these cases are recorded, it involves the Commission in a great deal of work which it has to do quickly, and has to take precedence over its other work. The Commission has only meagre resources relative to its statutory duties. In consequence, it relies a good deal on the co-operation of other public bodies and on local civic and archaeological groups who supply it with records, photographs and other material. Its Commissioners were appointed by the Crown, chosen on the basis of high academic distinction, and had its own expert staff of around 150.

Despite a similarity of name, and the fact that their headquarters shared the same building, RCHME was quite distinct from the Historic Buildings and Monuments Commission (English Heritage). In its evidence to the House of Commons Select Committee on the Environment (1986-7) RCHME wrote:

> *"Put very simply, the distinction is that the Royal Commission identifies what sites and buildings are important and why. English Heritage decides what should be preserved and how."*

However, despite RCHME's advice to the contrary, the Select Committee recommended in 1987 that the two bodies be merged. For more than ten years the recommendation was ignored, but was finally acted upon by the DCMS in 1998 and administratively (but not legally) implemented from April 1999.

The National Heritage Memorial Fund

The National Heritage Memorial Fund (NHMF) was created in 1980 to provide financial assistance towards the acquisition, maintenance and preservation of buildings, land, works of art and other important objects or structures of outstanding interest and of importance to the national heritage.

The NHMF replaced the National Land Fund, which had been the brainchild of Hugh Dalton, Chancellor of the Exchequer in the post-war Labour Government. His idea had been to create a large fund from the sale of surplus military stores to be used for the purpose of buying beautiful countryside, buildings and works of art for public enjoyment as a permanent memorial to the dead of two World Wars. The National Land Fund was created in 1946 and endowed with £50 million.

Unfortunately very little of the money was spent on the purposes for which the Fund had been created because successive governments diverted the money for their own use. By 1980 the accumulated fund should have been worth some £650 million, but all that was left was less than £12 million. There was much controversy over the misuse of the money which came to a head in 1977 when the government failed to purchase the country estate of Mentmore in Buckinghamshire, rejecting the Earl of Rosebery's asking price. The estate was sold elsewhere and its contents dispersed. However, such was the public outcry that the government felt obliged to pay for the purchase of some particularly valuable items for several millions of pounds: more in fact than it would have cost to buy the house and all its contents in the first place.

The Mentmore fiasco led to an inquiry which recommended the setting up of a new fund entirely independent of the government. The National Heritage Act 1983 which followed created the NHMF under the control of an independent body of eleven trustees who were given complete control of the £12.4 million left over from the National Land Fund to spend or invest as they chose. In addition, the NHMF receives grants from the DCMS. These varied from year to year, since the Fund was conceived originally as essentially a safety net to save treasures that are on the verge of being sold abroad or otherwise lost, and is therefore not in a position to plan its expenditure like other public bodies. In the first six years of its existence, the Fund benefited from government grants of over £40 million, and the government was in fact quite generous with this particular public body. Its grant funding has now fallen to £3.5 million in 2000/01 for reasons which will be explained.

The most spectacular purchases made possible through the government NHMF funding have been three major country houses, with their estates and treasures: Kedleston Hall in Derbyshire, Nostell Priory in Yorkshire and Weston Park in Staffordshire. Other purchases included the Abernathy Forest Lodge Estate for an RSPB bird sanctuary; land in the West Country to secure the habitat of the greater horseshoe bat; manuscripts of British writers, such as Walter Scott, from foreign owners; early steam vehicles, trade union banners and paintings by Cranach, Renoir and Picasso that had been part of British collections (not foreign works purchased abroad). One of the favoured use of funds is a loan to help a local conservation group to purchase a derelict house, which is then restored, sold to someone who will put it to useful purpose and look after it, and then the initial loan is returned for use elsewhere.

The Impact of the National Lottery

The original source of funding, however, is now totally overshadowed by the fact that, under the National Lottery Acts 1993 and 1998, it now also controls the distribution of the 'heritage good cause' share of the National Lottery proceeds. In the period up to the end of June 2000, this enabled grants totalling almost £1.5 billion to be awarded (England £1,165 million; Scotland £172m; Wales £67m; Northern Ireland £44m; more than one region £36m).

Charities and Churches are biggest recipients (45%), followed by local authorities (27%), central government and other public sector bodies (26%), and private owners (2%).

The total value of awards can be divided by type of heritage work:

- Museums and collections   40%

- Historic buildings and sites   28%

- Countryside and nature conservation   18%

- Documentary   8%

- Industrial, maritime and transport   6%

The Neptune Hall project in the Greenwich National Maritime Museum received over £12 million, while the third Wisbech Scout and Guide Groups were awarded £87,000 to repair and refurbish a Grade II listed building.

Government and State Buildings

The government itself owns and uses a vast range of buildings, many of which are of great historic interest. All such buildings, including the royal palaces, were the responsibility of the Department of the Environment through its Property Services Agency (PSA), until in the early 1990s when the system was drastically restructured over a number of years. The occupied royal palaces were made the responsibility of the DCMS (originally the DNH), together with the newly created Historic Royal Palaces Agency and Royal Parks Agency. The palaces occupied by the Royal Family are principally Buckingham Palace, St James's Palace, Windsor Castle, the Private Apartments at Kensington Palace and Sandringham. The rest are unoccupied and the DCMS is responsible for keeping them open to the public. These include the Tower of London, the Banqueting Hall in Whitehall, Hampton Court Palace, the State Apartments at Kensington Palace, Kew Palace and Queen Charlotte's Cottage in Kew Gardens, and Osborne House on the Isle of White (currently used as a convalescent home.) It also has ultimate responsibility for Apsley House (home of the great Duke of Wellington), Somerset House in the Strand, and the former Royal Naval College at Greenwich. The DCMS has thus found itself supervising (rather reluctantly) a somewhat diverse historic property portfolio, much of it in London. Some of these buildings may be devolved to the new Greater London Authority.

As to other buildings, those in central London are now the responsibility of the government departments concerned, while most of the rest of the PSA's work has been privatised. One particular concern for conservationists has been the Ministry of Defence (MOD). The MOD has a large number of buildings of great historical and architectural value, some of which, for security reasons, have been hidden from the public and the conservationists for a great many years. Because of cutbacks following the end of the Cold War, and some degree of privatisation, some of these buildings are beginning to become accessible for the first time. Buildings by some of our great architects, such as Sir John Vanbrugh, are coming to light for the first time. What is also coming to light is the dilapidation and neglect that some have suffered. Some valuable buildings have even been demolished. Now that attention has been brought to these buildings it is hoped that some may soon be accessible to the public, while others will be better treated in the future.

The Churches Conservation Trust

The Redundant Churches Fund was set up in 1969 to preserve those churches no longer used for worship but which are of historic or archaeological interest. It was renamed the Churches Conservation Trust in April 1994. The members of the Trust are appointed by the Queen on the advice of the Archbishops of Canterbury and York. Some 300 churches are presently in the care of the Fund, the cost of which is borne jointly by the DCMS (60%) and the Church Commissioners (40%). In total this comes to about £5 million per year. Grants for repair to churches in use come from English Heritage.

The Voluntary Sector

The protection of our heritage is a subject about which many people feel strongly. It has, in consequence, inspired a very large number of voluntary organisations and pressure groups, both national and local. Some are based on particular classes of building, while others are based on regions or towns or a particular set of buildings.

The more established and prestigious of the national groups are members of the Joint Committee of the National Amenity Societies which meets regularly to co-ordinate the work of the following bodies:

- Ancient Monuments Society

- Civic Trust

- Council for British Archaeology

- Council for the Protection of Rural England

- Georgian Group

- National Trust

- National Trust for Scotland

- Society for the Protection of Ancient Buildings

- Victorian Society.

The Joint Committee is an effective pressure group. Among the concessions it has gained is the statutory right of appropriate member groups to be automatically notified of a request for planning permission to demolish any building or monument in which they may have an interest. There is only room here to consider a couple of these groups.

The National Trust

The National Trust for Places of Historic Interest or Natural Beauty was founded in 1895 by Octavia Hill, the social reformer and pioneer of decent housing for the poor, together with Sir Robert Hunter and Canon Hardwicke Rawnsley, who created the Trust as a non profit-making company. Later the Trust was incorporated by Act of Parliament in 1907. It operates in England, Wales and Northern Ireland. Because of a different legal system and laws relating to property, there is a separate National Trust for Scotland, founded in 1931.

The Trust is the largest private landowner and largest conservation society in Britain. Under the National Trust Act of 1907 it has the right to declare its land or buildings inalienable. That is, they can never be sold or mortgaged without express consent of Parliament. The Trust also has a special right of appeal direct to Parliament if any of its property is threatened with compulsory purchase (such as part of an estate to make way for a motorway).

A number of National Trust Acts, beginning in 1907, have laid down the constitution of the Trust. Under these Acts, the Trust is governed by a Council of 52 members. Half of these are elected by the members and half are appointed by various bodies relevant to the work of the Trust, including: the Society for the Protection of Ancient Buildings, Royal Academy of Arts, English Nature, British Museum, Victoria and Albert Museum, National Gallery, Ramblers' Association and the Council for British Archaeology. The Council appoints an Executive Committee of 30 Trust members (half from the Council) to conduct the Trust's affairs on a day-to-day basis. This Executive Committee, together with a system of specialist committees and panels, supervises the work of a large full time staff employed in London and in sixteen regional offices.

The Trust is a charity. It receives no direct government grant and is reliant on the contributions of the public and its members, who now number over 2.5 million. The Trust is in receipt of substantial grants from government agencies, such as English Heritage and the Countryside Agency, for individual projects. Some of its recent initiatives have received National Lottery funding, either from the Heritage or the Millennium funds. Further substantial income comes from bequests, gifts and donations, from business sponsorship and the activities of the Trust's commercial organisation called National Trust Enterprises.

The Civic Trust

The Civic Trust was founded in 1957 by Duncan Sandys, a distinguished Conservative Cabinet Minister, as a charity with the purpose of stimulating interest in, and action to improve, the environment in both town and country. The Trust does not have individual members, but works in close co-operation with local amenity societies and building preservation trusts of which there are about 1,000 with a combined membership of approximately 300,000. The trust gives advice and support to local groups, and stimulates activities through annual 'Pride of Place' Competitions and 'Environment Weeks'. These groups organise tree plantings, 'clean-up' campaigns, etc. It has played a leading role in establishing annual weekends for free access to historic properties (often not normally open to the public) which take place in September. The much-prized Civic Trust Awards are given for good quality planning, design, restoration and new building. The Trust also administers the Architectural Heritage Fund (AHF), a charity created in 1976 following European Architectural Heritage Year. The AHF provides low interest loans for the purchase and restoration of old buildings deserving conservation. About £4 million was given in loans in the Fund's first five years. The Department of the Environment matches whatever the Fund can raise itself. The DoE also nominates half the Fund's members, with the Civic Trust nominating the other half.

The Trust has inspired a good deal of legislation to promote environmental improvement, especially in towns. The best known is The Civic Amenities Act of 1967 (a Private Members Bill promoted by Duncan Sandys) which introduced Conservation Areas. It also largely drafted The Town and Country Amenities Act of 1974, which extended the powers of local authorities in those areas. The Trust is regularly consulted by government on matters related to planning law and conservation.

Just under half of the Trust's income comes from covenants and donations, about one quarter from a government grant and the rest from business sponsorship, fees for consultancy work, etc. However, the Trust has long suffered from lack of the funds it needs to do the work it wants to do.

Issues in the Field of Heritage

Current problems for museums

However, set against these developments there are problems. There are pressures on local authorities to make financial cut-backs and contract out services. These may involve losing carefully built up expertise in the heritage conservation field. There are consequent pressures to charge and make profits and turn museums into entertainments rather than educational experiences. Some have even argued that e are turning Britain into a kind of museum, only giving a cosy and false image of the past, to please tourists. (See, for example, Robert Hewison's *The Heritage Industry: Britain in a Climate of Decline*) Local authority-run museums can be a boon, but more often a financial liability. Many have suffered severe cuts and there have been some closures. Government cuts have also posed a serious threat to medical museums, which some hospitals have, regimental museums, and university museums. Even the Ashmolean Museum at Oxford and the Fitzwilliam at Cambridge, two of the finest museums in the country, have faced severe financial problems.

Special problems face the great national museums and galleries which are the direct responsibility of the government. They are funded directly by the DCMS and have been subject to cuts in real terms in their expenditure. Businessmen, and others with no connection with the world of arts or scholarship, have been given seats on their boards. They have been forced to find more of their own money; to be more cost-minded and entrepreneurial. In consequence, it is argued, there has been a diminution of the work of scholarship and preservation in the interests of saving money, and a preoccupation with money-making schemes that are inappropriate to the kind of institutions they are. There is little money for new acquisitions, and it has even been suggestion that museums and galleries sell off some of their less important treasures to pay for the upkeep of the others.

An example of what has been happening is shown by the controversy which developed surrounding the V & A. Like some of our other national museums, the Victoria and Albert is one of the great museums of the world but it has severe financial problems. It occupies a vast building with a tendency to deteriorate with a roof which leaks (there has been severe flooding in the cellars); it has massive collections of materials such as paper and fabrics that are prone to deterioration; there is a huge backlog of restoration work; and there is a large staff to pay. As a result the museum felt forced to take drastic action of various kinds. This included restricting opening hours; asking visitors to pay £3 per visit (voluntarily but under some pressure); promoting the museum restaurant on TV; and financial deals with commercial firms to exploit the museum's design collection, e.g. in textiles and wallpapers. There were controversial changes in management in order to reorganise the staff in a more streamlined way and involving the redundancy of some senior curators, all of whom were scholars of international reputation. This created an uproar in the whole museum world. To many it seemed that a great museum was being ruined for no sound reason. Another example was the Science Museum which in late 1993 was forced to cut nearly 30 posts, prompting curators to take industrial action, which is virtually unheard of in the museum world.

In some ways museums and galleries are flourishing, yet many (especially the public ones) are beset by problems. Government policy from the mid 1980s encouraged museums and galleries to be more commercial and to find ways of attracting more customers. This has provoked furious debate in the museum world for many years. Traditionalists argue that it means turning over some of our greatest institutions to the entertainment industry: sacrificing scholarship for show business. This is probably the predominant view; but some leading figures in the museum world (for example, Sir Neil Cossens, director of the Science Museum and now Chairman of English Heritage) have insisted that there is no necessary conflict between scholarship and making museums more entertaining, informative and enjoyable places. It is certainly true that many museums seem to be more to do with entertainment than education, but as in many things it is a question of balance.

Admission Charges

A controversial issue for many years has been whether our great national museums and galleries should charge people for admission. The long-standing tradition of free admission was broken by the Conservative government of Edward Heath. The museums and galleries concerned had not been consulted about the change of policy and were duly outraged. There were legal obstacles, but these were removed by The Museums and Galleries Admission Charges Act of 1972. There was a great deal of opposition from many quarters before charges were introduced on 1st January 1974. However, within three months there had been a General Election resulting in a change of government and the charges were quickly dropped. The Act itself was not repealed; it was simply not implemented.

The early 1980s was a period of economic recession and government cutbacks in many areas, and it was against this background that the issue was revived. In 1982 the House of Commons Select Committee on Education, Science and Arts published a report, *Public and Private Funding of the Arts* in which the issue was discussed. The Committee took the view that it should be up to the individual museum or gallery whether or not to charge:

> *"Accordingly, we recommend that museums and galleries should be encouraged to expand all available sources of income. If their trustees or managers should decide to charge entrance fees, then they should arrange for at least two "free days" of entry each week at all times and for free admission for bona fide scholars and students, and those in receipt of*

pensions and other long-term benefits. They should have total discretion over the expenditure of sums generated in this way and, furthermore, such funds should not be offset against any public subvention."

Following this report admission charges were introduced in a number of national museums. The National Maritime Museum was the first in April 1984, followed by several other national museums in the following year. Various provincial outstations also had charges (e.g. the Tate Gallery on Merseyside and the National Museum of Photography, Film and Television, which is a branch of the Science Museum, in Bradford). The V & A introduced a voluntary donation scheme, where visitors are invited to contribute £3 per head, in November 1985. Others charge for special exhibitions. The Conservative government's consistent policy on this matter, as expressed by the Minister for the Arts, was to let each museum and gallery make up its own mind.

Introduction of admission charges, whether compulsory or voluntary, did involve a drastic drop of attendances. When the National Museum of Wales introduced charges in 1988 the fall was of the order of 85%. Others have been less spectacular, but nonetheless severe. The Science Museum introduced charges in 1985 and attendances fell from 2.7 million to 1.3 million by 1994; the attendances at the Natural History Museum which introduced charges at the same time, fell from 2.6 million to 1.7 million; while the V&A's voluntary scheme cost it more than half a million visitors. The same was true of museums up and down the country. The British Museum and the Tate and National Galleries, on the other hand, did not introduce charges and enjoyed record attendances.

In 1989 the House of Commons Education, Science and Arts Committee looked at the question again and concluded that admission fees were not wrong in principle and recommended that all national institutions should consider introducing compulsory admission charges. However, this conclusion was only supported by the majority of government MPs on the committee. The opposition MPs voted against. It remained, therefore, a highly contentious issue.

Those against charges point to Britain's strong and pioneering tradition of free access to all, which has been followed in other countries, such as the USA. Attendance by as many people as possible is an aim agreed by everyone, which charges clearly diminish. Furthermore it is wrong to deny cultural experiences to people simply because they cannot afford it. In its evidence to the Committee, the National Gallery spoke, in a sense, for all the free access institutions:

"The function of the National Gallery is essentially to educate and inspire: it is predicated on the belief that familiarity with great paintings is as important a part of education and discovery as is familiarity with literature or music ....the main aim of the Gallery must therefore be to allow the fullest possible access to the paintings compatible with their

safe-keeping, so that the public may come to see for themselves....our policy is not only to have as many visitors as we can, but to persuade them to come as often as they can and to spend as long as they can looking at particular objects. We are persuaded that a charge is a very serious impediment in the fulfilling of that aim, which was the aim of Parliament in setting up the National Gallery in the first place."

Even those which do charge agree that ideally there should be no charge, and only impose one because, as they see it, they are forced to by inadequate government funding.

In favour of admission charges are those who believe that the disciplines of the market are as applicable to museums and galleries as anything else: consumers should pay for what they want, and if customers are satisfied because of good quality and value for money, then the enterprise will thrive. It is argued the public is perfectly prepared to pay for museums such as the Tower of London, Ironbridge and Beamish, all highly successful; so why not the great national collections? Besides, foreign visitors (who flock to the London institutions in particular) are used to paying at home and do not pay British taxes for their upkeep.

The debate is set to continue, but probably with declining vigour. The election of the Labour government in May 1997 raised hopes among supporters of free entry, since in opposition the party had always been very hostile to charges. However, since the government and the Chancellor of the Exchequer took over the previous Conservative government's spending limits the scope for change was limited. Gradually funding for national museums and galleries has increased. Increased access to the arts and combating social exclusion were key elements in the DCMS strategy, and discussions started about possible abolition of the charging regimes. One complication arose from a strange feature of the VAT rules, which allowed institutions which charged for entry to reclaim certain VAT payments. If they ceased charging, these repayments would no longer arrive, and in spite of being compensated by the government for the loss of income from the entry charges, might still face an overall loss. The compromise which has been reached with the national charging institutions is an increase in funding, confirmed in the 18 July Treasury Spending Review 2000, which will guarantee free access for children and pensioners, and a flat-rate £1 fee for all others from September 2001.

How to Conserve Our Heritage?

Many of the conflicts and dilemmas facing the world of museums and galleries also face those committed to conserving our ancient monuments and historic buildings. On the one hand, there has never been more interest in the built heritage, as can be seen in membership of the National Trust and similar bodies, attendances at historic sites, etc. On the other hand, money is short and organisations like English

Heritage are encouraged to be more commercial and entrepreneurial. The distinction between providing an educational service and being part of the entertainment industry seems increasingly blurred. It is not obvious to everyone that, for example, English Heritage ought to be organising jousting matches and other 'mediaeval events' at its castles in order to attract customers and raise money for its work.

In order to make limited funds stretch further, English Heritage has been undergoing changes. In the summer of 1992 the government appointed Jocelyn Stevens as its director; a man with a fearsome reputation as a ruthless and confrontational manager ('piranha teeth' and 'Terminator 3' were some of the nicknames acquired in previous appointments). To some people, English Heritage was a rather stuffy, overstaffed and bureaucratic organisation, and Stevens could be expected to shake it up and strip it down to its essentials. Within months, and apparently consulting nobody, Stevens produced a radical plan entitled *Managing England's Heritage: Setting our priorities for the 1990s*, although usually referred to as the 'forward strategy'.

One controversial proposal was the privatisation of the direct labour force. That is, the body of craftsmen and specialist workers who repair the buildings and objects in the organisation's care. But the most contentious idea was that many of the sites in the organisations care could be hived off to LAs, voluntary organisations and other local bodies, in order to concentrate time and resources on major sites. There was outrage at this suggestion, which was characterised by some as "selling off" our heritage. However, the controversy somewhat subsided as the details of the proposal became clearer. The idea is to have management agreements with local organisations, such as local authorities, voluntary bodies or National Park authorities, for a limited period, and after English Heritage had satisfied itself that the sites would be well looked after. A number of such agreements were negotiated, and in fact no serious problems arose in their working.

What to Conserve in Our Heritage?

Another problem that faces conservationists is just how much and what to conserve. The late 1980s building boom certainly put pressure on what might be preserved, especially in places like London, and many felt the planning system was not strong enough to resist determined developers. An excellent example was the discovery of the foundation of the Rose Theatre, the only remains ever discovered of a theatre of Shakespeare's period. But the remains were not scheduled and a skyscraper was built over them.

At the same time, conservation has undoubtedly become fashionable in recent years. No doubt the 'nostalgia boom' will pass, but while it is with us it is a natural instinct for those concerned with conservation to secure as much of what is valuable while they can. This has happened to such an extent that some, even firm advocates of conservation in principle, have argued that perhaps too much is being conserved and that not enough attention is being paid to new architecture of quality. In fact the DCMS has established a new quango, the Commission for Architecture and the Built Environment (CABE) with this brief. It takes over some architectural functions from the Arts Council and the Royal Fine Arts Commission.

One might hope that we can conserve what is valuable and distinctive from the past without worshipping old things uncritically. It is important to keep creating today what future generations will wish to conserve as part of their heritage. The level of funding for such purposes which the National Lottery has made available should make this possible. The very successful 'Tate Modern' project is a recent hopeful sign. This started with a derelict power station on the south bank of the Thames opposite St Paul's Cathedral. The Bankside station (not to be confused with Battersea power station further up river) was owned by one of the electricity generating companies who wanted to either sell it or pull it down. The building was in fact designed by a famous architect, Sir Giles Gilbert Scott, and experts regard it as a magnificent piece of industrial architecture. The idea was to turn it into an art gallery to house the Tate's modern collection, leaving its other great collection of British art at its present site. A new Bankside complex could be made to link with the existing South Bank arts complex a few hundred yards up river, creating a huge cultural centre at the heart of the capital.

The Tate Modern, having received £8 million in Lottery funding, opened in early summer 2000, to rave reviews from the critics and an enormous response from the public - both young and old. At the same time, some 200 miles away in the picturesque small Devon coastal town of Budleigh Salterton, one of the Tate's well known nineteenth century pictures was going on display in a local museum and arts centre run entirely by volunteers. The 'Boyhood of Raleigh' by the great Victorian artist John Millais was being displayed in simple surroundings only a few yards from the scene it portrays and where it was painted. Heritage can be modern metropolitan-chic and professional, or modest, quiet and amateur (in the proper sense of the word.) But both need to be fostered.

Bibliography

Many of the institutions and organisations discussed in the text produce written materials, and especially annual reports and accounts. Some of these are listed below. In recent years the easiest way to read them (unless you have access to a very large library) is often on their websites, a number of which are given in the sections at the end of the bibliography.

Books and Printed Materials

Appleyard, Bryan (1984) *The Culture Club: Crisis in the Arts*. Faber & Faber.

Arts Council, (1985) *A Great British Succcess Story: An Invitation to the Nation to Invest in the Arts*; Arts Council.

Arts Council (2000) *Annual Review 1999*; Arts Council.

Audit Commission (1989) *Sport for Whom?: Clarifying the Local Authority Role in Sport and Recreation*. HMSO.

Audit Commission (1990) *Local Authority Support for Sport: A Management Handbook*. HMSO.

British Broadcasting Corporation (1999) *Public Service Broadcasters Around the World: a McKinsey Report for the BBC*. BBC, January.

British Broadcasting Corporation (1992) *Extending Choice: The BBC's role in the new broadcasting age*. BBC.

British Broadcasting Corporation (2000) *Annual Report and Accounts 1999-2000*. BBC.

British Film Institute (1993) *Film and Television Handbook 1994*. BFI.

British Tourist Authority (1998) *Annual Report and Accounts 1997-98*. BTA.

Brooke, Peter (1992) *Shaping Our Heritage*. Department of National Heritage.

Bruton, M. & Nicholson, D. (1987) *Local Planning in Practice*. Hutchinson.

Burkart, A. J. & Medlik, S. (1981) *Tourism: Past, Present and Future*. Heinemann, second edition.

Bussey, G. & Geddes, K. (1986) *Television: The First Fifty Years*. National Museum of Photography, Film & Television.

Cabinet Office, (1999) *Modernising Government*. Stationery Office, March (Cm 4310).

Cabinet Office (1985) *Pleasure, Leisure and Jobs: The Business of Tourism*. HMSO.

Cabinet Office (1997) *Scotland's Parliament*. Stationery Office, July (Cm 3558).

Cabinet Office (1997) *A Voice for Wales*. Stationery Office, July (Cm 3718).

Callaghan, Paul (ed) (1989) *Travel and Tourism*. Business Education.

Caygill, Marjorie (1992) *The Story of the British Museum*. British Museum Publications, second edition.

Central Office of Information (1993) *The Arts*. HMSO.

Central Office of Information (1994) *Sport and Leisure*. HMSO.

Coalter, F. et al. (1986) *Rationale for Public Sector Investment in Leisure*. Sports Council & ESRC.

Countryside Agency, *The State of the Countryside 1999*. Countryside Agency, Cheltenham.

Countryside Commission (2000) *Annual Report and Accounts 1998-99*. Countryside Commission, (HC 325).

Countryside Commission (1991) *Fit for the Future:Report for the National Parks Review Panel*. Countryside Commission. ['The Edwards Report']

Cullingworth, J. B & Nadin, V. (1997) *Town and Country Planning in England and Wales*. Routledge, twelfth edition.

Davidson, Andrew (1992) *Under the Hammer: The ITV Franchise Battle*. Heinemann.

Department For Culture, Media And Sport (1999) *Public Service Agreement 1999-2002; High Level Business Plan 2000-2001*. DCMS.

Department For Culture, Media And Sport (2000) *A Sporting Future for All*. Stationery Office, April.

Department For Culture, Media And Sport (1999) *Tomorrow's Tourism*. Stationery Office, February.

Department For Culture, Media And Sport (1999) *The Future Funding of the BBC: Report of the Independent Review Panel, Chairman Gavyn Davies*. DCMS.

Department For Culture, Media And Sport (2000*) The Funding of the BBC: the Government Reponse to the Third Report of the Culture, Media and Sport Committee 1999-2000*. Stationery Office March (Cm 4674).

Department Of Employment (1992) *Tourism in the UK: Realising the Potential.* HMSO.

Department Of The Environment (1972) *The New Local Authorities: Management and Structure.* HMSO, ['The Bains Report']

Department Of The Environment (1980) *Urban Renaissance: A better life for towns.* HMSO.

Department Of The Environment (1985) *Caring for the Past.* HMSO.

Department Of The Environment (1989) *Developing Sport and Leisure: Good Practice in Urban Regeneration.* HMSO.

Department Of The Environment (1996) *Circular 12/96: Environment Act 1995, Part III National Parks.* DOE.

Department Of The Environment, Transport And Regions (1999) *Access to the Countryside in England and Wales: the Government's Framework for Action.* Stationery Office, March.

Department Of The Environment, Transport And Regions (1999) *Local Leadership, Local Choice.* Stationery Office, March (Cm 4298).

Department Of The Environment, Transport And Regions (1998) *Modern Local Government: In Touch with the People.* Stationery Office, July (Cm 4014).

Department Of The Environment, Transport And Regions (1997) *New Leadership for London.* Stationery Office, July (Cm 3724).

Department Of National Heritage (1996) *Sport:Raising the Game, the first year report.* HMSO.

Department Of National Heritage (1992) *The Future of the BBC.* HMSO (Cm. 2098)

Doulton, Anne-Marie (1989) *The Arts Funding Guide.* Directory of Social Change.

Dunleavy, Patrick et al (eds.) (1997) *Development in British Politics 5.* Macmillan.

English Heritage (1992) *Managing England's Heritage: Setting Our Priorities for the 1990's.* English Heritage.

English Heritage (1999) *Report and Accounts 1998-99.* English Heritage.

English Tourism Council (1999) *Focus on the English Tourism Council.* ETC, July.

English Tourist Board (1993) *Annual Report 1993.* ETB.

European Parliament (1992) *Tourism in Europe.* European Parliament.

Forestry Commission (1999) *Annual Report and Accounts 1998-99.* Forestry Commission.

Henry, Ian (1993) *The Politics of Leisure Policy.* Macmillan.

Hewison, Robert (1997) *Culture and Consensus: England, Art and Politics since 1940*. Methuen, second edition.

Hewison, Robert (1987) *The Heritage Industry: Britain in a Climate of Decline*. Methuen.

Home Office (1986) *Report of the Committee on Financing the BBC*. HMSO. (Cmnd.9824) ['The Peacock Report']

Home Office (1988) *Broadcasting in the 90's: Competition, Choice and Quality*. HMSO. (Cm 517)

Horrie, Chris & CLARKE, Steve (1994) *Fuzzy Monsters: Fear and Loathing at the BBC*. Heinemann.

House Of Commons (2000) *Fourth Report from the Culture, Media, and Sport Committee 1999-2000 Wembley National Stadium*. Stationery Office.

House Of Commons (2000) *Fifth Report from the Culture, Media, and Sport Committee 1999-2000 Marking the Millennium in the United Kingdom*. Stationery Office.

House Of Commons (1998) *Ninth Report from the Culture, Media, and Sport Committee 1997-1998 The Future of News at Ten*. Stationery Office.

House Of Commons (1982) *Eighth Report from the Education, Science and Arts Committee 1981-2 Public and Private Funding of the Arts, Vols. I-III*. HMSO.

House Of Commons (1989) *First report from the Education, Science and Arts Committee 1989-90 Should Museums Charge?: Some Case Studies*. HMSO.

House Of Commons (1986) *Second report from the Environment Committee 1985-6 Sports Council*. HMSO.

House Of Commons (1987) *First report from the Environment Committee 1986-7 Historic Buildings and Ancient Monuments, Vols. I-III*. HMSO.

House Of Commons (1994) *Third Report of the National Heritage Committee 1993-4 Our Heritage: Preserving it, Prospering from it, Vols. I-II*. HMSO.

House Of Commons (1985) *First Report from the Trade and Industry Committee 1985-6 Tourism in the UK, Vols. I-II*. HMSO.

House Of Commons (1986) *Sixth Special Report from the Trade and Industry Committee Tourism in the United Kingdom: The Government's Reply to the Committee's First Report in Session 1986-86*. HMSO.

Independent Television Commission (1999) *Annual Report & Accounts 1998*. ITC, March.

Jenkins, Hugh (1979) *The Culture Gap: An Experience of Government and the Arts*. Marion Boyars.

Jones, Bill (ed.) (1999) *Political Issues in Britain Today*. Manchester UP, fifth edition.

Jones, Bill et al (eds.) (1998) *Politics UK*. Prentice Hall, third edition.

Kavanagh, Denis (2000) *British Politics: Continuities and Change*, Oxford UP.

Lambert, Stephen (1982) *Channel Four: Television with a Difference?* British Film Institute.

Leach, Steve (1996) *Enabling or Disabling Local Government*. Open UP.

Macewan, Ann and Malcolm (1987) *Greenprints for the Countryside?: The Story of Britain's National Parks*. Allen & Unwin.

Mcnaughton, Neil (1999) *Local and Regional Government*. Hodder & Stoughton.

Madge, Tim (1989) *Beyond the BBC: Broadcasting and the Public in the 1980s*. Macmillan.

Mason, Douglas (1987) *Expounding the Arts*. Adam Smith Institute.

Mason, Tony (1999) *Sport in Britain since 1945*. Blackwell.

Miall, Leonard (1994) *Inside the BBC*. Weidenfeld & Nicolson.

Minihan, Janet (1977) *The Nationalisation of the Arts: The Development of State Subsidies to the Arts in Great Britain*. Hamish Hamilton.

Museums And Galleries Commission (1984) *Review of Area Museum Councils and Services*. HMSO.

Museums And Galleries Commission (1988) *The National Museums*. HMSO.

Museums & Galleries Commission (1997) *Report 1996-7*. M&GC.

National Heritage Memorial Fund (1993) *Annual Report 1992-93*. NHMF.

Northern Arts (1998) *Annual Report 1998-99*. Northern Arts.

Northumberland National Park Authority (2000) *Best Value Performance Plan*.

Nugent, Neil (1999) *The Government and Politics of the European Union*. Macmillan, fourth edition.

Office Of Arts And Libraries (1984) *Public and Private Funding of the Arts: Observations by the Government on the Eighth Report from the Education, Science and Arts Committee. Session 1981-82*. HMSO. (Cmnd 9127)

Pearce, David (1989) *Conservation Today*. RKP.

Pick, John (1980) *Arts Administration*. Spon.

Pick, John (1991) *Vile Jelly: the birth, life and lingering death of the Arts Council of Great Britain*. Brynmill.

Redcliffe-Maud, Lord (1976) *Support for the Arts in England and Wales*. Calouste Gulbenkian Foundation.

Redhead, Brian (1988) *The National Parks of England and Wales*. The Oxford Illustrated Press.

Redundant Churches Fund (1990) *Churches in Retirement: a Gazetteer*. HMSO.

Rodgers, Peter (1989) *The Work of Art*. Policy Studies Institute/Calouste Gulbenkian Foundation.

Runyard, Sue (1994) *Museums & Galleries Commission: The Museum Marketing Handbook*. HMSO.

Rural Development Commission (1993) *The Countryside Means Business*. The Rural Development Commission.

Shaw, Sir Roy (1987) *Arts and the People*. Jonathan Cape, 1987.

Sinclair, Ian (1995) *Birth of the Box: the Story of Television*. Sigma Leisure.

Sport England Lottery Fund (1999) *Investing for Our Future. Sport England Lottery Fund Strategy 1999-2009*. Sport England.

Travers, A. S. et al (1981) *The Role of Central Government in Relation to the Provision of Leisure Services in England and Wales*. University of Birmingham (Centre for Regional Studies).

Torkildsen, George (1992) *Leisure and Recreation Management*. Spon, third edition.

Stewart, J. Leach, S. & Walsh, K. (1994) *The Changing Organisation and Management of Local Government*. Macmillan.

Stoker, G (ed). (2000) *The New Politics of British Local Governance*. Macmillan.

Wallace, H. & W. (eds). (2000) *Policy Making in the European Union*. Oxford UP, fourth edition.

Wilding, Richard (1989) *Supporting the Arts: A review of the structure of arts funding*. Office of Arts And Libraries.

Wilson, D. M. (1989) *The British Museum: Purpose and Politics*. British Museum Publications.

Wolfenden Committee (1960) *Sport and the Community*. CCPR.

World Wide Web Sites

Government: National Departments and LAs

Prime Minister, 10 Downing St	www.number-10.gov.uk
Cabinet Office	www.cabinet-office.gov.uk
Culture, Media and Sport (DCMS)	www.culture.gov.uk
Environment, Transport & Regions (DETR)	www.detr.gov.uk
Trade and Industry (DTI)	www.dti.gov.uk
Agriculture, Fisheries & Food (MAFF)	www.maff.gov.uk
Education and Employment (DfEE)	www.dfee.gov.uk
European Union (EU)	www.europa.eu.int
Local Government Information Unit (LGIU)	www.lgiu.gov.uk
Durham County Council	www.durham.gov.uk

National Lottery and Millennium

National Lottery Commission	www.natlotcomm.gov.uk
New Opportunities Fund	www.nof.org.uk
National Endowment for Science, Technology & the Arts (NESTA)	www.nesta.org.uk
National Lottery Charities Board	www.nlcb.org.uk
Heritage Lottery Fund	www.hlf.org.uk
Millennium Commission	www.millennium.gov.uk

Broadcasting

British Broadcasting Corporation (BBC)	www.bbc.co.uk
Independent Television Commission (ITC)	www.itc.org.uk
Channel 4	www.channel4.com
Channel 5	www.channel5.co.uk
Radio Authority	www.radioauthority.org.uk
Broadcasting Standards Commission	www.bsc.org.uk

Arts

Arts Council of England (ACE)   www.artscouncil.org.uk

Arts Council of Wales   www.ccc-acw.org.uk

Scottish Arts Council   www.sac.org.uk

Film Council   www.filmcouncil.org.uk

British Film Institute (BFI)   www.bfi.org.uk

National Training Organisation for   www.metier.org.uk
The Arts & Entertainment Industries (Metier)

Arts & Business   www.aandb.org.uk

British Museum   www.british-museum.ac.uk

Countryside

Countryside Agency   www.countryside.gov.uk

Environment Agency   www.environment-agency.gov.uk

English Nature   www.english-nature.org.uk

Forestry Commission   www.forestry.gov.uk

Peak District National Park Authority   www.peakdistrict.org

Northumberland NPA   www.nnpa.org.uk

Sport

English Sports Council (Sport England)   www.english.sports.gov.uk

UK Sport   www.uksport.gov.uk

Sport Scotland   www.ssc.org.uk

Sports Council for Wales   www.sports-council-wales.co.uk

Sports Council for Northern Ireland   www.sportscouncil-ni.org.uk

National Playing Fields Association   www.nfpa.co.uk

National Training Organisation for Sport,   www.sprito.org.uk
Recreation & Allied Occupations (Sprito)

Tourism

English Tourism Council (ETC)	www.englishtourism.org.uk
Scottish Tourist Board	www.holiday.scotland.net
Northern Ireland Tourist Board	www.ni-tourism.com
Wales Tourist Board	www.tourism.wales.gov.uk
Northumbria Tourist Board	www.ntb.org.uk

Heritage

English Heritage (HBMCE)	www.english-heritage.org.uk
Heritage Lottery Fund	www.hlf.org.uk
Resource: Council for Museums, Archives and Libraries	www.resource.gov.uk
Commission for Architecture & the Built Environment (CABE)	www.cabe.org.uk
British Library	www.bl.uk
National Trust	www.nationaltrust.org.uk

Index